TRUMP'S FIRST YEAR

MILLER CENTER STUDIES ON THE PRESIDENCY
Marc J. Selverstone, Editor

The First Year Project

TRUMP'S FIRST YEAR

MICHAEL NELSON

UNIVERSITY OF VIRGINIA PRESS

Charlottesville and London

University of Virginia Press

Printed in the United States of America on acid-free paper

First published 2018

9 8 7 6 5 4 3 2 1

Library of Congress Cataloging-in-Publication Data
Names: Nelson, Michael, 1949–
Title: Trump's first year / Michael Nelson.
Description: Charlottesville : University of Virginia Press, 2017. | Series:
Miller Center Studies on the Presidency | Includes bibliographical references.
Identifiers: LCCN 2017055597 | ISBN 9780813941448 (pbk. : alk. paper) |
ISBN 9780813941431 (e-book)
Subjects: LCSH: Trump, Donald, 1946– | United States—Politics and
government—2017–
Classification: LCC E912 .N45 2017 | DDC 973.933—dc23
LC record available at https://lccn.loc.gov/2017055597

Cover art: President-elect Donald Trump walks to take his seat for the inaugural swearing-in ceremony at the U.S. Capitol in Washington, DC, Friday, January 20, 2017. (Official White House Photo by Shealah Craighead)

TO MY BELOVED WIFE, LINDA

CONTENTS

ACKNOWLEDGMENTS

Trump's First Year is infused with and inspired by the extensive and excellent work of the First Year Project of the University of Virginia's Miller Center. The ripe fruits of that project may be plucked at its website, firstyear2017.org, as well as in various ebooks that have been published by the University of Virginia Press and a new bound volume edited by me, Stefanie Georgakis Abbott, and Jeffrey L. Chidester. *Crucible: The President's First Year* includes project-commissioned essays by renowned scholars and practitioners such as H. W. Brands, Gary Gallagher, William Galston, David Greenberg, Melvyn P. Leffler, Sidney M. Milkis, Jeff Shesol, Stephen Skowronek, Alan Taylor, and Peter Wehner. My work on that book inspired this one. Particular thanks go to William J. Antholis, Director of the Miller Center and founder of the First Year Project; Barbara A. Perry, the Center's Director of Presidential Studies; and, at the University of Virginia Press, Richard Holway, Senior Executive Editor, History and Social Sciences; copy editor Susan Murray; project editor Morgan Myers; marketing and sales director Jason Coleman; and publicity and social media director Emily Grandstaff. I am also grateful to my friend and colleague Air Force Captain Bradley DeWees of Harvard's Kennedy School of Government for giving the manuscript such a thorough and helpful read, as well as to Stephen Skowronek of Yale University and Bruce Miroff of SUNY Albany, who reviewed it for the Press.

TRUMP'S FIRST YEAR

INTRODUCTION

Donald Trump was fortunate to take office when he did. Unlike Abraham Lincoln, he did not have to deal with the secession of seven states during the period between his election and inauguration.[1] Unlike Richard Nixon, he did not inherit a war in which more than a half-million American soldiers were bogged down. Unlike Franklin D. Roosevelt and Barack Obama, he did not take the oath of office in the midst of a massive financial crisis. Although the world had its share of problems when the Trump presidency began on January 20, 2017, they were ongoing, not new or urgent. The domestic economy had been growing, slowly but steadily, for all but one of the previous twenty-three quarters. The annual rate of inflation was about 2 percent, and unemployment had recently dipped below 5 percent. The percentage of Americans who regard themselves as middle- or upper-class had reached 62 percent, a greater share than before the 2008–9 economic meltdown.[2] The stock market was booming: from a modern low of 6,547 in March 2009, the Dow Jones Industrial Average had nearly tripled to 18,332 by Election Day. Unlike all of his recent Republican predecessors during the past three-fourths of a century, Trump took office as the head of a united party government, with a GOP majority in both the House of Representatives and the Senate. Strong corporate earnings, along with investor confidence that Republican-sponsored tax cuts and deregulatory policies were in the works, helped trigger an additional surge in the stock market, which rose by 1,473 points (8 percent) between the election and inauguration.

The outlook for the Trump presidency was considerably less bright by November 8, the anniversary of his election. To be sure, the year was not devoid of accomplishments. Congress passed more than a dozen laws rolling back specific regulations issued late in the Obama administration. Most of them had been opposed by the business community, as were the many more regulations that several of Trump's cabinet members and agency heads took steps to repeal. Trump was able to replace the late Justice Antonin Scalia on the Supreme Court with another respected conservative jurist, Neil Gorsuch, and his administration moved steadily to fill the more than one hundred vacancies he inherited on the lower federal courts. Trump's handling of the damage caused by Hurricane Harvey and Hurricane Irma, which battered southern Texas and Louisiana in late August and Florida and neighboring states in early September, was generally applauded.

These successes were far outnumbered by Trump's first-year failures. In the international arena, both allies and adversaries were bewildered by the president's erratic policies and pronouncements. North Korea's rapid advances in weapons technology meant that it was at least close to being able to launch ballistic missiles armed with nuclear weapons at its Asian neighbors and even the United States. The Republican president and Republican Congress failed to enact a single piece of significant legislation until September, when crises as varied as hurricanes and a looming shutdown of the federal government forced their hand. Federal courts struck down various administration actions. Several state and local governments openly defied some of Trump's policies, especially concerning undocumented immigrants. His White House staff underwent unprecedented turnover, as members fell out with the president, each other, or both. Vacancies in important positions in the executive branch were filled at a glacial pace, slowing the administration's efforts to direct the activities of the departments and agencies. Leaders in the business community, an important Republican constituency, resigned en masse from two presidential advisory boards. High-ranking military officers openly disputed some of the president's words and actions. Democrats and even a few Republicans in Congress raised the possibility of removing Trump from office, either through the impeachment process or on grounds of psychological inability. A special counsel investigated possibly illegal actions involving the Russian government and the president, his family members, and close associates. Trump's public approval rating sank below 40 percent within months of his taking office and remained at historically low levels for an elected first-year president for the remainder of the year.

Trump's First Year reports and analyzes the president's conduct during the twelve months (and a few weeks beyond) that followed his election. More than that, it embeds his first year in the larger context of the American political system, whose leading feature is fragmented power. After recounting Trump's background and election in chapter 1 and laying the theoretical groundwork for assessing his presidency in chapter 2, the book chronicles and analyzes the formation (and ongoing re-formation) of the Trump administration (chapter 3) and his unusually early reliance on unilateral executive action (chapter 4). Subsequent chapters treat the president's relations with other constitutional actors: the courts and the states and cities (chapter 5) and Congress (chapter 6). Chapter 7 concerns presidential communications under Trump, chapter 8 his foreign policies, and chapter 9 the discussions, unprecedented for a newly elected president, of removing him from office. The book concludes with an overall assessment of the remarkable year that followed Trump's election, as well as a broader consideration of the contemporary American presidency.

1 ★ TRUMP IS ELECTED

Donald Trump won an astonishing victory in the 2016 presidential election. At each turn of the electoral calendar, from June 16, 2015, when Trump announced he was running, until well into the evening of Election Day—November 8, 2016—political analysts of every stripe were confident that he would not be the forty-fifth president of the United States. Trump's candidacy would not last long enough even to contest the Iowa caucuses and New Hampshire primary, many experts said. The world's leading political betting firm made him a 100-to-1 long shot on the day of his announcement. The *New York Daily News* added a red nose and mouth to his photograph on its June 17 front page with the headline, "Clown Runs for Prez."[1] The Huffington Post refused for months to "report on Trump's campaign as part of [our] political coverage. Instead we will cover his campaign as part of our entertainment section."[2] Democratic nominee Hillary Clinton, who knew Trump from her years representing New York in the Senate and had attended his (third) wedding in 2005, wrote, "When Trump declared his candidacy for real in 2015, I thought it was another joke."[3] Election-eve forecasts placed his chances of victory at 2 percent (HuffPost), 1 percent (the Princeton Election Consortium), or even 0 percent (the celebrated Democratic strategist David Plouffe).[4] "In a mood of 'at long last' and, yes, celebration," *New Yorker* editor David Remnick wrote an election-night article on "the first woman president" to be posted on the magazine's website as soon as Clinton was declared the winner.[5] One prominent political scientist whose statistical model forecast months before the election that the Republican nominee would win because the economic and political fundamentals were so favorable decided that Trump was such a bad candidate that the model did not apply.[6]

The presidential election was not the only one whose outcome surprised the experts. Most forecast that the results of the Senate elections, in which the Republicans were forced to defend more than twice as many seats as the Democrats, would turn over control of that chamber from the Republican to the Democratic Party. Wrong again. The Democrats gained just two seats, not the five they needed to secure a majority. Senatorial elections were on thirty-four state ballots in 2016, and for the first time in history, the same party whose presidential nominee carried each state also won its Senate contest. As Trump prevailed in all but twelve of these states, so did the Republican candidates for senator. Predictions for the House elections generally were that the Democrats would add fifteen to twenty seats, bringing them within striking distance of a majority. That didn't happen either. With a near-record 98 percent of House incumbents reelected, Democrats gained a paltry six seats, leaving the Republicans in charge of a united party government—a newly inaugurated president and a majority of both houses of Congress—for the first time since Dwight D. Eisenhower was elected in 1952. Not many Republicans owed their election to Trump. Eighty-six percent of the party's victorious House candidates ran ahead of him in their districts, and only 8 percent won by less than 10 percentage points. Even the six successful Senate candidates whom Trump outpolled in their states won landslide victories.[7]

Although surprising in its result, the 2016 election was less remarkable in its magnitude. It was not, as Trump claimed, "a massive landslide victory, as you know, in the Electoral College," much less "the biggest Electoral College win since Ronald Reagan."[8] From 1788 to 2012, forty-five of fifty-seven presidential elections were decided by a larger electoral vote majority than Trump's 306–232 victory over Clinton (304–227 after seven "faithless electors" voted for different candidates than the ones to whom they were pledged).[9] In the seven elections that followed Reagan's landslides in 1980 and 1984, the winning candidate outdid Trump in the Electoral College five times. In only four elections in two and a quarter centuries did the winner fail to secure more votes from the people than his opponent. Yet Trump ran a record 2.9 million votes behind Clinton in the national popular tally, and his postelection claim that "between three and five million illegal votes [for Clinton] caused me to lose the popular vote" was completely unsubstantiated by evidence.[10]

Similarly, although the election gave Trump a united party government, the Republican majority in both congressional chambers was perilously thin. In the House of Representatives, Republicans outnumbered Democrats by 241 to 194, and in the Senate by 52 to 48. In the face of cohesive Democratic opposition, this meant that any legislative proposal opposed by just 10 percent of Republican House members was unlikely to be enacted. Republican leaders would have to keep the party's extremely conservative, nearly three dozen–strong, and highly unified Freedom Caucus on board in order to prevail, without alienating Tuesday Group moderate conservatives, greater in number but less disciplined.[11] In the filibuster-prone Senate, where it takes sixty votes to pass most legislation, the barrier to passage was yet higher. To enact even those few measures that require only a simple majority, all but two Republican senators would need to vote together.

An additional complication for President Trump arose from the nature of the election campaign waged by Candidate Trump, which was marked by name-calling and extravagant promises. He branded the leading Democratic contenders, Senator

Bernie Sanders of Vermont and former secretary of state Clinton as "Crazy Bernie" and "Crooked Hillary," respectively, and led chants of "Lock her up!" at campaign rallies. He challenged President Barack Obama's bona fides as a natural-born citizen and, when Obama produced proof that he was born in Hawaii, suggested that the "birth certificate is a fraud."[12] Most astonishing, in a video-recorded 2005 conversation with *Access Hollywood* host Billy Bush that became public one month before the election, Trump bragged that when he saw beautiful women, "I just start kissing them. . . . And when you're a star they let you do it. You can do anything. Grab 'em by the pussy."[13]

Nor did Trump spare Republican rivals Ted Cruz and Marco Rubio, whom he dubbed "Lyin' Ted" and "Liddle Marco" (Trump's spelling).[14] He dismissed Republican senator John McCain of Arizona, an authentic hero of the Vietnam War who endured unending torture as a prisoner of war rather than be released before his fellow captives, as "not a war hero. . . . I like people who weren't captured."[15] Ignoring aides' advice to apologize, Trump's first campaign manager, Corey Lewandowski, recalled, "Donald Trump does what Donald Trump always does, which is he doubles down," calling a press conference to repeat his attack.[16] Neither McCain nor any of the other four living former Republican nominees for president regarded Trump as fit to hold the office. Former president George W. Bush let it be known that he would not vote for Trump, and his father, former president George H. W. Bush, called him a "blowhard" and voted for Clinton.[17] The party's 2012 nominee, Mitt Romney, publicly excoriated Trump's bankruptcies in business as well as his "personal qualities, the bullying, the greed, the showing off, the misogyny, the absurd third-grade theatrics."[18] All of the leading conservative publications actively opposed Trump.[19]

The release of the *Access Hollywood* recording raised the level of intraparty opposition to Trump. Senator McCain, the Republican candidate for president in 2008, called on him to withdraw from the election, as did Republican National Committee (RNC) chair Reince Priebus, Senator John Thune of South Dakota, Senator Kelly Ayotte of New Hampshire, and other party leaders. Trump doubled down once again, dismissing his vile language as "locker room banter" and attacking former president Bill Clinton as "the greatest abuser of women in the history of American politics" and Hillary Clinton as "an enabler" who "attacked the women who Bill Clinton mistreated afterward."[20] Trump even brought four of President Clinton's accusers to the second presidential debate. He then threatened to sue (but never did) the more than a dozen women— all of whom he said were "horrible, horrible liars"—who came forward to accuse him of grabbing their breasts, putting his hand up their skirt, kissing them aggressively, or other sexual misconduct.[21] One result of Trump's tawdry campaign was that he took office with almost no support from his party's elected leadership that was rooted in anything deeper than short-term political expedience, chiefly their fear of alienating his followers.

Trump's campaign promises stretched far beyond realism. Concerning the economy, he pledged to create 25 million jobs in ten years and to eliminate the $19 trillion national debt two years sooner than that, historically unprecedented targets that somehow would be reached while reducing taxes, increasing defense spending, and "sav[ing] Medicare, Medicaid, and Social Security without cuts."[22] The hourly minimum wage would be raised "to at least $10."[23] He would not only "build a great, great wall on our southern border," Trump promised, but also "have Mexico pay for that wall."[24] Of the "at least 11 million people that came in this country illegally," he said, "they will go out."[25] "We're going to win so much," Trump declared, "you're going to be so sick and tired of winning, you're going to come to me and go, 'Please, please, we can't win any more.'"[26] Some Democrats were so offended by Trump's policies and demeanor that they organized a postelection campaign to persuade electors to deny him a majority of electoral votes and throw the election into the House.[27]

THE REPUBLICAN NOMINATION

The same freewheeling and aggressive style that alienated Democrats during the election solidified Trump's support among many Republican voters, who regarded his rhetorical excesses as evidence of authenticity, undiluted by the normal social constraints that Trump dismissed as "political correctness." As the political scientists John Sides, Michael Tesler, and Lynn Vavreck have argued, Trump's campaign for the Republican nomination "became a vehicle for a different kind of identity politics" than that centered on groups historically oppressed by race, gender, or sexual orientation. It was instead "oriented around white Americans' feelings of marginalization in an increasingly diverse America."[28] Supporters cheered when Trump said that Mexican immigrants were "bringing drugs, they're bringing crime[,] they're rapists"[29] and when he called for a "total and complete shutdown of Muslims entering the United States."[30] They nodded approvingly when Trump claimed that former president George W. Bush "lied" about weapons of mass destruction as a pretext for the "big, fat mistake" of waging war against Iraq.[31] In the global war on terror, Trump declared: "Torture works. . . . Waterboarding is fine, but it's not nearly tough enough."[32] "We're gonna be saying 'Merry Christmas' at every store," he offered; "You can leave 'Happy Holidays' at the corner."[33] Trump roared through the Republican primaries, readily disposing of seemingly formidable opponents such as Governor Scott Walker of Wisconsin, Governor Chris Christie of New Jersey, former governor Jeb Bush of Florida, Governor John Kasich of Ohio, and Senators Cruz of Texas and Rubio of Florida. He wrapped up the nomination by handily defeating the last rivals standing, Cruz and Kasich, in the May 3 Indiana primary, five weeks sooner than Clinton was able to defeat Senator Sanders for the Democratic nomination.

In addition to his freewheeling views, Trump's voters also valued his experience as a businessman rather than a politician. Historically, nearly everyone elected or even nominated by a major political party for president has been a current or former senator, governor, vice president, general, or cabinet member. In the quarter century after World War II, senators and vice presidents (most of whom had been senators) dominated presidential elections because Cold War–era voters trusted the federal government and valued their experience dealing with national security issues. Then, in the aftermath of the Vietnam War and the Watergate scandal, the electorate turned to state governors, who were untainted by the incompetence and corruption now associated with a Washington-based political career: Jimmy Carter of Georgia in 1976, Ronald Reagan of California in 1980, Bill Clinton of Arkansas in 1992, and George W. Bush of Texas in 2000.

The ascendant Tea Party movement that helped the Republican Party win control of the House in 2010 and the Senate in 2014, however, was not just anti-Washington but antigovernment in all its forms. Seven current or former Republican governors battled Trump for the Republican nomination, including large- or swing-state chief executives Bush, Kasich, Walker, Christie, George Pataki of New York, and Jim Gilmore of Virginia. None of them came close. On the eve of the primary campaign, 58 percent of Republicans said they would prefer "someone from outside the existing political establishment" to "someone with experience in how the political system works."[34] As a candidate who had never held public office, Trump appealed to many voters as a complete outsider who would "drain the swamp" in Washington.[35] "The problem with politicians," he told a rally: "[they're] all talk and no action. It's true. All talk, and it's all bullshit."[36] He knew politicians could be bought, Trump claimed, because he had bought some of them himself as a cost of doing business. "When I need something from them—two years later, three years later," he said, "they are there for me."[37]

Trump also understood something that his rivals and other party leaders did not: most Republican voters do not share their consistently conservative ideology. For years, Republican leaders had pursued an agenda that favored free trade, reduced spending on Social Security and Medicare, cuts in federal discretionary programs, and a path to legal status for undocumented immigrants. Many rank-and-file Republican voters favored none of these things. In parallel 2014 surveys of Republican voters and elites, for example, 62 percent of voters but only 26 percent of elites said that spending on Social Security should be increased. Seventy-two percent of voters said "immigrants and refugees coming to the U.S." pose a "critical threat" to the country, compared with 22 percent of elites. By vowing to protect Social Security and Medicare, deport illegal immigrants, introduce protectionist trade policies, and ramp up spending on infrastructure programs, "Trump simply met many Republican voters where they were," Sides, Tesler, and Vavreck argue, "tapping into longstanding but often unappreciated, sentiments."[38]

THE RISE OF DONALD TRUMP

The seeds for the seventy-year-old Trump's rise to national prominence were planted decades before his election. After graduating from the New York Military Academy, where he was a star athlete and was promoted to company captain, and the University of Pennsylvania's Wharton School, Trump joined his father's Brooklyn- and Queens-centered real estate business. Lifted up the ranks of the highly profitable family concern, Trump moved to Manhattan in 1971, at age twenty-five, aiming to enter the island's brutally competitive building market. Four years later he bought the run-down

Commodore Hotel in a blighted neighborhood near Grand Central Station and, with help from City Hall, transformed the property into the Grand Hyatt. Trump Tower soon followed, instantly becoming a midtown Manhattan landmark. In a futile quest to own a National Football League team, in 1983 Trump bought the New Jersey Generals in the newly formed United States Football League (USFL), pressured his fellow owners to file an antimonopoly lawsuit against the NFL in the hope of forcing it to merge with the USFL, and then watched the league collapse in 1986 when the lawsuit failed.[39] A year later Trump published *Trump: The Art of the Deal,* a secrets-of-my-success book that sold more than a million copies in hardcover. He married a glamorous model, Ivana Winklmayr, in 1977 but let neither the marriage nor the birth of his first three children (Ivanka, Donald Jr., and Eric) stand in the way of his growing notoriety. People "didn't think he was a snooty guy," said Ed Kosner, who as editor of *New York* magazine and the *New York Daily News* found that his readers loved reading stories about Trump: "They thought he was a regular guy who's made a lot of money."[40] Trump "had just the requisite touch of Elvis vulgarity to endear him to the common man," wrote Liz Smith, whose gossip column featured him for years.[41]

Trump cultivated a reputation as a lothario ("Best Sex I've Ever Had," the *New York Post* blared on its front page, quoting model Marla Maples, who became his second wife in 1993) and a successful businessman. His growing "network of ventures in gambling, sports, beauty pageants, television . . . sent the message that *Trump* meant ambition, wealth, and a distinctly personal expression of success," observed biographers Michael Kranish and Marc Fisher.[42] As a result, even when Trump's Atlantic City casinos and some of his other properties went bankrupt, "his creditors believed his name still had enough value to keep him in charge."[43] Over time, Trump was able to make money from others' business ventures simply by licensing his name to help them establish their brand of clothing, fragrances, eyeglasses, even mattresses. After years in the spotlight, he proved a natural when the producer Marc Burnett signed him in 2004 for his new NBC program *The Apprentice*. Trump improvised his lines—including the trademark, "You're fired!"—while advancing his image as the epitome of entrepreneurial success and glamor. The network's original idea was for Trump to turn over the reins after one year to another well-known business owner, but he was such an audience favorite that his run lasted fourteen years. Various Trump ventures might fail, including the Plaza Hotel, Trump Airlines, and Trump University, but *The Apprentice* helped to keep the association between Trump and success alive in the public mind.

Trump's wealth became a major part of his allure when he ran for president in 2016. Other candidates were "controlled by those people," he averred, referring to wealthy individuals and interest groups: "I'm not controlled. . . . I'm using my own money. I'm not using the lobbyists. I'm not using the donors. I don't care. I'm really rich."[44] He added, "Do you want someone who gets to be president and that's literally the highest-paying job he's ever had?"[45] According to Lewandowski, Trump disdained Romney's 2012 campaign for pulling into towns "in a Chevy pickup and pretend[ing] he wasn't as rich as he really is. Trump says, 'No, no. I'm going to pull up in my 757 . . . and we're going to have the most expensive cars.' "[46] He bragged that he was worth $10 billion, about three times more than *Forbes* magazine estimated.[47] He was able to buck Republican orthodoxy on issues like free trade and immigration because "not having donors allowed him the freedom to go and say and do things that others couldn't say or wouldn't do," Lewandowski added.[48] And because Trump was such an unlikely candidate, refused to make public his recent tax returns, and was expected until the end to lose the election, his extensive financial dealings drew far less media scrutiny than Clinton's more modest ones.

In addition to being a businessman and the best-selling author of self-glorifying books, Trump was a celebrity in every sense of the word. Even before *The Apprentice*, he built a large local and then national audience as a frequent talk-show guest. David Letterman had him on more than thirty times, and he was a regular on Howard Stern's raunchy radio program. Trump was a fixture on tabloid front pages and on magazine covers for his many romances. He married his third strikingly beautiful wife, Melania Knauss, in 2005, with Bill and Hillary Clinton in attendance.[49] He later became a guest battler in pro wrestling spectacles, bragging salaciously that with his "Trump Tower" he would dominate WWE owner Vince McMahon's "grapefruits." On television he starred in not just *The Apprentice* but also its popular successor, *Celebrity Apprentice*, which ran until he announced for president in 2015.[50]

Trump began flirting with a presidential candidacy long before running. In September 1987, at age forty-one, he took out a full-page ad in the *New York Times* and other major newspapers charging that the American economy was stunted "by the cost of defending those that can easily afford to pay us for the defense of their freedom," singling out Japan and Saudi Arabia: "Let's not let our great country be laughed at anymore."[51] Hinting that he might seek the 1988 Republican nomination, he went to New Hampshire in October and told an enthusiastic audience: "We have had enough of the men who say, 'Vote for me because I am nice.' I have nothing against nice people, but I personally have had enough of them."[52] Trump decided not to run and, in the years to come, changed parties seven times before returning to the GOP in 2012. Along the way he hosted a fund-raiser for Clinton's first Senate campaign and said of her husband: "I think Bill Clinton is terrific. I think he's done an amazing job."[53] Hillary Clinton, Trump said, was a "terrific woman" who "does a great job."[54] In 2000 Trump spent several months seeking the Ross Perot–founded Reform Party's nomination for president. His platform included universal health care and allowing gays and lesbians to serve openly in the military.[55] He withdrew in February but won the Reform primaries in Michigan and California, where his name remained on the ballot. After flirting with another candidacy as a Republican in 2012 and then campaigning for Romney, Trump applied to the Patent and Trademark Office for ownership of a phrase: Make America Great Again.[56]

HOW TRUMP WON

Trump's unconventional background and iconoclastic style struck strong chords with an angry electorate when he sought the presidency for real in 2016. Remarkably, on Election Day 20 percent of the voters who said Trump lacks "the temperament to serve effectively as president" voted for him anyway, along with 18 percent of those who said he is not "qualified to be president."[57] So repelled were these roughly 12 million voters by Clinton that they held their noses and cast their ballots for Trump. Although Trump scored the lowest of any candidate in the forty-eight-year history of the American National Election Studies "feeling thermometer" (38 on a 100-point scale), Clinton was second from the bottom, with 44.[58] According to interim Democratic National Committee chair Donna Brazile, Clinton was so "anemic" a candidate, both politically and, at times, physically, that Brazile actually considered trying to replace both her and her running mate, Senator Tim Kaine of Virginia, with a ticket of Vice President Joe Biden and New Jersey senator Corey Booker.[59]

Other than capitalizing on these elements of his appeal and many voters' intense dislike of Clinton—her coziness with Wall Street, her misuse of a private e-mail account to send and receive messages that included classified material while serving as secretary of state, her close embrace of race- and gender-based identity politics, her longtime status as a political insider, and, for some, her sex—how did Trump win?

Geographically, Trump tore a large hole through the Democrats' "blue wall," the nineteen states with 242 electoral votes that had voted Democratic in all six presidential elections since Bill Clinton won his first victory in 1992. Three of these states, all of them in the Rust Belt, cast their combined 46 electoral votes for Trump: Michigan, Pennsylvania, and Wisconsin—each by less than 1 percent, with Trump's margin of victory provided by defecting Sanders supporters.[60] Three other states that supported Obama in 2008 and 2012—Ohio, Florida, and Iowa, with 53 electoral votes—also voted for Trump. As Clinton lamented in her postelection memoir, Sanders's "attacks caused lasting damage, . . . paving the way for Trump's 'Crooked Hillary' campaign."[61] Sanders's populist ire was aimed at Wall Street, Trump's at Washington. But by associating Clinton with both domains, Sanders inadvertently led some who shared his resentment of concentrated power away from her and toward Trump.

Although Sides, Tesler, and Vavreck have shown that Trump was already gaining on Clinton before FBI director James Comey's announcement that the bureau was investigating a new batch of Clinton's e-mails just eleven days in advance of the election, FiveThirtyEight's Nate Silver is among several experts (along with Clinton herself) who argue that the news tipped enough voters in Trump's direction to cost her the presidency.[62] Seizing on the announcement less than an hour after Comey made it, Trump declared: "Hillary Clinton's corruption is on a scale we have never seen before. We must not let her take her criminal scheme into the Oval Office."[63] Between then and the election, nearly half of the lead stories on the three broadcast networks' evening news programs dealt with her e-mails.[64]

Clinton added to the list of causes for her defeat the misogyny of some voters, the media's excessive fascination with Trump, her focus on policy in a year of bluster, some missteps on her part, "the godforsaken Electoral College," and Russia's efforts on Trump's behalf.[65] Russia secretly placed anti-Clinton posts and ads on American social media that may have reached as many as 157 million users during the campaign. It engineered WikiLeaks' release of thousands of Democratic Party e-mails, some of which highlighted the national committee's bias toward Clinton over Sanders in the nominating contest and all of which placed "Clinton" and "e-mails" back in the headlines alongside each other.[66] At a minimum, revelations in July 2017 about Donald Trump Jr. and son-in-law Jared Kushner's meeting with Russian representatives the previous June, along with special counsel Robert Mueller's subsequent conviction of foreign policy advisor George Papadopoulos for lying to the FBI about his own role in Russian efforts to share "dirt" about Clinton, revealed the Trump campaign's unsavory openness to how Russia might help him win the election.[67] With Paul Manafort, who worked for a pro-Russia political party in the Ukraine before serving as Trump's second campaign manager, overseeing the Republican National Convention, it surely was no coincidence that the one change in the party platform made at the Trump campaign's behest was to remove a plank urging that Ukraine be rearmed to resist Russian aggression. Yet, as the political scientists Steven Schier and Todd Eberly point out, although "there can be no doubt that Russian agents interfered in the election," it was "less clear is whether that interference substantively affected the outcome."[68]

Others credit Trump's victory to his more disciplined campaign style as Election Day drew near, as well as to Clinton's overconcentration on inner cities and university towns. Certainly Clinton's overweening confidence that she could not possibly lose to someone she disrespected as much as Trump clouded her understanding of his support, half of which she labeled a "basket of deplorables."[69] She and her husband actually bought the house next to the one they own in Chappaqua, New York, to host the Secret Service agents they assumed would surround her as president. After a quarter century as first lady of Arkansas and then of the United States, senator from New York, secretary of state, and an extravagantly paid ($20 million in all, by one account) maker of speeches to Wall Street financial institutions, Clinton had been "a resident of a bubble of power since her days in the Arkansas governor's mansion."[70]

Nationally, blue-collar whites, who roughly correspond to the category "non–college educated" in polls, tipped the balance to Trump by turning out to vote at a higher rate than in 2012 and giving him 66 percent of their votes.[71] As many as 10 percent of the electorate were "Obama-Trump" voters, Democrats who switched parties from 2012 to 2016 because their economic plight seemed to be getting worse.[72] Sixty percent of military veterans voted for Trump, choosing to overlook his avoidance of service during the Vietnam War. And so great was white evangelical Christians' concern about Clinton's social liberalism and the left-wing Supreme Court justices they expected her to appoint that a record 81 percent of them cast their ballots for the thrice-married, notoriously unfaithful, casino-owning Trump. The election was not "for Sunday School teacher or pastor," conservative Christian leaders like Liberty University president Jerry Falwell Jr. told fellow evangelicals.[73] Asked in 2011 if they thought "an elected official who commits an immoral act in their private life can still behave ethically and fulfill their duties in their public and professional life," only 30 percent of evangelicals said yes. Enamored of Trump when asked the same question in 2016, 72 percent answered in the affirmative.[74]

Meanwhile, despite many Republican leaders' unhappiness with their nominee, Trump secured a solid 90 percent of GOP voters. Indeed, if the only information one had about the election was the pattern of voting revealed in exit polls, one might well conclude that it had pitted a mainstream Democrat (which was true) against a mainstream Republican (which was not). To be sure, Trump's unusually great support among working-class whites is what enabled him to tear down the Democrats' blue wall, but it mostly extended a trend toward the Republican Party in presidential elections that, although accelerated during the Obama presidency, has been under way since Richard Nixon's victories in 1968 and 1972.[75] And as Trump gathered electoral votes by carrying key states narrowly, Clinton racked up her national popular vote plurality by inefficiently running up the score in states like California, which she won by 4.1 million votes, and New York, where her victory margin was 1.7 million.

Taken together, these aspects of the 2016 election were enough to get Trump elected but augured poorly for his first year as president. Not once has the economy gained 25 million jobs in ten years. Nor has the national debt ever shrunk at a rate anywhere close to $2.5 trillion per year over two four-year terms. As William Safire observed, presidents who promise rain will be held responsible for the droughts that inevitably come.[76] Further, surprising as Trump's victory was, it was modest in magnitude. His party's other leaders felt no sense of personal loyalty to him, and the opposition party was determined to see him fail. Trump earned none of the goodwill from people who voted against him that traditionally sets the stage for a first-year honeymoon. On top of that, as the political scientist Stephen Skowronek has pointed out, Trump took office at the same late stage of "political time" as did Franklin Pierce at the tail end of the Jacksonian era and Jimmy Carter in the waning years of New Deal liberalism. Like these two hapless predecessors, Trump faced the challenge of holding together a crumbling party coalition.[77] In his case the coalition included blue-collar Republicans motivated by conservative social views but opposed to free trade and reductions in (some) entitlement programs, as well as white-collar Republicans who were little concerned about social issues but cared deeply about these conservative economic policies. Most important, perhaps, Trump had been elected by harshly attacking the opposition, not by offering a positive program for governing.

2 ★ A CYCLE OF DECREASING INFLUENCE *AND* DECREASING EFFECTIVENESS

New presidents normally undergo what the political scientist Paul Light has called a "cycle of increasing effectiveness." Because no previous position entirely prepares one for the unique challenges of the presidency, much of the president's training is necessarily on-the-job. Over time, Light observes, "the presidential information base should expand; the president's personal expertise should increase. As the president and staff become more familiar with the working of the office, there will be a learning effect. They will identify useful sources of information; they will produce effective strategies."[1] In other words, presidents typically get better at the job by doing it.

The history of the presidency is rich with examples of presidents becoming more effective with the passage of time. Four months after taking office, George Washington brought some ideas for a treaty to the Senate to seek its advice. After a confusing and disjointed discussion ensued, he reportedly fumed that he'd "be damned if he ever went there again!" and submitted treaties only after they were negotiated.[2] Abraham Lincoln deferred to the less-than-competent military leadership he inherited during the early stages of the Civil War before devising a strategy for victory and finding generals who would execute it. Franklin D. Roosevelt was determined to balance the federal budget when he became president; only from experience did he decide that deficit spending would do more to stimulate the depressed economy than fiscal austerity. John F. Kennedy uncritically approved a dubious CIA plan to help depose Cuban leader Fidel Castro at the Bay of Pigs. Eighteen months later, when Soviet nuclear missiles were discovered in Cuba, he subjected the experts' judgments to much greater scrutiny before deciding how to back down the Soviet Union short of war. Ronald Reagan tried to reduce Social Security benefits six months into his first term, was rebuffed by a unanimous Senate, and then forged a more constructive path by appointing a bipartisan commission. Bill Clinton thought he could open the military to gays and lesbians with the stroke of a pen, met strong resistance, and turned to Congress and the Joint Chiefs of Staff in pursuit of a compromise measure.[3]

Learning from experience to become a more effective president is essential because it helps to offset the simultaneous "cycle of decreasing influence" that presidents undergo during their tenure in office. When expectations raised during the campaign cannot all be met, some because they are excessive and others because they are contradictory, people become disappointed. As a former Gerald Ford aide observed: "Each [presidential decision] is bound to hurt somebody. . . . He will satisfy one group but anger three others."[4] Thomas Jefferson famously lamented that every appointment he made to federal office earned him *un ingrat and cent enemis.*"[5] Consequently, presidents experience what the political scientists Paul Brace and Barbara Hinckley have labeled a "decay curve," a decline in public approval that normally begins about halfway through the first year of the term and lasts well into the third year, "independently of anything the president does" and "irrespective of the economy . . . or outside events."[6]

One vital element of presidential influence in the months before the decay curve bends downward is the president's status as not just the nation's chief of government—its political leader as the head of the winning political party and thus an inherently divisive figure—but also its chief of state, the living symbol of national unity. Without even thinking about it, Americans tend to associate each newly elected president with his long line of predecessors, many of them memorialized in monuments, currency, place-names, museums, and lore. Iconic trappings of the presidency—the White House, Air Force One, Camp David, "Hail to the Chief"—underscore this association, which reaches an early culmination in the grand ceremony of national unity that takes place on Inauguration Day.

By virtue of the chief-of-state role, newly elected presidents normally enjoy a postelection increase in public approval that represents the vote of confidence granted to anyone who ascends to the office. This is the basis of the traditional "honeymoon" period, which usually lasts well into the president's first year and can readily be converted into a governing asset in the form of increased influence in Congress.[7] Even the media, however critical of the president they were during the election campaign when he was a mere candidate, initially tend to pull their punches, offering admiring profiles of the president's family, appointees, and planned initiatives.[8]

According to Light, one implication of the "race against time" that inevitably marks the cycle of decreasing influence is that "the first year offers the greatest opportunity" for achievement.[9] "I know the honeymoon won't last," said Lyndon B. Johnson; "Every day I lose a little more political capital."[10] "When an administration really makes great successes," observed veteran Republican senator Roy Blunt of Missouri a half century later, "it's usually in that first year—and more importantly, in the first seven months of that first year" before Congress begins its month-long summer recess.[11] Historically, much of the landmark legislation for which presidents such as Woodrow Wilson, Franklin Roosevelt, Lyndon

Johnson, and Ronald Reagan are remembered was enacted early in their tenure, before the decay curve set in.

To be sure, in the contemporary era of polarized partisan politics, in which many Democratic and Republican voters regard each other not as friendly rivals but as enemies,[12] presidential honeymoons have grown shorter and less idyllic. In the history of polling from Dwight D. Eisenhower to Barack Obama, every president's initial job approval ratings exceeded his share of the popular vote in the election that brought him to power.[13] The increase represented a surge of goodwill toward the new chief of state even among those who wished that his opponent had been elected. But the surge has been shorter and less steep for recent presidents like George W. Bush and Obama than it was for earlier modern presidents such as Eisenhower and Kennedy.

Donald Trump's brutalistic campaign aggravated this trend toward diminished honeymoons and assured that he would not have one at all. His 46 percent level of support on Election Day began declining almost immediately. Public protests broke out the next day. Nearly 5 million people—4.3 million of them within four days of the voting—signed an online change.org petition "calling on 'Conscientious Electors' to protect the Constitution from Donald Trump" and vote instead for Clinton, "the national popular vote winner."[14] Trump's inaugural address, with its theme of "American carnage," was as dark and divisive as any of his campaign speeches. On January 21, 2017, the day after the inauguration, more than 3 million women marched in dozens of cities and towns, collectively the largest mass protest in American history. Trump's Gallup approval rating the week after his inauguration was 45 percent, the lowest ever recorded for a new president.[15] Monthly YouGov/ *Economist* surveys showed no measurable increase from Election Day onward in the public's assessment of Trump's "qualifications to be president," "temperament to be the president," or "honesty and trustworthiness."[16]

Pressure from the Democratic grassroots (Trump's approval rating among Democrats was less than 10 percent) further undermined any claim the new president may have made to being a unifying chief of state.[17] From the start, groups such as Indivisible, Swing Left, and #KnockEveryDoor were formed by party activists for the purpose of making clear to Democratic leaders in Congress that cooperation with Trump would not be tolerated on any terms other than complete presidential surrender.[18] As late as mid-September, Hillary Clinton said she would not "rule it out" when asked if she would question "the legitimacy of this election if we learn that Russian interference is even deeper than we know now."[19]

Nothing degraded the president's ability to bring the country together more than Trump's own words and actions, which were designed to unify his base of supporters in opposition to his critics. For example, on September 22, 2017, he took a customary ceremonial action performed by all modern presidents as part of being chief of state—welcoming championship sports teams to the White House—and withdrew it from the National Basketball Association champion Golden State Warriors in a petulant tweet: "Stephen Curry is hesitating, therefore invitation is withdrawn!"[20] That night, Trump launched the first of a series of attacks on National Football League players who refused to stand for the national anthem. "Wouldn't you love to see one of these NFL owners, when somebody disrespects our flag, to say, 'Get that son of a bitch off the field right now, out, he's fired?'" Trump asked a rally in Huntsville, Alabama. Dozens of tweets on the subject followed. Bishop Sankey, a running back for the Minnesota Vikings, responded with a tweet of his own: "It's a shame and disgrace when you have the President of the US calling citizens of the country sons of a bitches."[21]

One aspect of the president's chieftainship of state is his conduct as "consoler-in-chief" or "comforter-in-chief" in times of tragedy.[22] People look to the president to speak the words and make the gestures that provide meaning and reassurance in the wake of a national disaster. As the political scientist Barbara Perry has written, "A secular liturgy has formed around the modern presidential response: a formal condolence statement from the White House, followed by a sacramental ritual of visiting survivors and victims' loved ones and participating in public memorials."[23] Notable examples include Reagan's speech in the aftermath of the *Challenger* space shuttle explosion in 1986, Clinton's remarks when a domestic terrorist killed 168 Americans in an Oklahoma City federal office building in 1995, George W. Bush's dramatic trip to Ground Zero three days after foreign terrorists flew airplanes into New York City's World Trade Center in 2001, and Obama speaking (and singing) at a memorial service for nine African American church people slain by a white racist in 2015. In every instance, the president's subdued, heartfelt, and nonpartisan expression of hope tempered by grief not only rang true but raised his overall approval rating from the American people.

Trump had multiple occasions to act as consoler-in-chief during a six-week period in his first year. His performance was mixed at best. As discussed in chapters 3 and 7, the president's worst moment came after a woman was killed and more than a dozen people injured on August 12 when a racist demonstrator in Charlottesville, Virginia, drove his car into a group of counterprotesters. Adopting the farthest thing from a unifying stance, Trump spent several days equating the two sides in ways designed to rally his political base rather than unify the country. Then, between August 25 and September 19, a series of three massive hurricanes rocked the coasts of Texas, Louisiana, and Florida and decimated Puerto Rico, an American territory whose residents are citizens of the United States. Trump traveled to all four sites, met with victims and local leaders, promised assistance, and even participated in relief efforts by unloading crates, handing out sandwiches, and tossing rolls of paper towels into a crowd.

In all his visits, however, Trump leavened expressions of sympathy with inappropriately self-glorifying rhetoric. "What a great job we've done," "we have done an incredible job," "we get an A-plus," he boasted.[24] Worse, his visit to Puerto Rico was preceded by a series of tweets and remarks that criticized islanders who "want everything to be done for them" and the mayor of San Juan for displaying "such poor leadership ability" and being "nasty to Trump."[25] "Look at a real catastrophe like Katrina," he told the people of Puerto Rico, who lacked electricity, water, shelter, medical care, and other basic needs; "What is your death count as of this moment? . . . Sixteen people versus in the thousands?"[26] One week later Trump impatiently tweeted, "We cannot keep FEMA, the Military, & the First Responders . . . in P.R. forever!"[27] Only on October 4, when he visited Las Vegas three days after a gunman killed fifty-nine concertgoers and wounded more than five hundred, did Trump confine himself to consolation undiluted by preening. "We cannot be defined by the evil that threatens us or the violence that incites such terror," he said, sticking to his prepared text. "We are defined by our love, our caring, and courage."[28]

Trump also saw a well-intentioned effort to console the widow of one of the four soldiers killed that same day in an ISIS raid in Niger turn controversial. Two weeks later, on October 18, Florida Democratic congresswoman Frederica Wilson complained that in his phone call to the widow of Sergeant La David Johnson, Trump insensitively said, "he knew what he signed up for."[29] Trump tweeted that the "Democrat Congresswoman totally fabricated what I said . . . Sad!," to which she responded: "This man is a sick man. He's cold-hearted and feels no pity or sympathy for anyone."[30] Her account rang true to Trump's critics, who recalled his dismissal of Senator John McCain as "not a hero" and his public feuding with the Khan family, Muslim Americans who lost a son in combat in Iraq and criticized Trump at the Democratic convention for his disparaging comments about Muslims. The president's chief of staff, John F. Kelly, a Marine Corps general who had also lost a son in combat, then muddied the waters further. Kelly had witnessed the president's call to Myeshia Johnson and, while commending him as one who "very bravely does make those calls" and criticizing Wilson as part of the "long tradition of empty barrels making the most noise," did not dispute that Trump made the comment Wilson found objectionable.[31] Kelly also inaccurately charged that Wilson had claimed credit for funding a new FBI building in Miami. The controversy lasted more than a week, with Wilson attacking the White House as "full of white supremacists," the president calling Wilson "Wacky Congresswoman Wilson," the widow saying Trump "made me cry because I was very angry at the tone of his voice," Trump denying the charge, and so on.[32]

As the journalist Peter Baker pointed out, fostering division over unity, sometimes unintentionally but usually not, was nothing new for Trump. It had been his strategy since he announced his candidacy in 2015. "As a president and as a candidate for president," Baker wrote, "Mr. Trump has attacked virtually every major institution in American life: Congress, the courts, Democrats, Republicans, the news media, the Justice Department, Hollywood, the military, NATO, the intelligence agencies," and others.[33] His supporters relished these attacks, which Trump "thinks make him look strong," but the rest of the country did not.[34]

For all these reasons, the normal months-long honeymoon that a new president enjoys by virtue of his status as chief of state did not occur before the historically predictable cycle of decreasing influence kicked in. To be sure, as would be expected for any president, Trump's influence in most matters of politics and governance diminished over time. But it did so not after the customary six months or so but at a pace that accelerated from the very beginning. By the anniversary of his election, Congress had not enacted even one of the ten legislative items on the "Contract with the American Voter" that constituted Trump's "100-Day action plan to Make America Great Again." Nine of the ten had not even been introduced.[35] This was especially noteworthy because Trump frequently had said that major accomplishments would occur "soon" or "very soon" after he took office. In January and February of 2017 alone, he promised: "Obamacare will be repealed very soon," "We're going to start building the wall very soon," "We're going to be doing tax policies very soon," "Announcing very, very big infrastructure projects soon," and so on. None of these things happened even remotely soon, if ever.[36]

Trump's job approval rating at the six-month mark was 39 percent, the lowest of any newly elected president in the history of opinion polling, and his disapproval rating was 55 percent, the highest. They remained within a point or two of those levels for months to come, even as public regard for his handling of specific matters such as terrorism and health care continued to decline.[37] The average net approval rating—that is, the percentage approving minus the percentage disapproving—for the nine elected presidents from Eisenhower to Obama was +36 percent after six months. Trump's was −16 percent.[38] Trump's low standing with the American people was even more exceptional in light of the favorable economic conditions that prevailed during his first year. Drawing on four decades of data, the political analyst Harry Entman calculated that based on the strength of the economy Trump's approval rating should have been at least 10 percentage points higher than it actually was.[39] To be sure, as 2017 wore on, most of those who identified themselves as Republicans or Trump voters in 2016 remained steadfast in their support. But the number of people who professed to being Republicans declined.[40] At the start of the Trump presidency, 31 percent of voters surveyed in the Gallup Poll identified with the GOP. By October, only 24 percent did.[41]

Nor would Trump find—or even seek—a way to counterbalance his immediate loss of influence by accelerating the cycle of increasing effectiveness. Instead, he learned little about how to be president from the experience of being president. Once in office, "I will be more effective and more disciplined," Trump had mused during the campaign;[42] "At the right time I will be so presidential that you'll call me and you'll say, 'Donald, you have to stop that'" because "you will be so bored."[43] As of December 2017, no one had called President Trump out of boredom to tell him he was being too presidential. Trump himself decided that although, "with the exception of the late, great Abraham Lincoln, I can be more presidential than any president who has ever held this office, . . . that's not going to get it done."[44]

But what did "get it done" mean? As the chapters that follow show, Trump wasted much of the ten-week transition period, tossing aside the months of planning and research his team had done. He eschewed intelligence briefings. "I'm, like, a smart person," Trump said, dismissing the daily postelection sessions that all of his predecessors had found necessary; "I don't need to be told the same thing in the same words every single day for the next eight years."[45] Important positions in the executive branch remained unfilled after a year had passed, and the White House staff was in recurring turmoil. Promised legislative initiatives were slow to materialize, and when they did, Trump often seemed uninformed about their contents. Carefully planned efforts by his subordinates to focus the nation's attention on administration priorities were undone by Trump's impulsive remarks on whatever subject happened to rouse his ire while he watched television. Thoughtful written speeches read by the president one day were undermined by his controversial tweets or ramblings the next. Only the Trump administration's careful attention to filling judicial vacancies and its ongoing assault on Obama-era regulations aligned with the cycle of increasing effectiveness that marks the typical president's first year. "We're not getting the job done," Trump said on October 16; "And I'm not going to blame myself."[46]

3 ★ FORMING (AND RE-FORMING) THE ADMINISTRATION

Donald Trump's good fortune in taking office when he did spanned the nation and the globe. Crises, foreign or domestic, have not been unusual occurrences during presidents' first years, but in the thirteen months after Trump's election, none occurred. The world was free of major wars. Even North Korea's rapid advances in nuclear weapons and the missiles with which to deliver them were only the latest iterations of developments that dated back to the early 1990s. At home, inflation, unemployment, and interest rates remained low. The stock market continued to soar. Median household income reached an all-time high even when adjusted for inflation, and the percentage of Americans lacking health insurance fell to an all-time low. The annual rate of GDP growth rose to 3.0 percent in the second and third quarters of 2017.

Even presidents as fortunate as Trump in the circumstances of their taking office need to accomplish multiple tasks in the aftermath of their election. None is more essential than forming the administration. The dozen or so people whom the president places in vital positions on the White House staff and the hundreds who are nominated to fill important policy-making positions in the departments and agencies either will serve the newly installed chief executive ably and faithfully or will fail to do so, with grievous consequences for presidential influence and effectiveness.

Because he had never served in government, Trump knew very few people who were prepared by virtue of knowledge or experience to occupy the most important positions in his administration. Nor, as a businessman who had run his own moderately sized private company for several decades, had he ever had to answer to shareholders or a board of directors not dominated by himself.[1] (He "personally didn't like answering to a board of directors," Trump wrote.)[2] Instead, during decades as a real estate developer and franchiser of hotels, resorts, and casinos, Trump had grown used to acting on his own surrounded by a handful of family members and loyal subordinates. As the political scientist James Pfiffner has observed, Trump's "style of management during his real estate career was personal and informal," marked by "selective micro-management" and "a high premium on personal loyalty."[3] Nothing in his professional experience or presidential campaign made Trump think he needed to do things any differently as president. His campaign staff was not only small and loosely organized, it was "the Bad News Bears of Politics," in NBC correspondent Katy Tur's apt phrase, "the people the other candidates didn't pick."[4] But like the kids' baseball team of movie fame, they overcame long odds to win the election, contributing to Trump's sense that what had worked for him all his life would work in the White House as well.

It soon became clear that it would not, any more than the Bears' success at baseball meant they would have been a winning basketball team. For starters, Trump's ad hoc style ("I prefer to come to work each day and just see what develops," he wrote in his most famous book, *Trump: The Art of the Deal*) did not match up well with the body of law and tradition concerning transitions from one president to another that had developed since Congress passed the Presidential Transition Act in 1963.[5] The act, as amended in 1998, 2000, and 2016, directs the Government Services

Administration to provide office space, funding, and access to government services to each major-party nominee for president well in advance of the election. It also enjoins the outgoing president to appoint transition councils six months before the election to begin smoothing the way for the incoming administration. President George W. Bush's unprecedented helpfulness after Barack Obama was elected in 2008 inspired Obama to be equally solicitous to both Trump and Hillary Clinton once they secured their party's nominations in 2016. In addition, two donor-supported projects, the Center for Presidential Transitions of the Partnership for Public Service and the First Year Project of the University of Virginia's Miller Center, were formed to help whichever candidate was elected make a smooth and productive transition from election to inauguration.

On May 9, 2016, Trump appointed Governor Chris Christie of New Jersey to lead an intensive transition planning process that would generate a list of able candidates for each appointed position and help Trump flesh out his campaign promises with detailed advice from policy experts. On November 11, three days after the election, the president-elect fired Christie, who had been leading a team of more than one hundred. The governor, Trump thought, was trying to slip too many of his own people into the administration; he also had been judged insufficiently loyal in the aftermath of the *Access Hollywood* affair and was immersed in a political scandal of his own in New Jersey.[6] Not just Christie but also the extensive body of research his team had completed concerning policy and administration were tossed out.[7] As a result, the new president took office knowing little about what the executive branch does or who could run it on his behalf. When it comes to future presidential transitions, the political scientist John Burke concluded, "Donald Trump's experience will likely provide the textbook case on what not to do."[8]

STAFFING THE WHITE HOUSE

One consequence of Trump's lack of preparation was that, not having many ideas of his own about how the White House should be organized, he accepted the "institutional presidency" as he inherited it from his recent predecessors: a chief of staff with two deputies, a National Security Council (NSC) advisor and staff, a National Economic Council (NEC) director and staff, a Domestic Policy Council (DPC) director and staff, a communications director and press secretary, a White House counsel, a political director, a public liaison, and so on.[9] Unusually, Trump made the political strategist Steve Bannon "equal partners" with the chief of staff and awarded "assistant to the president" status (the highest rank on the White House staff) to twenty-nine individuals, considerably more than any recent new president.[10]

Trump's major intended organizational innovation was to create a new National Trade Council headed by trade hard-liner Peter Navarro, on an equal footing with the NSC, NEC, and DPC. Trump initially wanted to do so for the same reason previous presidents created new staff units: to underscore how important a matter they had emphasized during the campaign was to their governing agenda. But before launching the new council he was persuaded to downgrade it to a small Office of Trade and Manufacturing Policy. In September Navarro was further demoted when his office was folded into the NEC, which meant he was now reporting to NEC director Gary Cohn, the leading advocate within the White House of preserving multilateral trade agreements.[11]

Vice President Mike Pence had been the sort of running mate whom any Republican presidential nominee might have chosen; he was experienced as the third-ranking Republican in the House of Representatives and as governor of Indiana and enjoyed support from social, economic, and national security conservatives. Once in office, Trump assigned Pence all of the perquisites and responsibilities that vice presidents had been accumulating since the 1970s: a West Wing office, a professional staff, ready access to the president, and a wide-ranging role as senior advisor on virtually every issue.[12] Having gotten to know his colleagues well as a House leader, including several members who had been elected to the Senate by the time he became vice president, Pence also was Trump's most effective liaison to Republicans on Capitol Hill. He repaired (or at least patched) the previously testy relationship between the president and Speaker of the House Paul Ryan and worked to shepherd nominations and other measures through the congressional process.[13] In public Pence was perhaps more deferential to the president than any vice president in history.[14]

A second, less fortunate consequence of Trump's lack of relevant experience was that he filled most White House positions by drawing from the small circle of people with whom he became acquainted during his election campaign. These included Republican National Committee chair Reince Priebus as chief of staff, foreign policy advisor Michael Flynn as national security advisor, campaign spokesman Sean Spicer as press secretary, senior campaign strategist Bannon as senior political strategist, senior campaign policy advisor Stephen Miller as senior White House policy advisor, and election lawyer Donald McGahn as White House counsel. Not knowing these individuals very well, Trump also brought his daughter Ivanka Trump and her husband, Jared Kushner, into the West Wing as free-floating advisors. As the political scientist Paul Quirk has pointed out, despite having no experience in government, Kushner was charged with "possibly the most diverse substantive policy jurisdiction ever seen in the White House," including "lead responsibility for the Arab-Israeli conflict, governmental efficiency reforms, criminal justice reform, and the opioid crisis." Ivanka Trump pursued causes that captured her interest, such as persuading her father to propose paid family and medical leave and support a World Bank initiative to help woman entrepreneurs.[15] Abilities aside, Ivanka and Kushner's status made it awkward for staff members who lacked their strong personal connection with the president to disagree with them.

A third consequence of Trump's unfamiliarity with both staffing in general and his own staff (his daughter and son-in-law aside) in particular was that he placed aides in unusual relations to each other. Bannon was granted a seat on the NSC's Principals Committee, for example, but the chairman of the Joint Chiefs of Staff and the CIA director were assigned a merely advisory role. As Bannon's equal partner, Priebus was denied real authority to direct and discipline the rest of the staff. Spicer was undermined by Trump's barely concealed scorn for his handling of the press.[16] Lines of responsibility were notoriously unclear in the Trump White House. Factions formed based on ideological differences and personal rivalries. Staff members leaked disparaging comments about each other to the press corps.

Leakers from the Trump White House sometimes were publicly identified by name, with disastrous consequences for those who failed to make clear to journalistic confidants that their remarks were off the record. On July 26, 2017, five days after becoming Trump's second communications director, Anthony Scaramucci unleashed an obscenity-laced tirade in a phone call to the *New Yorker* reporter Ryan Lizza. He called Priebus a "f—ing paranoid schizophrenic" and said Bannon was "trying to build [his] own brand off the f—ing strength of the President." Within the White House, Scaramucci claimed, "me and the president" are the only "two fish that don't stink."[17] Priebus was let go the following day; four days after that, on July 31, Scaramucci's eleven-day tenure as communications director ended when he was fired as well. On August 15 Bannon told *American Prospect* editor Robert Kuttner that certain White House aides and State and Defense department officials were "wetting themselves" at the thought of invoking trade sanctions against China; he also bragged: "I'm changing out people at East Asian Defense; I'm getting hawks in. I'm getting [acting director of Bureau of East Asian and Pacific Affairs] Susan Thornton out of State." Bannon, whose portrayal in the media as Trump's puppet master was resented by the president and whose remark to Kuttner that "there's no military solution [to North Korea's nuclear threats]—forget it" infuriated Priebus's successor as chief of staff, four-star Marine Corps General John F. Kelly, was shown the door four days later.[18]

Talented prospective appointees, turned off by the ongoing turmoil, declined to join Trump's staff. A general air of chaos prevailed. By the end of Trump's second hundred days as president, the White House had seen the firing or resignation of his first national security advisor, chief of staff, deputy chief of staff, chief strategist, press secretary, and other aides, notably two communications directors. Additional removals, including the head of the Office of Public Liaison and another deputy chief of staff, soon followed. By November, most of Trump's original staff was gone. "I'm doing a great job, but my staff sucks," he complained.[19] "No modern presidency, going all the way back to FDR's, experienced so much and so early change in personnel," according to Burke.[20]

Even while still on the job, Spicer, Priebus, and others were so widely rumored to be on the chopping block that they were rendered ineffectual. Trump made his dissatisfaction with Spicer obvious to the point that he was unable to represent the president effectively to the White House press corps. More significantly, Priebus was never empowered to perform the core functions— so essential to the smooth functioning of an administration—of a chief of staff. In the consensus view of presidential scholars and former occupants of the position, a chief of staff must be able to shape the flow of advice and information to the president in a way that faithfully represents the range of perspectives within the administration, as well as to communicate, monitor, and enforce the president's decisions to the staff and cabinet once he has made them. End runs around the chief of staff by others in the White House who put their own memos on the president's desk or drop by the Oval Office to bend his ear—and then leak their displeasure to reporters if their advice is not followed—are anathema to a smoothly functioning presidency. As a longtime party apparatchik, Priebus lacked the stature with Trump to impose these strictures on a former businessman whose style was to "leave my door open. You can't be imaginative or entrepreneurial if you've got too much structure."[21] Nor did Trump or those around him who had served loyally during the election campaign fully trust Priebus, who as RNC chair had advised him to abandon his candidacy after the *Access Hollywood* tape was released. Trump also resented Priebus's strategy of slow-walking the president's impulsive orders to, for example, impose steel tariffs on China or fire Attorney General Jeff Sessions until cooler heads could prevail.[22]

As a former general and the administration's highly successful secretary of homeland security until becoming White House chief of staff on July 31, Kelly had the stature Priebus lacked in Trump's eyes. He was able to persuade the president that despite his claims of "No White House chaos!" and "The White House is functioning beautifully," some sweeping changes were needed to align the staff with the best practices of previous administrations.[23] As was the case in other recent presidencies, either Kelly or one of his deputies (typically, staff secretary Robert Porter) would review all briefing materials before they went to the president.[24] At the heart of the process were "decision memos" that integrated the perspectives of the relevant departments, agencies, and staff members only after passing through the appropriate policy council: NEC, NSC, or DPC. Kelly decided which staff members would meet with Trump and when, as well as who would attend the mandatory meetings of various staff units. "When we go in to see him now, rather than onesies and twosies, we go in and help him collectively understand what he needs to understand to make these vital decisions," Kelly said.[25]

At Kelly's direction, executive orders were widely vetted within the administration before being issued.[26] The authority of Flynn's replacement as national security advisor, three-star army General H. R. McMaster, to fire staff members such as Bannon favorites Ezra Cohen-Watnick and Sebastian Gorka was buttressed. Undisciplined aides, notably Scaramucci and Bannon himself, were dismissed. Miller, a close Bannon ally, remained, however, both as the policy advisor to whom the DPC reported on important issues and as the president's chief speechwriter. His influence with Trump, to whom he was fiercely loyal, grew steadily, especially on matters related to immigration and refugees.[27] For example, in summer 2017 Miller for the first time involved the DPC in the decision to set the number of refugees admitted into the United States in the coming year, traditionally an NSC decision. Under Miller's influence, the number was reduced by more than half.[28]

Less clear was how sustainable Kelly's model, tried and tested as it was in multiple previous administrations, would be over time. Staff members Kushner and Ivanka Trump promised that they would not take advantage of their family connection to the president by operating outside the structure, and Kushner's long list of duties gradually was reduced to a more realistic level, with a particular focus on the Middle East.[29] Trump reportedly said, "I now have time to think."[30] Shrewdly, Kelly resolved from the start that he would confine his changes to the staff, not the president, who would be free to watch cable news programs, tweet, and make public comments as he wished. "I was not brought to this job to control anything but the flow of information to our president," said Kelly—certainly not to "control him."[31] Without success, Kelly did ask Trump to allow aides to vet his tweets before posting them.[32] Even Trump's lawyers were unable to restrain him from posting indiscreet tweets that, as shown in chapter 7, could later be used in court to discredit his motives for certain executive actions.[33]

As Kelly and others found, the long-term reining in of a seventy-one-year-old man who rose high in the business and entertainment worlds and was elected president by doing things in a loose, personal, and spontaneous way was not easy to accomplish. Offhandedly, with Kelly present but not consulted, Trump publicly reacted to a North Korean missile test on August 9 by threatening to rain down "fire and fury like the world has never seen."[34] Advised six days later not to take questions from the press after reading a statement about his plans for an infrastructure program, Trump not only took questions but made provocative remarks about the previous weekend's riot in Charlottesville that seemed to equate racist demonstrators with those who were protesting their appearance, thereby sparking controversy for weeks and completely overshadowing everything he came to say about the need to repair the nation's highways and bridges. Offered a carefully written speech urging national unity for an appearance in Phoenix one week later, Trump lurched instead from attacks on the state's Republican senators to hints that he would pardon a controversial convicted sheriff to complaints that the press corps were "truly dishonest people."[35] Longtime Trump associate Roger Stone warned: "General Kelly is trying to treat the president like a mushroom. Keeping him in the dark and feeding him shit is not going to work. Donald Trump is a free spirit."[36] Kelly himself attracted controversy in October when, stepping into the spotlight, he made off-the-mark comments about matters such as Trump critic Representative Frederica Wilson and the origins of the Civil War.[37] "He violated the first basic rule of the chief of staff, which is not to make yourself the news of the day," said former Clinton chief of staff Leon Panetta, an admirer of Kelly.[38]

Trump's Charlottesville remarks rippled out through his administration. His leading economic advisor, NEC director Cohn, seriously (and publicly) considered resigning in protest but decided that "as a patriotic American, I am reluctant to leave my post."[39] Trump did not like it, but he could not help but take note that the stock market dropped nearly 300 points on rumors that Cohn might quit. Leading business executives resigned from two presidential advisory councils, the Strategic and Policy Forum and the American Manufacturing Council. To prevent others who intended to resign from carrying out their plan, Trump disbanded the councils. In an implicit rebuke of their commander in chief, the four-star officers who lead every branch of the military—army, navy, marines, air force, coast guard, and national guard—publicly expressed their distaste for racism and extremism. All sixteen members of the President's Committee on the Arts and the Humanities resigned. For a Republican president to lose the support of generally left-leaning artists, actors, and authors was unremarkable. But to be publicly reproached by the corporate sector, a leading GOP constituency, and the military was unprecedented. The depth of disapproval by the generally conservative Republican officer corps was especially unusual. A November poll found that only 31 percent of officers approved of Trump's performance as president.[40]

An axiom of staffing for presidents who lack experience in the federal government is to stock the White House with people who have that experience and then rely on their judgment. Trump took a different approach. The result was that a president who had never spent a day in office was surrounded by advisors who had never spent a day in office—with consequences that were all too predictable.

CHOOSING THE CABINET

Trump was equally unfamiliar with the talent pool from which presidents usually draw cabinet members and their high-ranking subordinates: the secretaries, deputy secretaries, undersecretaries, and assistant secretaries who do the real work of leadership in the executive branch. Without them, the change-resistant (especially to Republican changes) permanent civil service, few of whose members voted for Trump, would be free to keep doing things as they had under his Democratic predecessor.[41] In filling the most important executive positions, Trump was drawn to people who had succeeded in domains he respected—business (ExxonMobil chief executive Rex Tillerson as secretary of state, investor Steven Mnuchin as secretary of the treasury, and former Lilly USA president Alex Azar as his second secretary of health and human services) and, in a carryover from his years as a student at the New York Military Academy, the military (four-star army General James Mattis as secretary of defense, General Kelly as secretary of homeland security and, six months later, as White House chief of staff)—as well as to the small set of Republican politicians who had supported him in the election, notably Senator Jeff Sessions as attorney general and Ben Carson, who sought the party's presidential nomination before dropping out and endorsing Trump, as secretary of housing and urban development.

Most of Trump's other cabinet appointees were members of Congress or political figures whose names he got from Pence.[42] As Bannon recalled, immediately after winning the election Trump was "thinking, 'Hey, I've got to put together a government. I've got to really staff up something. I need to embrace the establishment.'" In Bannon's view, shared by few others, that was "the original sin of the administration."[43]

Pence was exceptionally well-wired in established conservative circles, and his recommendations reflected that. Several cabinet nominees were actively hostile to their new departments and agencies. As a House member from Georgia, Tom Price had strongly opposed the Affordable Care Act; as secretary of the Department of Health and Human Services (HHS), Obamacare was part of his jurisdiction. Azar, Price's successor, was one of several HHS appointees whom Pence knew well from Indiana. Trump's nominee for secretary of the interior, Representative Ryan Zinke of Montana, was less interested in preserving the 500 million acres of mostly western federal land that the department manages than in opening parts of it to mining, grazing, and oil and gas exploration. Scott Pruitt, whom Trump appointed as director of the Environmental Protection Agency, had sued to overturn EPA regulations multiple times as attorney general of Oklahoma. On more than one occasion when Pence was governor, Indiana had joined the suits. Famously, former Texas governor Rick Perry placed the Department of Energy on the list of three federal departments he wanted to abolish while seeking the 2012 Republican presidential nomination—only to forget its name in a debate ("Sorry. Oops.").[44] Perry became Trump's choice as secretary of energy. Representative Mick Mulvaney of South Carolina, a Freedom Caucus stalwart in the House, regarded his appointment as director of the Office of Management and Budget as an opportunity to abolish or shrink a range of mostly domestic federal programs.[45] In late November Mulvaney earned double duty as Trump's choice to temporarily head the Consumer Financial Protection Bureau, which he had described as a "sick, sad case" while serving in Congress.[46]

As discussed in chapter 8, early tensions arose between the president and Secretary of State Tillerson on several foreign policy matters, including NATO, Qatar, and Iran, as well as about Trump's comments after the violence in Charlottesville. Tillerson's experience as the head of a major publicly traded corporation, in which he was accountable to a board of directors and shareholders, headed a complex organizational hierarchy, and embraced diversity in hiring and promotion, was very different from the president's background in business. Trump and Secretary of Defense Mattis butted heads concerning what to do in Afghanistan and how to handle transgender men and women in uniform, although Mattis's four stars and affable demeanor kept him in the president's good graces. Trump rebuked HHS secretary Price for his use of expensive charter flights to travel around the country. "I am not happy about it, and I let him know it," the president said on September 27.[47] Price resigned two days later.

Relations grew especially acid between Trump and Sessions over the attorney general's decision to recuse himself from any Justice Department investigation of Russia's role in the election after it was revealed during his Senate confirmation hearings that he had falsely denied having "communications with the Russians." Sessions had no choice in the matter: his department's regulations require that "no employee shall participate in a criminal investigation or prosecution if he has a personal or political relationship."[48] But in an Oval Office meeting in May, Trump called Sessions an "idiot" and demanded that he resign.[49] Aides talked him out of accepting the resignation letter Sessions sent, but two months later, in tweets and interviews, the president publicly decried Sessions as "VERY weak" and "disappoint[ing]," declaring that he wished he had "picked someone else."[50] Outside of his immediate family, loyalty was something Trump demanded but did not give. He did not even meet with his cabinet until June 12. At that televised gathering, participants tried to overcome their uncertain status with the president by vying to outdo each other in professing the "honor," "blessing," and "privilege" they felt at serving him. Only Mattis declined to join in, professing instead his "honor to represent the men and women of the Department of Defense."[51]

Urged on by grassroots Democrats who were reflexively against everything Trump was for, Democratic senators assumed an unprecedentedly adversarial stance in the Senate confirmation process that presidential nominees for positions outside the White House must undergo. Democratic National Committee chair Thomas Perez set the tone by rousing his party to hit Trump "between the eyes with a two-by-four."[52] All but five Senate Democrats voted against the relatively uncontroversial Tillerson, the most opposition any nominee for secretary of state has ever received. All but one voted against Sessions, whom most Democrats knew as a friend and fellow senator; breaching protocol toward a senator nominated to a cabinet post, a fellow senator, Democrat Cory Booker of New Jersey, testified against his nomination. Betsy DeVos, whose longtime support for private-school vouchers made her anathema to the public-school teachers unions that are a bedrock of the Democratic coalition, was confirmed as secretary of education only because Vice President Pence broke a tie Senate vote, the first time this had ever happened for a cabinet nominee. Because the Democrats had abolished the filibuster for all but Supreme Court appointments in 2013, when they controlled the Senate and Obama was president, Trump was able to form his cabinet with Republican votes. But Democratic delaying tactics meant that the confirmation process for cabinet members took much longer than in the past, an average twenty-five days each compared with two days for Obama's nominees, one day for Clinton's, and zero days for Bush's.[53]

Trump's main problem in forming an administration, however, was not the Democrats but rather his own slowness in filling most of the hundreds of subcabinet positions that department heads rely on to help lead their organizations. As late as the end of July, Trump had failed to nominate candidates for 379—more than two-thirds—of 566 key positions in the executive branch, hampered by a selection process that valued loyalty above competence and gave a half-dozen quarreling White House aides veto power over possible nominees.[54] Tillerson, for example, after firing most of Obama's high-ranking appointees from the State Department, was stymied in his efforts to replace them with experienced Republicans by staff members' objections on grounds of disloyalty to Trump. Tillerson in turn found the staff's suggested nominees unacceptable on grounds of incompetence. The root of the problem was that almost the entire Republican foreign policy community had publicly opposed Trump's election, which meant that the mutually acceptable talent pool was virtually dry.[55] So thin was the bench of Trump supporters that when he introduced his small foreign policy team to reporters during the campaign, it included one who was later brought before a grand jury investigating Russian involvement in the election (Carter Page), another who later pleaded guilty to lying to the FBI about his contacts with the Russians (George Papadopoulos), and a third, General Flynn, who was fired after twenty-four days as national security advisor for misleading the vice president about his own contacts with Russians.[56]

Overall, only 49 of Trump's 187 actual nominees—just 26 percent—had been confirmed by the Senate by late July, compared with 201 at the midpoint of Obama's first year and 185 at Bush's first-year midpoint.[57] Ten of fifteen cabinet departments lacked a deputy secretary (second in the departmental chain of command), and 163 of 169 undersecretary and assistant secretary positions remained unfilled. Kelly's move from the cabinet to the White House left the Department of Homeland Security without a secretary for seven weeks until Trump nominated Kirstjen Nielsen, Kelly's closest aide both at the department and in the White House, to succeed him in mid-October.[58] Price's firing left HHS unled for seven weeks until Trump nominated Azar to succeed him. As with the staff, numerous potential candidates for departmental leadership posts, turned off by the perceived chaos within the Trump White House and by the president's humiliation of Sessions, refused to be considered. Instead, Trump assigned junior White House staff members to each department to monitor the secretaries' behavior.[59] Confirmed nominations rose only to 152 by early October, compared with 334 for Obama and 355 for Bush at an identical point in their first years.[60]

Many of Trump's early innovations when forming the administration were soon abandoned. After Flynn was forced out as national security advisor, his successor, General McMaster, insisted not only that Bannon be removed from the NSC's Principals Committee but also that Joint Chiefs chairman Joseph Dunford and CIA director Mike Pompeo be added.[61] Cabinet members ignored the junior staffers sent to their departments; when one of them told Secretary of Transportation Elaine Chao that he needed to sign off on her decisions, she asked, "What's your name again?"[62] Eventually the junior staffers were withdrawn.

Trump never did understand that his disinclination to fill many executive jobs was only making his cabinet members and agency heads more dependent on the permanent civil service, which felt no loyalty to him. In February he said, "I look at some of these jobs and . . . I say, 'What do all these people do?' "[63] Eight months later he was just as oblivious: "I'm not going to make a lot of these appointments that would normally be—you don't need them."[64] On the eve of a twelve-day trip to Asia in November, Trump said, "I'm the only one that matters. . . . I'm a business person, and I tell my people, when you don't need to fill slots don't fill them," a fine sentiment for the hands-on leader of a small operation but, for the president, a certain formula for bureaucratic inertia.[65] On October 26, for example, when Trump officially proclaimed the nation's opioid addiction crisis a public health emergency, the effort to combat it was hamstrung by the absence of an HHS secretary, a Drug Enforcement Administration director, an Office of National Drug Control Policy director, and a homeland security secretary.[66] Quietly, to break the logjam, Kelly began delegating the power to make subcabinet appointments to cabinet members.[67]

In developing domestic and foreign policies in his first year, Trump was frequently surprised to learn that impressions he had formed outside government were misplaced. "Nobody knew that health care could be so complicated," he said, a turnabout from his claim during the campaign that "nobody knows more about health care than Donald Trump."[68] Mattis quickly convinced Trump to defer to the general's view that torture is ineffective.[69] The Chinese were "not currency manipulators," as Trump often had charged, and they lacked the power to dictate policy to North Korea, another assumption abandoned. "After listening [to Chinese president Xi Jinping] for ten minutes," the president said, "I realized that it's not so easy."[70] During the campaign Trump promised, "My Number One priority is to dismantle the disastrous nuclear deal with Iran."[71] Twice during his first six months in office he certified that Iran was fulfilling its pledge not to build nuclear weapons. Secretary of Agriculture Sonny Perdue initially backed Trump off his campaign promise to abandon the North American Free Trade Agreement by showing him a map of where export-dependent farmers live. "It shows that I do have a very big farmer base," the president replied. "I'm going to help them."[72] He also confessed, "This is more work than in my previous life. I thought it would be easier."[73]

4 ★ EXECUTIVE ACTION

In the modern era, presidents—especially those whose party controls Congress—usually have turned to unilateral executive action as the primary means of pursuing their goals only after their efforts to secure legislation have failed. Bill Clinton, George W. Bush, and Barack Obama, for example, all came to rely heavily on executive action late in their tenure, after Congress fell into the hands of the opposition party. But each began with a chiefly legislative strategy to achieve major policy goals: the Family and Medical Leave Act and a major deficit-reduction plan (Clinton); a massive tax cut and the No Child Left Behind Act (Bush); and the American Recovery and Reinvestment Act and the Affordable Care Act (Obama).

Donald Trump chose not to adhere to this pattern. As a candidate he had complained that Obama was "a president who can't get anything done, so he just keeps signing executive orders all over the place.... I want to do away with executive orders for the most part."[1] Trump's main bastion of institutional support in Washington when he took office was the Republican Congress. During his first year, most congressional Republicans were reluctant to oppose the president and thereby invite primary challenges from ambitious contenders who shared their Republican constituents' enthusiasm for Trump. Among Republican voters he retained a job approval rating above 80 percent even as his overall rating slid below 40 percent in mid-May and settled at that level for months to come.[2] The executive branch was initially less reliable. Trump's White House staff was inexperienced and divided. Except for cabinet members, the top layers of the executive departments and agencies were mostly unoccupied throughout nearly all of his first year. This left both staff and cabinet unusually dependent on career civil servants, who in most cases (Immigration and Customs Enforcement and Border Patrol excepted) were unsympathetic to the new president's agenda.[3]

Yet instead of turning to Congress with most of his major policy initiatives—the equivalent in the world of publicly traded corporations of securing approval from a board of directors—Trump's very different business experience in private companies prompted him to issue a flurry of executive orders and take other unilateral actions throughout his first year. He detached himself from his majority party in Congress not at the end of his tenure, but from the beginning.[4] In a press release issued at the end of his first one hundred days in office, the White House bragged about what Candidate Trump had decried, that he had signed more executive orders than any president since Harry S. Truman.[5]

The appeal of executive action is that it lies within the president's own authority. In some cases this authority is constitutionally grounded in Article II clauses, especially the vesting clause ("the executive Power shall be vested in a President of the United States of America"); the take-care clause ("he shall take Care that the Laws be faithfully executed"); and the pardon clause ("he shall have Power to grant Reprieves and Pardons for Offenses against the United States, except in cases of Impeachment"). In a wide range of other instances, legislation passed by Congress has authorized the president to act according to his discretion in applying the law. With cameras present, Trump was able to sign a series of executive actions—orders, proclamations, memorandums, and, in one case, a pardon—without having to wait for Congress to enact new laws and send them to his desk.

Executive actions entail certain disadvantages, which is why presidents usually turn to them as a last rather than a first resort. For one thing, an executive order can be undone by another order by a subsequent president. Starting with Ronald Reagan in 1981, for example, every change of party in the White House has witnessed the immediate issuance of an executive order that either forbids (Reagan and his Republican successors, including Trump) or allows (Clinton and his Democratic successor) giving foreign aid to nongovernmental agencies that offer women abortion counseling or referrals.

For another, such actions often are of limited effectiveness. An order cannot repeal a regulation that already has undergone the Administrative Procedures Act's lengthy "notice-and-comment" process. All the order can do is launch a new, equally onerous notice-and-comment process aimed at undoing the regulation, and even then the new process must result in what the Supreme Court has called "a reasoned basis" to explain why the old regulation was wrong and the new one is right.[6] Trump took aim at Obama's 2015 anti-coal Clean Power Plan, for instance, but to undo it will entail a years-long process, an alternative plan for reducing carbon emissions, and a series of legal challenges—with no guarantee of success.[7] When EPA director Scott Pruitt moved to suspend a regulation that restricts methane emissions from new oil and gas wells, a federal appeals court voided his decision as "unreasonable," "arbitrary," and "capricious" and said that he would have to launch the required notice-and-comment process to have any chance of prevailing.[8]

In many cases, however, executive actions by the Trump administration were effective in advancing his goals. For example, Trump signed an order redirecting $100 million from existing federal job-training funds to new apprenticeship programs.[9] Many more such initiatives were aimed at rolling back Obama-administration regulations, sometimes through legislation (see chapter 6) but more often through executive action. Trump issued a freeze on federal hiring that made exceptions for "national security or public safety," thereby allowing the parts of the executive branch that Republicans favor—namely the Departments of Defense and Homeland Security—to grow while shrinking the work force in the domestic agencies favored by Democrats.[10] "Indeed," wrote the political scientist Daniel W. Drezner, "this might be the Trump administration's most significant policy achievement to date," at least in comparison to its other, mostly limited achievements.[11]

The range of the administration's executive actions against decisions made by its predecessor was wide. In foreign policy, Trump abandoned the Trans-Pacific Partnership and curtailed aspects of Obama's outreach to the Cuban government.[12] On June 1 he announced that the United States would withdraw from the two-hundred-nation Paris climate accord negotiated by Obama and "see if we can make a deal that's fair. And if we can, that's great. And if we can't, that's fine."[13] In any event, withdrawal from the accord was a three-year process that, after Nicaragua signed it in October and Syria did so in November, would leave the United States the only nonsignatory country in the world. Trump knew that any effort to persuade Congress to repeal the 2010 Dodd-Frank Act would be thwarted by a Democratic filibuster in the Senate, but his treasury secretary, Steven Mnuchin, quickly targeted nearly ninety banking and financial regulations issued under the law for repeal or reassessment.[14] Secretary of Transportation Elaine Chao withdrew an Obama-administration plan to allow cities to reserve jobs on federally funded public works programs for local residents.[15]

Trump's Department of Health and Human Services (HHS), initially led by the ardent Affordable Care Act (ACA) opponent Tom Price, shrank the advertising budget for encouraging people to enroll by 90 percent, reduced grants to nonprofit "navigators" that help smooth the enrollment process for potential beneficiaries by 43 percent, posted anti-Obamacare videos on its website, and tweeted messages such as "Obamacare is flawed, failing, and harming the American people."[16] With an eye toward giving states the enhanced control of Medicaid administratively that the failed Obamacare-repeal effort in Congress had tried to give them legislatively, Price and the Center for Medicare and Medicaid Services administrator Seema Verma also targeted a host of Obama-era regulations imposed on doctors, hospitals, insurers, and nursing homes.[17] And on October 6, with Price fired and not yet replaced, HHS restricted an Obama-administration requirement that employers and insurers provide free birth control coverage to women by creating exceptions based on "sincerely held" religious beliefs or moral convictions.[18]

Trump's assault on the ACA was relentless but only partially effective. On October 12 he signed an executive order telling three departments to develop plans to allow small businesses of a similar kind to band together in "association health plans" and offer policies with fewer benefits at a lower cost than Obamacare required. Such plans could also be sold across state lines, something the ACA forbade. Workers who were between jobs would be able to buy short-term insurance for nearly a year at a time, not the three months allowed by the ACA. Both new plans would be freer from state and federal regulation than had previously been the case, and critics warned that as younger and healthier people flocked to them in order to reduce their premiums, health insurance costs would rise for the remaining population of older and sicker individuals.[19]

The next day the administration announced that it would discontinue about $9 billion in "cost-sharing reduction" subsidies for health insurance companies to help cover the out-of-pocket expenses of about 6 million low-income people, claiming that the Obama administration had no legal authority to initiate the program under which these payments were made.[20] Absent the subsidies, premiums were expected to rise still more and some insurance companies seemed likely to withdraw from Obamacare unless a legislative remedy was found.[21]

On the eve of issuing his Obamacare-related orders, Trump grandly tweeted, "Since Congress can't get its act together on HealthCare, I will be using the power of the pen to give great HealthCare to many people—FAST."[22] The reality was less impressive. The ACA remained the law of the land in most respects. Most people, including employees of large companies, universities, and nonprofits; government at all levels; and those covered by Medicare and Medicaid, would not be affected by Trump's proposed changes. The elimination of subsidies to insurance companies was offset to some extent by tax credits that continued to help low-income people pay their insurance premiums—if the cost of insurance rose, so would the size of the credits.[23] Other changes would have to wait on the extended notice-and-comment process that was guaranteed to ensue, as departments drafted new rules and a lengthy public comment period followed. Litigants immediately lined up to challenge Trump's new orders in court.

Not all of the rules issued by the Obama administration had taken the form of formal regulations. Some were "guidances," which technically are not binding because they have not been through the notice-and-comment process but often are treated as such by those at whom they are aimed. Trump's labor secretary, R. Alexander Acosta, withdrew some of his predecessor's recent guidances, including one that extended minimum wage and overtime pay to Uber-style "gig-economy" workers whom companies treat as independent contractors rather than employees.[24] In a widely reported speech in late September, Secretary of Education Betsy DeVos took strong exception to the Obama-era Education Department's guidance to colleges and universities that when adjudicating claims of sexual assault they eschew mediation in favor of formal hearings and use a "preponderance of evidence" standard of judgment, sometimes described as "50 percent plus a feather."

Arguing that this had led institutions of higher education to create "kangaroo courts" unfairly stacked against the accused, DeVos opened a public comment period as a step on the way to issuing a new set of formal rules.[25] Later that month, her department's civil rights office rescinded the Obama-administration guidance, freeing institutions of higher education to employ a "clear and convincing evidence" standard and allow for mediation while the new rules were being formulated.

Despite Trump's resentment of him for allowing the special counsel to be appointed, no one pursued the president's agenda more faithfully and effectively than Attorney General Jeff Sessions. He reversed an Obama-administration guidance to U.S. attorneys and federal agencies that employers could not discriminate against transgender individuals.[26] At Sessions's initiative, the Justice Department also changed its position in multiple cases before the federal courts. Justice lawyers would defend, not attack, Texas's voter identification law, for example, as well as oppose an Army Corps of Engineers ban on firearms on Corps property. A Trump executive order directing Sessions to issue guidelines for protecting religious liberty led him to argue in a workplace discrimination case that the Civil Rights Act of 1964 does not protect workers on the basis of sexual orientation.[27] In addition, according to the attorney general's interpretation, the act's protections against discrimination on the basis of sex would be enforced only for men and women, not transgender individuals. Nonetheless, Trump said he was "very frustrated" to learn that on criminal matters the president was "not supposed to be involved with the Justice Department. I'm not supposed to be involved with the FBI." His frustration was chiefly rooted in the appointment of a special counsel to investigate Russian involvement in his election campaign and in the department's unwillingness to continue "going after Hillary Clinton."[28] "Everybody is asking why the Justice Department (and FBI) isn't looking into all the dishonesty going on with Crooked

Hillary & Dems," he tweeted with considerable exaggeration on November 3.[29] Days later, Sessions asked career prosecutors in his department whether he should appoint another special counsel to do so, in apparent violation of the long-standing democratic norm that those who win elections should not use the power of the state to seek revenge against their defeated opponents.[30]

Sessions aside, few Trump cabinet members were more ardent in their assault on regulations issued by their Democratic predecessors than EPA director Pruitt and Interior Secretary Ryan Zinke. Pruitt, who as attorney general of Oklahoma had come to know the agency well by filing fourteen lawsuits against it, sought to replace dozens of regulations that the president's business and agricultural supporters disliked. These included repealing the Waters of the United States rule, which had expanded the list of waters protected by the EPA to include not just large ones like the Mississippi River and Chesapeake Bay but also the wetlands and tributaries that flow into them; lifting the ban on offshore oil drilling in the Arctic, Atlantic, and Pacific Oceans; and delaying and potentially reducing fuel-efficiency standards for motor vehicles.[31] In response to an executive order by Trump that the lands presidents had made national monuments during the previous twenty years be reviewed, Zinke proposed removing monument status from parts of at least four large pieces of western territory to free them up for grazing, logging, and mining.[32] He also called a halt to a study of the health risks of coal mining that involves mountaintop removal, which Obama had ordered.[33] In early October the *New York Times* counted twenty-five environmental rules that the Trump administration already had overturned and twenty-seven more repeal efforts that were under way.[34]

Several of these executive actions concerning the environment —or sometimes just the prospect of them—provoked opposition in the courts. On three occasions during the Trump administration's first nine months, federal judges overturned EPA or

Department of the Interior initiatives for short-circuiting the notice-and-comment process; on three others, the administration backed off as soon as a lawsuit was filed.[35] Dissent also arose within the departments and agencies, where civil servants consulted outgoing Obama appointees about how to push back against the new president's directives.[36] The legal scholar Jack Goldsmith reported that "online guides for how to 'resist from below' or to 'dissent from within'" were posted immediately after the election. Twitter accounts with anonymous tags like @alt_labor and @Rogue_DoD appeared as vehicles for sharing damaging information about the administration.[37] Numerous civil servants in the EPA, State Department, and Justice Department resigned rather than pursue the new president's policies, even as Hillary Clinton urged them to remain in the agencies "being targeted by the administration" because "the country is going to need you."[38] Still others stayed in place while leaking information about controversial policies and practices to supportive interest groups, congressional staff members, and reporters. For example, in August complete transcripts of Trump's phone calls with the leaders of Mexico and Australia were leaked to the *Washington Post*, which posted them.[39] Equally without precedent, information gathered by the National Security Agency in the course of surveilling Russian officials, including information incidentally collected about American citizens, was made public. Trump's first national security advisor, General Michael Flynn, was undone by a leak that revealed his discussions about sanctions with the Russian ambassador, quickly leading to his dismissal.

Resistance also came in the form of endless meetings, reports, and consultations within the departments. "You're going to see the bureaucrats using time to their advantage," a Justice Department official told the *Washington Post* in late January.[40] Long-serving civil servants, experts in the work of their agencies, almost never said no to an order from Trump's appointees. Instead, they said

words to the effect of, "we're on it but it's complicated." In desperation Zinke, who told an audience of oil and gas executives, "I got
30 percent of the crew that's not loyal to the flag," moved about
fifty high-ranking Senior Executive Service officials to different
positions so he could replace them with more cooperative executives, provoking an investigation by the department's inspector
general.[41] With so few subcabinet appointees in place to direct the
permanent government's efforts, it sometimes was hard for cabinet members to follow through successfully on their and the president's bold orders.

A remarkable outbreak of open resistance occurred when, in
a series of tweets on July 26, 2017, Trump responded impulsively
to pressure from some House Freedom Caucus members and
reversed a year-old Obama-administration order by declaring,
"After consultation with my Generals and military experts, please
be advised that the United States Government will not allow Transgender individuals to serve in any capacity in the U.S. Military."[42] It
was not clear who "my Generals" were. Neither retired U.S. Marine
general and Secretary of Defense James Mattis nor national security advisor and army general H. R. McMaster knew what Trump
intended to do until the day before he did it.[43] The head of the
Coast Guard vowed to "not break faith" with his service's transgender members. The chairman of the Joint Chiefs of Staff pointed out
that a tweet had no legal status.[44] Retreating while trying to save
face, Trump issued a formal order to Secretary Mattis on August 25
to conduct a six-month study of the issue while leaving currently
serving transgender soldiers, sailors, and airmen at least temporarily in place. The order granted Mattis wide discretion concerning how these individuals should be treated in the future. The
president huffed that he wanted to prevent additional transgender
people from enlisting, but only if Mattis did not "provide a recommendation to the contrary that I find convincing."[45] In any event,
on October 30 a federal district court judge in Washington, D.C.,

Colleen Kollar-Kotelly, stayed the ban on constitutional grounds, and two weeks later the Pentagon approved gender-reassignment surgery for transgender service members.[46]

In other instances events caused the Trump administration to reconsider orders it had issued. In mid-August, as part of an order to streamline the approval process for new roads, bridges, pipelines, and other infrastructure projects, the administration repealed the Obama-issued Federal Flood Risk Management Standard that required federally funded roads and houses to be built high enough off the ground to withstand the flooding expected from the stronger storms that climate change augured.[47] Two weeks later, Hurricane Harvey battered Texas and Louisiana with rain, wind, and massive flooding, followed in short order by Hurricane Irma, which did similar damage to Florida and parts of neighboring coastal states, and Hurricane Maria, which devastated Puerto Rico. Trump benefited from the much-improved capabilities of the Federal Emergency Management Agency (FEMA) since its ineffective response to Hurricane Katrina in 2005, as well as the close coordination between FEMA and the affected state and local governments, which had badly bungled Katrina relief in New Orleans. As for his order lifting the ban on low-level construction in floodplains, that would now be reconsidered.[48]

Trump's most controversial executive action came on August 25, when he pardoned Joe Arpaio, the former sheriff of Maricopa County, Arizona. Arpaio had recently been convicted of criminal contempt by a federal judge for refusing to obey an order to stop detaining immigrants without cause and was awaiting sentencing. Trump had clear constitutional authority to issue this pardon; as the Supreme Court ruled in *Ex Parte Garland* in 1866, the pardon power "is unlimited" and therefore "not subject to legislative control."[49] Most presidential pardons are the product of a lengthy and elaborate process that culminates in an expression of remorse by the recipient and a recommendation by the Justice Department's Office of the Pardon Attorney. This one was impulsive on the president's part and unaccompanied by remorse from Arpaio. But other recent presidents had acted on their own soon after taking office, including Gerald R. Ford, who pardoned former president Richard Nixon, and Jimmy Carter, who pardoned more than twelve thousand draft evaders in the Vietnam War. Both presidents paid a political price for their action, but each thought it essential to national healing in the aftermath of Watergate and Vietnam. Critics of Trump's action saw in it no civic purpose and concentrated on the sheriff's status as a law enforcement official who refused to enforce the law, which made his pardon appear a betrayal of the president's constitutional duty to "take Care that the Laws be faithfully executed."[50] Trump seems to have been motivated by loyalty to a political supporter who had endorsed his candidacy and even his anti-Obama birther campaign, as well as by a desire to reinforce his public stance in opposition to illegal immigration and in favor of tough policing.

Trump campaigned for president in 2016 by promising to drive out the "at least 11 million people that came in this country illegally," including children smuggled into the United States by their parents. In 2012, after failing to persuade Congress to pass the DREAM Act, which would have granted these children legal status, Obama had issued an executive order to create the Deferred Action for Childhood Arrivals (DACA) program. Under DACA, most "Dreamers" could obtain work permits that were valid for two years and renewable based on good behavior. By the time Trump took office, more than seven hundred thousand permits had been granted, mostly to childhood immigrants now in their twenties. An additional Obama order in 2014 to create the Deferred Action for Parents of Americans (DAPA) program was overturned by federal courts the following year, and Trump revoked it in June 2017. Although DACA remained in place, nine conservative state attorneys general told Sessions that they intended to file a lawsuit against it on September 5 unless the administration agreed to end the program.[51] All were from states that Trump had carried overwhelmingly in the election.

Sessions, who strongly opposed DACA and encouraged the state attorneys general, told Trump that the Justice Department would not defend in court what he regarded as the unconstitutional executive order with which Obama created it. He also predicted that the lawsuit would succeed because the courts would find the program to be in violation of existing immigration law.[52] Although Trump's attitude toward the Dreamers had softened—he said in April that they could "rest easy" because he was "not after the Dreamers, we are after the criminals"—and multiple Republican corporate and party leaders urged him to leave DACA in place, the president authorized Sessions to announce on September 5 that the program would end in six months, a deadline that Trump later seemed open to extending.[53] If Congress wanted to preserve DACA, it would have to enact legislation to do so. The president indicated that he would be favorably inclined to sign such a law, at least in principle. He also undercut Sessions by tweeting that if Congress did not act, "I will revisit this issue!" rather than automatically end the program.[54]

On the broader subject of immigration, one of the first executive orders Trump issued after becoming president was his least successful in one way but perhaps his most successful in another. One week after taking office, he issued an order to ban entry to the United States to visitors, even those with a visa, from seven predominantly Muslim nations for 90 days and to ban all refugees from entering the country for 120 days. Devised entirely within the White House, with no advice from the agencies that would have to interpret and enforce it, the order created chaos at airports around the world as officers tried to make sense of what it required. As discussed in chapter 5, lower federal courts undid the original order as well as a revised one, ruling that they exceeded the president's legal authority and violated the First Amendment's establishment clause by discriminating against people on the basis of their religion. The judges cited statements Trump made as a candidate as evidence of the orders' true intent, including his oft-repeated call to bar all Muslims from entering the country. Trump's executive order "speaks with vague words of national security, but in context drips with religious intolerance, animus and discrimination," the Fourth Circuit Court of Appeals ruled.[55]

The real effect of Trump's orders, however, was not their legal standing but rather the message they sent to many Muslims and Latin Americans who were thinking of coming into the country: in a word, don't try. Arrests of undocumented immigrants already within the United States rose by more than 40 percent during the president's first year even as arrests at the nation's southern border—a useful index of how many people are trying to cross into the United States illegally—plummeted to their lowest level in nearly a half century.[56] The number of visas the State Department issued to residents of the countries named in Trump's executive order fell by 55 percent from the previous year.[57] Fifty-nine thousand Haitian refugees who had been admitted to the United States under the Temporary Protected Status program after an earthquake hit the island in 2010 were told they would need to leave by 2019, along with 2,500 Nicaraguan refugees.[58] Absent a physical wall along the southern border, the Trump administration was building a "virtual wall" in the eyes of critics.[59]

On September 24 the president issued a third executive proclamation concerning travel that tried to address the courts' concerns about his first two. The ban applied to eight countries, two of them (Venezuela and North Korea) not majority Muslim. The "objective criteria" for choosing these countries were that they did not share information with the United States about potential travelers' criminal history or connection with terrorists. The ban was permanent, not temporary, but countries could remove themselves from the list if they changed their policies and practices. Equally important, the proclamation emerged from a thorough process that included the Departments of State and Homeland Security as well as various intelligence agencies.[60] Critics argued that the new proclamation was fruit of the poisoned tree, just another version of the original travel ban that courts had disallowed, and judges in Hawaii and Maryland agreed on October 17–18, with further litigation to follow. But in response to the proclamation, on September 25 the Supreme Court canceled the scheduled oral argument on the earlier orders.[61] One day later, the Trump administration announced that, exercising its responsibility under the Refugee Act of 1980 to determine the maximum number of refugees who could be admitted to the United States in the fiscal year that began on October 1, the ceiling would be reduced from 110,000 in fiscal year 2017, a number set by President Obama, to a record-low 45,000 in fiscal year 2018.[62] On December 4, the court allowed enforcement of the third travel ban to go forward while its legality was being litigated.

5 ★ LOCI OF OPPOSITION
The Courts and the States and Cities

Conflict with the courts is atypical of presidents' first years but not unexpected in circumstances like those faced by— and, to a great extent, created by—the Trump administration. In sixteen of the twenty-four years before Donald Trump took office, federal judges had been appointed by Democratic presidents Bill Clinton and Barack Obama, including four of the eight justices on the Supreme Court. (Obama tried to fill the ninth seat during his final year in office, but Senate Republicans thwarted him.) When Trump became president in January 2017, nine of the thirteen federal courts of appeals (all but the Fifth, Sixth, Seventh, and Eighth Circuits) had Democrat-appointed majorities. Well over half of the 673 judges on the nation's ninety-three federal district courts were Democratic appointees. Trump's heavy reliance on unilateral executive actions, unusual for a president in his first year, assured that his administration would frequently be challenged in court. Some of these actions originated in an inexperienced White House staff led by an inexperienced president, further aggravating the potential for carelessness and legal vulnerability.

State governments—at least the minority of them controlled by Democrats—and the strongly Democratic larger cities within most Republican states were another source of early opposition to the new president. In 2016 Hillary Clinton carried most of the nation's metropolises, state capitals, and college towns, but Trump won the election by dominating its rural and exurban counties and small cities. State Republican parties did even better. After the election, thirty-four states had Republican governors, thirty-three states had Republican legislatures, and twenty-six states had both. In contrast, just fifteen governorships and fifteen legislatures were controlled by the Democrats, and in only eight states were the Democrats entirely in charge. (In the other sixteen states neither party was.) Democrats improved their position slightly in the November 2017 elections, winning the New Jersey governorship from the Republicans and taking control of the legislature in Washington State. But even before then enough states had Democratic attorneys general and enough urban jurisdictions had Democratic city attorneys to mount multistate legal challenges to Trump-administration actions, following the lead of Republican state attorneys general during the Obama years.[1] The rising ideological polarization in Washington and across the nation in recent decades increasingly had led state and local governments to pursue their policy agendas by filing lawsuits as a first, not a last resort.

With the Republicans in control of the two elected branches in Washington, much of the early resistance to the Trump presidency centered in the third branch of the federal government and in the nation's states and cities. Although the degree of conflict during Trump's first year was unusual, the fact of it was not. The Constitution was explicitly designed to slice and dice power both within the nation's capital and among the levels of government that constitute the larger federal system. And just as it left the president's opponents enclaves from which to challenge him, it also left the president tools to resist those challenges, especially his power, buttressed by a supportive Republican majority in the Senate, to change the composition of the federal judiciary.

THE COURTS

During the presidential campaign Trump attacked the courts regularly, even claiming on June 2–3, 2016, that the Indiana-born Gonzalo Curiel, the federal judge who ruled against Trump University in a lawsuit, was "a hater of Donald Trump, a hater" who was biased by his "Mexican heritage."[2] Far from denying that he would apply a "litmus test" to judicial nominees, Trump pledged as a candidate that his appointees would "automatically" overturn *Roe v. Wade*, the Court's landmark abortion decision. "I am pro-life and I will be appointing pro-life judges," he promised in his final debate with Hillary Clinton.[3] Relying on suggestions from the conservative Heritage Foundation and Federalist Society, Trump released two lists of judges—a list of eleven on May 18, 2016, and an additional list of ten on September 23—from which he said he would choose his Supreme Court nominees, an unprecedented action by a presidential candidate. More than a year later, on November 17, 2017, he added five more names.[4] Evangelical Christians strongly supported Trump in the election and during his first year in office based largely on his commitment to a conservative judiciary.

Looming over nearly the entire election year, for the first time since George Washington was chosen as president in 1789, was the certainty that if Trump were elected, he would have an immediate opportunity to nominate someone to the Court. No sooner had Justice Antonin Scalia died on February 13, 2016, than Senate Republican leader Mitch McConnell vowed that the vacancy would "not be filled until we have a new president" because "the American people should have a voice in the selection of their next Supreme Court justice."[5] McConnell was gambling that Clinton would not win the election and choose someone more liberal than Merrick Garland, Obama's fairly moderate nominee. With four Republican justices balancing the four Clinton and Obama appointees, all knew that whoever was chosen to take Scalia's place would cast the decisive vote in many controversial cases.

Partisan conflict over judicial nominations was hardly a new feature of American politics by the time Trump became president. Trump's three predecessors, the Democrats Clinton and Obama and the Republican George W. Bush, had enjoyed great success winning confirmation for their nominees when their own parties controlled the Senate, but not later in their terms when the opposition party took control. Yet even as Senate Democrats, still in the majority, changed the chamber's rules in 2013 by removing the filibuster as a barrier to Obama's district and appeals court nominations, they left it unaltered for Supreme Court appointments. They also preserved the "blue slip" tradition that requires consent from both of a state's senators before the Senate Judiciary Committee will consider a nominee from that state for a federal judgeship, which meant that many Obama nominees from states with Republican senators were left to languish after the GOP won control of the Senate in the 2016 midterm election. The result was that not just a Supreme Court vacancy but also the opportunity to fill more than a hundred seats on lower federal courts awaited Trump when he took office.[6] Subsequent judicial retirements meant that by November 2017, there were 18 appellate court vacancies and 127 openings on the district courts even after more than a dozen of Trump's nominees were confirmed.

Because Scalia had been a leading conservative voice during his three decades on the Supreme Court, Trump's nomination of the equally conservative appeals court judge Neil Gorsuch to succeed him did not threaten to change the Court's ideological balance in the same way that replacing a liberal justice would. Gorsuch acquitted himself well during the confirmation process, demonstrating both a strong command of the law and a thoughtful demeanor. Even so, responding to continuing pressure from party activists, forty-five Senate Democrats opposed his nomination, enough to wage a filibuster that would have killed it under the chamber's existing rules. Senate Republicans then changed the rules, extending the prohibition against filibusters to all appointments, which made Trump the first president in history who could count on having his nominees confirmed by a simple majority vote. Gorsuch's nomination was approved on April 7 by a vote of 54 to 45, with Republican senators unanimous in their support and Democrats voting 42 to 3 against confirmation.

With three of the remaining justices in their late seventies or early eighties, it seemed possible that Trump would have other opportunities to add new members to the Supreme Court. Two of the three, Ruth Bader Ginsburg and Stephen Breyer, were among the Court's liberals, and the other, Anthony Kennedy, was a moderate conservative. Replacing any one of them with a Gorsuch-style strong conservative would move the narrowly divided Court squarely to the right and provoke fevered opposition from Senate Democrats. But with the filibuster gone and Republicans in control of the Senate (and likely but not certain to remain so after the 2018 midterm election, in which they must defend only eight seats compared with the Democrats' twenty-six), Trump wielded a strong hand in the politics of Supreme Court nominations.

The same was true of district and appeals court appointments. In contrast to the lagging pace of his executive branch nominations, Trump was relatively quick to send judicial nominees to the Senate, many of them not just conservative but also young. Planning began during the transition period, when White House counsel designee Donald McGahn led a team whose primary focus was on identifying appellate court nominees.[7] By mid-July, Trump was already "on pace to more than double the number of federal judges nominated by any president in his first year."[8] By October 1, he had made eighteen appellate and thirty-nine district court nominations.[9] By midmonth, seven had been confirmed, compared with three at the same point in Obama's first year.[10]

With many vacancies still to fill and a Republican Senate that shared his conservative judicial philosophy, Trump's prospects for altering the partisan balance on the federal courts were great. From the start, he used his election-year lists of twenty-one judges to stock the judicial shelves with potential Supreme Court nominees whose professional credentials would be difficult to challenge if they were on the appellate bench, as eight of the nine current justices had been.[11] By October, Trump had nominated five from his two lists to fill appeals court vacancies. Four already were serving on their states' supreme courts, and the fifth was a federal district court judge. All, like the forty-nine-year-old Gorsuch (the lists' first product), were in their forties or early fifties.

Two of Trump's early appeals court nominees were from states with Democratic senators, and in neither case did the Senate Judiciary Committee receive from them the blue slip that it traditionally requires before considering a nomination. In September, Minnesota Democrat Al Franken said that he would not return a blue slip for David R. Stras, the Minnesota Supreme Court justice whom Trump nominated for a seat on the Eighth Circuit Court of Appeals, and both Oregon senators, Ron Wyden and Jeff Merkley, announced that they would not return one for Ryan Bounds, an assistant United States attorney in their state and Trump's nominee for a Ninth Circuit judgeship.[12] As he had when the Democrats vowed to filibuster the Gorsuch nomination, McConnell indicated that rather than allow these and other appointments to fall by the wayside, he and his Republican colleagues would end the blue-slip tradition for appellate court nominations while preserving it only for the district courts. The difference, he said, was that district court judges operate within a single state whereas appeals court judges hear cases from all of the states within their circuit.

Senator Charles Grassley, the chair of the Judiciary Committee, was reluctant to move as summarily against blue slips as McConnell, but he and the majority leader agreed that the confirmation process had to proceed more swiftly. Even before Franken resigned from the Senate in response to sexual misconduct allegations, for example, committee hearings were scheduled for Stras in December. McConnell and Grassley regarded confirming lifetime appointments for judges as a more important goal for conservatives than confirming executive branch nominees, who serve only temporarily.[13] So did the president. Judicial appointments have "consequences forty years out, depending on the age of the judge—but forty years out," Trump marveled.[14] In addition, the phasing out of filibusters meant that the blue-slip tradition, which dated to the 1910s, probably was bound for obsolescence. If forty-one senators no longer could thwart a nomination, then allowing one or two senators to do so seemed especially anomalous.

Unlike federal judges, who under the Constitution enjoy lifetime tenure, United States attorneys—one for each of the ninety-three federal judicial districts—hold office at the pleasure of the president. Traditionally they have been replaced at a much slower pace than other executive branch appointees because they serve both the executive and the judiciary. The importance of U.S. attorneys lies at the intersection of their role in advancing the administration's prosecutorial priorities and the launching pad they provide for subsequent judicial or political careers. Within six weeks of Trump's taking office, forty-seven attorneyships became vacant because of resignations tendered either during Obama's last year or after the election. On March 10, 2017, Attorney General Jeff Sessions requested the immediate resignations of all forty-six remaining U.S. attorneys, and by mid-September the president had nominated forty-two replacements, compared with twenty at the same point in Obama's first term. When Preet Bharara, an aggressive prosecutor of political corruption and financial malfeasance as the U.S. attorney for the Southern District of New York, refused to resign, he was fired the next day.

Quick as he was to start filling judicial and other law-related vacancies, Trump could not do so fast enough to prevent federal courts from ruling against several of his early actions. On February 3, just two weeks after Trump took office, Judge James Robart of the federal district court in Seattle—a George W. Bush appointee—ruled that the administration's executive order banning travel to the United States by immigrants and refugees from several Muslim nations was unconstitutional. That night the White House issued a statement that it would appeal the judge's "outrageous order." Early the next morning Trump tweeted that "the opinion of this so-called judge . . . is ridiculous and will be overturned."[15] But he did not defy the order, instead issuing a revised travel ban in March, which also was blocked by district court judges in Washington State and Maryland. Both the Fourth and Ninth Circuit Courts of Appeals upheld these lower court rulings, despite Trump's lambasting one of the hearings as "disgraceful."[16] The Fourth Circuit Court based its judgment on a religious discrimination claim, the Ninth Circuit on Trump's having "exceeded the scope of the authority delegated to him by Congress."[17]

In June the Supreme Court complicated matters by accepting the cases on appeal while allowing parts of Trump's revised executive order to take effect temporarily. In doing so, however, the Court said that the government should let in travelers and refugees who had a "bona fide relationship with a person or entity in the United States." The administration interpreted "person" to include immediate family members but not grandparents, grandchildren, aunts, uncles, and cousins, and "entity" to exclude refugee resettlement agencies. Federal district court judge Derrick K. Watson of Honolulu ruled that this definition was too narrow, and on September 7 a three-judge panel of the Ninth Circuit agreed. Five days later the Supreme Court granted an administration request to stay the part of the ruling that dealt with refugee agencies—all this pending a thorough hearing on the travel ban on October 10. But after Trump issued yet another revised order in late September, the Court canceled the hearing on the grounds that the case had become moot. The justices then vacated the lower court rulings, which means that the opinions of the Fourth and Ninth Circuit Courts of Appeals were wiped off the books.

Trump kept trying—and judges kept resisting—new ways of banning travel from certain countries that he regarded as terrorist threats. As discussed in chapter 4, the third, late-September version of the order included two non-Muslim majority countries on the list of eight from which travel was forbidden, provided a way for countries to be removed from the list, and emerged from a deliberative process within the administration. Before the order could take effect as planned on October 18, however, Judge Watson and, in a less sweeping decision, Judge Theodore Chuang in Maryland determined that these were, in effect, distinctions without a difference and invalidated it.[18] This time the Ninth Circuit Court rejected part of Watson's decision when the case came before it on appeal, ruling that visitors from the affected countries without close American ties could legally be denied entry.[19] Once again the Supreme Court would eventually be asked to resolve the issue.

Along with these cases, a plethora of lawsuits were filed during the president's first year challenging other Trump-administration actions, including his order to bomb Syria and a host of executive orders to reduce environmental regulations and cut off federal aid to "sanctuary cities" that refuse to help federal agents arrest undocumented immigrants by holding them when they are released from jail until an Immigration and Customs Enforcement (ICE) officer can pick them up. Federal district court judge William Orrick ruled in favor of two sanctuary jurisdictions in California, citing Trump's comment that cutting off aid was "a 'weapon' to use against jurisdictions that disagree with his preferred policies of immigration enforcement."[20] The president's ban on transgender individuals in the military was successfully challenged on constitutional grounds.[21]

Trump also faced lawsuits filed by Citizens for Responsibility and Ethics in Washington (CREW), nearly two hundred Democratic members of Congress, and the Democratic attorneys general of Maryland and the District of Columbia urging courts to force his businesses to stop accepting payments from foreign governments. The legal basis of the suits was the Constitution's foreign emoluments clause, which forbids any "Person holding any office of Profit or Trust" from accepting "any present, Emolument, Office or Title, of any kind whatever, from any King, Prince, or foreign State." A second clause provides that beyond the salary, the president may not receive "any other Emolument from the United States, or any of them."

The clauses, which appear in Article I, section 9, and Article II, section 1, respectively, are obscure at best and subject to a wide range of interpretations. They were dusted off by the Democrats because Trump chose neither to sell his businesses when he became president nor put them into a blind trust. Instead he assigned his two adult sons to run them. Federal judges were asked to decide whether, for example, foreign governments renting rooms in the Trump International Hotel in Washington were conferring emoluments on the president, as well as whether courts should rule on the issue rather than leaving it to Congress. In a brief filed against the CREW suit, the Justice Department pointed out that George Washington continued to sell crops to foreign countries while he was president without facing charges that the proceeds of his private business pursuits constituted emoluments.[22] As with the Supreme Court, who the judges are that will rule on these and similar cases during the remainder of Trump's tenure in office will be a matter of urgent and ongoing interest for his administration. Robart excepted, nearly all of the jurists who ruled against him during his first year were appointed by Demo-cratic presidents. The Fourth and, especially, the Ninth Circuit Courts were particular bastions of judicial liberalism.

STATES AND CITIES

One day after Trump's inauguration, the rapidly organized Women's March protesting the president's victory drew not just a half-million marchers to Washington, but another 1.5 million to Chicago, Los Angeles, and New York and hundreds of thousands more to Boston, San Francisco, Madison, and scores of other cities. Other large-scale, multicity protests attacked aspects of Trump's presidency on a regular basis, including his unwillingness to release his tax returns on April 15 (Tax Day), his alleged resis-tance to science in a multicity March for Science the following week, his lack of concern for global warming in a People's Climate March in Washington the week after that, his order to ban trans-gender individuals from the military, and so on. From February to October, an average of 446 anti-Trump protests and demonstra-tions per month were held across the country.[23] During Congress's summer recess, constituents packed town hall meetings in loud defense of the Affordable Care Act, just as Tea Party supporters had packed similar meetings eight years before to protest passage of the act when Obama was president. This was no coincidence. As the political analysts E. J. Dionne, Norman Ornstein, and Thomas Mann note, four "former progressive congressional staffers who saw the Tea Party beat back President Obama's agenda" offered Tea Party–derived lessons about how to wage an effective grassroots protests in an online guide that went viral: *Indivisible: A Practical Guide for Resisting the Trump Agenda.*[24] By November, Indivisible claimed that more than 5,800 local groups were using the guide to hold their members of Congress accountable.[25] Postelection opposition to Trump generated much more activism than support for Clinton had during the campaign, in part because she was so widely expected to win.[26]

Official acts of state and local resistance also marked Trump's first year in office. As noted above, several dozen municipal governments declared themselves to be sanctuary cities whose police forces would not help federal authorities pursue undocumented immigrants, with support from the courts when the Trump administration tried to deny them federal aid in retaliation. Another federal judge enjoined the State of Texas from enforcing its own ban, despite the Justice Department's intervention on the state's side. In disregard of the conservative orthodoxy that the best governments are those closest to the people, multiple Republican-controlled state legislatures imposed similar restrictions on their more liberal, Democratic-dominated cities concerning matters as varied as minimum wage, transgender rights, drug enforcement, and statues honoring the Confederacy in the Civil War.

On September 18, Democratic governor Jerry Brown of California signed the California Values Act, passed two days earlier by his state's overwhelmingly Democratic legislature. The act made California a sanctuary state for its estimated 2.7 million undocumented immigrants, about one-fourth of all those in the country. One week later ICE agents launched Operation Safe Cities, a four-day sweep of multiple sanctuary cities in which 498 undocumented immigrants, 317 with criminal convictions, were arrested.[27] California also negotiated a "green technology" agreement with China after Trump moved to withdraw the United States from the Paris climate accord signed by Obama. More than three hundred mayors agreed to abide by the accord and "intensify efforts to meet each of our cities' climate goals."[28] Thirteen states joined California in the United States Climate Alliance by late September, and Brown and other governors met with diplomats at the UN General Assembly to underscore their commitment even though "we have a climate denier in the White House."[29] Twelve of the nation's fifteen Democratic governors were part of the Climate Alliance, but only two of the thirty-four Republican governors.[30] In November an informal delegation to the international climate summit in Bonn led by Brown, former vice president Al Gore, and billionaire Michael Bloomberg said that, taken together, the American states, cities, and businesses pledged to abide by the Paris climate accord constituted the third-largest economy in the world, behind only the United States and China.[31]

As with the legal challenges to the president's travel ban, which were initiated by the Democratic attorneys general of Washington and Maryland, fifteen state attorneys general contested his executive order in September to end the Deferred Action for Childhood Arrivals (DACA) program. Thirteen of them were from states Trump lost handily in the 2016 election. As with the earlier challenges, too, they grounded their appeal in statements Trump made as a candidate that disparaged undocumented Mexican immigrants as "criminals, drug dealers, rapists, etc."[32] Democratic state attorneys general filed an additional suit to prevent Secretary of Education Betsey DeVos from freezing an Obama-era regulation that would erase the federal debts of students whose colleges had acted fraudulently. Eighteen of them joined ranks in the hope of having Trump's October order to end cost-reduction subsidies to health insurance companies overturned in court.

States resisted Trump-administration initiatives in other ways as well. Even many Republican governors in the thirty-one states that expanded Medicaid under Obama's Affordable Care Act opposed Trump-supported efforts to reduce federal spending on the program and urged Congress to stabilize health insurance markets in their states by providing funds to subsidize insurance companies' underwriting of policies for low-income people. In July all but a handful of states—including most of those governed by Republicans—refused some or all of the Trump-formed Presidential Advisory Commission on Election Integrity's requests for information about their voters. In Texas, a state that wanted to share its voter rolls with the commission, a local judge ruled that it could not do so on privacy grounds in response to a lawsuit filed by the NAACP and the League of Women Voters.[33] Facing a number of other legal challenges, including one from a Democratic member, the commission went dark after meeting only twice after being formed in May.[34]

As in his dealings with the bureaucracy (see chapter 4) and the courts, Trump was unprepared for such resistance. Nothing in his long business career had required him to share power. With his absence of governing experience and lack of knowledge about American history and government, Trump had at best a dim understanding of the sharing of power mandated by the Constitution, both between the state and federal governments and among the branches within the federal government. Examples of his ignorance abounded. A week before the election, he oddly promised that he would convene a special session of Congress as soon as he was sworn in, even though Congress is always in session at that time of year.[35] Andrew Jackson, Trump said, "was really angry that he saw what was happening in regard to the Civil War."[36] (Jackson died sixteen year before the war.) Speaking of Abraham Lincoln, Trump asked, "Most people don't even know he was a Republican. Right? Does anyone know?"[37] (Every Republican who has ever claimed membership in the "party of Lincoln" does, which is pretty much every Republican.) "Frederick Douglass," Trump declared, as if speaking of a living person, "is an example of somebody who's done an amazing job."[38] At a July 8 meeting with House Republicans, Trump professed his devotion to the Constitution he had taken an oath to "preserve, protect, and defend" by saying of the document, "I want to protect Article I, Article II, Article XII— go down the list."[39] (There are seven articles, not twelve, much less a longer "list.") After mentioning William McKinley to a crowd in Youngstown, Ohio, he wondered, "Does anybody know who the hell he is?"[40] (President McKinley's birthplace is twelve miles away.) Weeks after Hurricane Maria wracked the Virgin Islands, Trump referred to "the president of the Virgin Islands" which, like all American states and territories, actually has a governor. The president of the United States is the Virgin Islands' president.[41]

6 ★ CONGRESS AND
DOMESTIC POLICY

"Welcome to the dawn of a new unified Republican government," declared Speaker of the House Paul Ryan in January 2017, while predicting that the 115th Congress would pass major health care, tax, and border wall legislation by August.[1] Senate Majority Leader Mitch McConnell told associates that because Donald Trump had few opinions about what he wanted Congress to do, he and Ryan would hold the reins of legislative power.[2]

Ryan and McConnell's optimism was understandable but unwonted. The Congress with which Trump entered office was far from a rubber-stamp body for him or his party's leaders. Trump's victory in the election had been narrow and carried no clear policy mandate. House Republicans could afford only a twenty-three-vote defection in the face of united Democratic opposition. The party's even slighter majority in the Senate allowed at most two defections on the limited number of bills, such as repealing and replacing the Affordable Care Act and enacting tax reform, that could be shoehorned into the filibuster-proof "reconciliation process" on the grounds that they were budget-related measures.[3] Even then, Vice President Mike Pence would have to break tie votes, as he did six times in his first eleven months as president of the Senate—almost as many as his two predecessors combined had in sixteen years. Other than appointments, most other measures required a

hard-to-attain sixty-vote majority to overcome a Democratic filibuster. Yet serious illnesses afflicting two older Republican senators, John McCain and Thad Cochrane; bitter presidential feuding
with two others, Bob Corker and Jeff Flake; and the loss of an Alabama Senate seat in a December 2017 special election made securing even fifty votes an uncertain thing.[4]

Depending on the issue, it was clear from the start that Republican defections might come from the party's moderately conservative Tuesday Group or, if its members' concerns were placated,
from the ultraconservative Freedom Caucus. Most Republican legislators in both chambers were economic conservatives who had
been elected on a less populist platform than Trump. One-fourth
of Republican senators did not support him against Hillary Clinton in the 2016 election, and only one-ninth of them were slated
to be on the ballot in 2018.[5] All but 34 of the 241 Republican representatives won a higher percentage of the vote in their districts
than Trump, and few shared his professed commitment to leave
the federal government's major entitlement programs—Social
Security, Medicare, and Medicaid—untouched.[6] As the political
scientists Theda Skocpol and Vanessa Williamson found, however,
Tea Party supporters in the electorate did share that commitment,
regarding these programs as benefits they had earned, as opposed
to "'unearned' entitlements handed out" to "freeloaders."[7] When
Mick Mulvaney, the South Carolina congressman Trump named
as director of the Office of Management and Budget, went to the
president and said, "Look, this is my idea on how to reform Social
Security," the president said, "No." "Well," Mulvaney continued,
"here are some Medicare reforms." "No," Trump said, "I'm not
doing that."[8] Medicaid, as expanded by the Affordable Care Act,
was a different matter.

As for the Democrats, even those who may have preferred to
vote for certain Trump-supported bills were hamstrung by grassroots party activists who insisted on unrelenting resistance. And

few were inclined to do so anyway. In both the House and the Senate, not a single Democratic member was more conservative than the most liberal Republican member, and the ideological gap between the parties was not only clear but vast.[9] Like congressional Republicans during the Obama years, congressional Democrats quickly became the "party of no."

The Republican majority on Capitol Hill with which Trump was elected was, like him, experienced in opposition but not in governing. The party won control of the House in the 2010 midterm election by opposing President Barack Obama; it captured the Senate by opposing him again in 2014. In both elections, Republicans succeeded by attacking not just the president but also the entire federal government, which made supporting a legislative program of any kind all the more difficult. This included Trump's ideas for an expensive wall along the nation's southern border; ramped-up infrastructure spending on roads, bridges, tunnels, transit systems, waterworks, and airports; and measures to "prime the pump . . . in order to get the economy going, and going big league."[10] "We were a ten-year opposition party," said Ryan, "where being against things was easy to do. And now . . . we actually have to get 218 people to agree with each other on how we do things."[11] "We just simply don't know how to govern," echoed Representative Steve Womack of Arkansas.[12] Trump did not help matters by sending only loosely formulated legislative proposals—or no proposals at all—to Capitol Hill.

The Republicans' success in passing a flurry of Trump-supported deregulation bills in the early months of his presidency was the exception that demonstrates the rule. They won vote after vote on measures passed under the Congressional Review Act (CRA) of 1996. That act granted Congress sixty legislative days (that is, days Congress is in session) to revoke new regulations issued by the executive branch, with no Senate filibusters allowed. Until 2017 it had been used only once. But, seeing the CRA as a way to continue opposing Obama's policies even after he left office, Congress passed and Trump signed bills to repeal fourteen late Obama-administration regulations, including one that would have prevented Internet service providers from selling their customers' data and another that authorized state governments to offer retirement accounts to private-sector workers. The tactic was entirely negative and served mostly as a short-term expedient. On May 11, 2017—less than four months into Trump's term—the deadline for using the CRA to undo Obama-era regulations was reached.

Rarely was the CRA invoked afterward, and even then only under unusual circumstances. In late October, Congress overturned a regulation that would have permitted class-action lawsuits against financial institutions. The regulation had just been issued by the Consumer Financial Protection Bureau (CFPB), an independent agency led by Richard Cordray, an Obama appointee. Corday resigned in late November, reportedly to run for governor in his home state of Ohio. But on his last day he elevated his chief of staff, Leandra English, to deputy director so that she could replace him until Trump could nominate and the Senate confirm a permanent director. Trump, refusing to accept the legality of this move, charged OMB director Mulvaney to take on an additional role as the CFPB's acting director. The contrast was sharp: English wanted to continue leading the bureau aggressively, while Mulvaney once had said, "I don't like the fact that CFPB exists." Conflicting statutes seemed to support both English's and Mulvaney's right to the position.[13] Although Trump's interpretation was supported by the Justice Department's Office of Legal Counsel and the CFPB's own general counsel, English immediately filed suit in federal court claiming to be the "rightful acting director."[14] A federal district court judge in Washington ruled against her.

By the anniversary of Trump's election, Congress had yet to pass a single piece of major administration-sponsored legislation, belying his claim that "we've signed more bills—and I'm talking about through the legislature—than any president, ever."[15] Of the forty-two he signed by the six-month mark (fewer than the average number signed by his six most recent predecessors), most were minor, including one to rename a federal courthouse in Tennessee and another three to add board members to the Smithsonian Institution. In October, after approving a few more bills, Trump made an equally empty boast: "I've had just about the most legislation passed of any president, in a nine-month period, that's ever served."[16] Congressional Republican difficulty in enacting a legislative program was aggravated by Trump's failure to provide effective leadership. He began by wasting the postelection transition period, which most new presidents use to begin developing detailed legislative proposals and staff the White House with at least some experienced veterans of Capitol Hill. Trump did neither.

Nor did Trump acquaint himself adequately with the contents of most of the policies he supported, which made his attempts to persuade members of Congress with evidence-based arguments risible. Although "the president tried to cajole and charm" legislators with dinners, rides on Air Force One, bowling nights at the White House, and the like, the political scientist George Edwards observed, considerable research has demonstrated that "schmoozing will not take the president far" toward winning votes in Congress. As House Freedom Caucus chair Mark Meadows said, "If this was about personalities, we'd already be at 'yes.' He's charming, and anyone who spends time with him knows that. But this is about policy."[17]

The author of *Trump: The Art of the Deal*, Trump prided himself on his ability to sway others to do what he wanted and promised voters during the campaign that he would use his business acumen to make favorable deals for the American people. But as the political scientist George Tsebelis has observed, the president can't deal with "an alternative Congress" the way a real estate developer can choose a different lender or contractor if the one he is negotiating with refuses to meet his terms.[18] As Trump's public approval rating quickly sank below 40 percent, his leverage on Capitol Hill declined further, despite his odd claim in July that "almost 40 percent is not bad at this time."[19] Reelection-seeking Democratic senators from states Trump carried handily, such as Joe Manchin of West Virginia and Heidi Heitkamp of North Dakota, breathed a sigh of relief when they saw how steeply his support in their states fell. Underlying all these sources of Trump's ineffectiveness with Congress was his lack, in the absence of factual knowledge about his own proposals, of consistent guiding principles that could make up for it, as they did for Ronald Reagan. On Capitol Hill, Trump increasingly was neither feared nor loved. Instead, with the passage of time, he was disrespected, even among Republicans. "The vast majority of our caucus," said Senator Bob Corker of Tennessee, "understand the volatility that we're dealing with and the tremendous amount of work that it takes by people around him to keep him in the middle of the road."[20]

Trump's major asset throughout his first year was that in addition to being the majority party in both the House and the Senate, congressional Republicans had long been united on two major issues: the evils of Obamacare—the label they attached to the Affordable Care Act—and the virtues of tax cuts. The challenge would be to take matters on which they agreed in general and turn them into legislation they could agree on in all its particulars.

REPEAL AND REPLACE OR . . . ?

From the beginning Republicans legislators united with the president in focusing relentlessly on their shared campaign promise to repeal and replace the Affordable Care Act (ACA). As was the case when Obama was president, Trump and his congressional party knew what they were against. Starting as soon as the Republicans won control of the House in 2010, that chamber voted to repeal or amend the ACA more than fifty times. When the Senate joined the House in doing so in 2015, Obama vetoed the measure, as they knew he would. During his presidential campaign Trump promised again and again "to end, terminate, repeal Obamacare and replace it with something really, really great that works."[21] But agreeing on what he and the Republican Congress were for was a challenge they were unprepared to meet, in part because his party's legislators had not expected Trump to win the election.[22]

With little guidance from the administration, Republican House leaders began 2017 by writing a bill that the nonpartisan Congressional Budget Office (CBO) estimated would leave 24 million more Americans uninsured in ten years than if Obamacare remained on the books. Ryan canceled a scheduled floor vote on March 24 when it became obvious that the bill would not pass. Freedom Caucus members objected to the measure's four-year extension of expanded Medicaid payments to the states even as Tuesday Group Republicans bridled at the proposed reduction in the size of those payments.[23] Ryan and his fellow party leaders then modified the measure somewhat, with Pence helping to broker a deal that placated conservatives by allowing states to opt out of certain provisions of the new bill and moderates by adding money to supplement coverage for individuals with serious pre-existing conditions.[24] Although the CBO estimated that 23 million more people would still be uninsured, the House passed the revised bill on May 4 on a 217–213 vote, with Democratic members unanimous in opposition.

The bill then went to the Senate, where it was modified further under McConnell's guidance (22 million more uninsured) but did not come close to uniting enough Republican senators to bring it to the floor. McConnell found that every moderate Republican vote he could attract by covering more people cost the bill a conservative Republican vote because of the added expense. Opposition from three conservative Senate Republicans doomed one version of the measure. When McConnell revised it to satisfy them, three moderate Republicans defected. Senate Democrats stood on the sidelines and, to a one, enjoyed watching the chamber's Republican majority refuse to cohere, leaving Obamacare legislatively intact. As for Trump, during the week in mid-July that these efforts failed, he took four positions in three days: first he supported the McConnell bill, then he proposed repealing the ACA without replacing it, then he suggested that Republicans "let Obamacare fail" by doing nothing, and finally he pressured Republican senators to replace it after all.[25]

Desperate to pass something, McConnell brought three measures to the Senate floor during the last week of the month. Republican defectors again doomed all three. Nine Republican senators voted against a repeal-and-replace bill, seven against a repeal-only measure, and three against a "skinny repeal" bill that preserved Obamacare while abolishing the mandate that individuals have and large employers offer health insurance. In mid-September, with the deadline for folding health care reform into the filibuster-proof budget reconciliation process looming on September 30, the last day of the fiscal year, Republican senators Bill Cassidy of Louisiana and Lindsey Graham of South Carolina tossed another proposal into the hopper. Their measure would have replaced Obamacare with block grants to the states. Frustrated that the Senate had at no point considered a reform bill with "regular order"—that is, "extensive [committee] hearings, debate, and amendment"— Senator McCain led a group of moderate Republicans in defeating the Cassidy-Graham version.[26]

Trump's interventions during the health care debate in the House were so clumsy ("I'm going to come after you," he emptily threatened Representative Meadows, who had won his North Carolina seat by a hundred thousand votes in 2016) that McConnell politely spurned his request to help out in the Senate.[27] Trump's public rhetoric was erratic, swerving from one petty complaint to another on Twitter instead of consistently rousing public opinion to support any of his policy proposals. Even when he did talk about health care, Trump veered from praising the House bill as a "great plan" that was "very, very, incredibly well-crafted" to condemning it as "mean" rather than "generous, kind, with heart."[28] Legislators seldom forget casting a tough vote in support of a president only to have him criticize them for it later.

Having worked exclusively with congressional Republicans in his effort to repeal and replace Obamacare, Trump blamed them, not himself, for his failure. "The only reason we don't have it [is] because of John McCain," he complained in a radio interview.[29] He attacked McCain's Arizona colleague, Jeff Flake, as "WEAK" and "toxic!"[30] Senator Graham, he tweeted, was "publicity seeking" and the purveyor of a "disgusting lie. . . . He just can't forget his election trouncing" by Trump in the 2016 South Carolina presidential primary.[31] Along with attacking Republican senators Dean Heller of Nevada, Lisa Murkowski of Alaska, and Susan Collins of Maine at various points in the health care fight, Trump went after the retiring Senator Corker in a series of October 8 tweets, inaccurately accusing Corker of having "begged" Trump to endorse his candidacy for reelection, having asked to be named secretary of state ("I said 'NO THANKS' "), and being "largely responsible for the horrendous Iran Deal!!!"

In a prophecy that was sure to be self-fulfilling at a time when he essentially had no Republican votes to spare on controversial measures, Trump predicted that during his remaining fifteen months in the Senate " 'Liddle' Bob Corker" would "be a negative voice and stand in the way of our great agenda."[32] Corker, who chairs the Senate Foreign Relations Committee, responded by comparing the Trump Oval Office to "an adult day care center" in which "every single day at the White House, it's a situation of trying to contain him." (He also created an #AlertTheDaycareStaff hashtag on Twitter.)[33] Trump's "volatility," Corker told the *New*

York Times, is "alarming" and "would have to concern anyone who cares about our nation.... [W]e could be heading towards World War III with the kinds of comments he's making."[34] Corker convened committee hearings on a Democratic bill to strip the president of the exclusive authority to launch a nuclear attack that had been granted in the Atomic Energy Act of 1946. In the course of defending Trump in July, the short-lived communications director Anthony Scaramucci essentially confirmed Corker's description of the White House. "There are people inside the administration that think it is their job to save America from this president," Scaramucci said.[35]

McConnell was another favorite target of Trump's ire. In general, Trump found both the Senate majority leader and Speaker Ryan ("does zilch!" Trump tweeted in 2016) to be too serious and policy-focused compared with the more affable "Chuck and Nancy," Senate Democratic leader Charles Schumer and House Democratic leader Nancy Pelosi.[36] In particular Trump was furious with McConnell for not getting a version of health care legislation through the Senate. "Can you believe that Mitch McConnell, who has screamed Repeal & Replace for 7 years, couldn't get it done?," Trump complained in one of a series of taunting tweets.[37] When McConnell told a Kentucky audience that because "our new president, of course, has not been in this line of work before, I think he had excessive expectations about how quickly things happen in the democratic process," Trump tweeted: "I don't think so. After 7 years of hearing Repeal & Replace, why not done?"[38]

Trump then unwittingly confirmed McConnell's diagnosis by complaining that "the Filibuster Rule" was impeding health care reform, which it was not because filibusters are not allowed in the budget reconciliation process under which reform was being considered. "If Republican Senate doesn't get rid of the Filibuster Rule . . . they are just wasting time!," Trump tweeted, irrelevantly.[39] With equal lack of insight into his role as chief legislator, the president said about his feuds with senators of his own party: "Sometimes it helps. Sometimes it gets people to do what they're supposed to be doing."[40] Senator Flake, announcing that he, too, was retiring after 2018, tore into Trump for "reckless, outrageous, and undignified" behavior.[41]

In desperation, Trump called Schumer on October 6, to see if "the Dems want to do a great HealthCare Bill," only to be told that "repeal and replace . . . is off the table."[42] Ten days later, the president issued an executive order ending Obamacare's cost-sharing reduction subsidies to health insurance companies, which had helped to defray the out-of-pocket expenses of low-income people, because the subsidies lacked specific authorization in law. That night, Republican senator Lamar Alexander of Tennessee and Washington Democrat Patty Murray, the chair and ranking member of the Senate Health, Education, Labor, and Pensions Committee, introduced a bill to continue the subsidies for two years while also giving states more flexibility to shape the menus of coverage they made available. As he had when the Senate was considering repeal and replace in July, Trump took three positions on the bill in less than two days: "we will get the votes" for it on Tuesday morning, October 17; "I can never support bailing out ins co's" early on Wednesday morning; and "if something can happen, that's fine" a few hours after that.[43] In less than a day, Alexander–Murray attracted twelve Republican and twelve Democratic cosponsors. Despite Trump's indecisiveness and a lack of initial support among House Republicans, its chances of passing increased in conjunction with the omnibus spending measures that, for reasons explained below, would have to be passed in December and January to keep the government open.

Trump's effort to repeal and replace Obamacare was dead by mid-October. A remnant of it would be revived a month later when Congress turned its attention to taxes, spending, and the national debt.

DEBT AND TAXES

While Congress devoted the first nine months of 2017 to the failed health care reform effort, other much-touted Trump legislative priorities, such as reforming taxes, enhancing the nation's infrastructure, building a border wall, and passing a budget were weakly developed and stuck in traffic. Nevertheless, although on issues such as trade and immigration the Republicans were a party divided, on tax cuts they traditionally have been a party united. After failing to repeal Obamacare, the GOP was under enormous pressure not to fail on taxes. "The 115th Congress, if we go oh for two, gets a failing grade," said Rep. Mark Walker, the chair of the conservative Republican Study Committee; "I think a lot of us may not come back."[44] If anything should have been legislatively straightforward during Trump's first year, it was reducing taxes on individuals and businesses. But straightforward it was not.

One reason is that taxes and spending are interwoven. When the latter outstrips the former in a fiscal year, a budget deficit arises and with it a further increase in the national debt. Despite the federal government collecting nearly $3.5 trillion in taxes in the fiscal year that ended on September 30, 2017, deficit spending added $666 billion to the national debt, raising it above the $19.808 trillion ceiling then allowed by law. The deadline for Congress to raise the debt ceiling was September 29, the date after which the federal government would no longer be able to pay its bills unless Congress acted, thereby roiling the global financial markets that count on Washington to be financially reliable. House Freedom Caucus Republicans vowed that they would not vote to raise the debt ceiling without exacting some concessions in return, especially cuts in federal domestic spending. Because, as the political scientist Frances Lee has shown, bills to raise the debt ceiling in times of united party government have always depended on the governing party to provide the necessary votes and the GOP was now unwilling to do so, Trump had to turn to Schumer and Pelosi.[45] On September 6, they agreed in an Oval Office meeting that Democrats would supply the votes but only to raise the debt ceiling for another three months and, even then, only if domestic spending was not reduced. "It's the first time I can recall we're increasing the debt ceiling without something conservative being attached to it," lamented Freedom Caucus chair Meadows.[46]

The Democratic leaders took advantage of another looming deadline to exact further concessions from the president. On September 30 the federal government would run out of money to meet its ongoing expenses and have to shut down all but essential activities unless additional funds were appropriated for the new fiscal year that began the next day. Like the Freedom Caucus members who had wanted spending cuts in return for raising the debt ceiling, Trump insisted that he would allow a shutdown to take place if the appropriations did not include $1.6 billion for a wall along the nation's southern border. "If we have to close down our government, we're building that wall," he thundered at an August 22 rally.

But like the Freedom Caucus, the president was unsuccessful. In truth, Trump had little leverage. The damage caused by the hurricanes that recently had rocked Texas, Louisiana, Florida, and Puerto Rico required an urgent federal response, and the president already had sent a $14.5 billion emergency relief bill to Congress, with tens of billions in additional requests soon to follow. The country would not understand or accept shutting down the government in the wake of a natural disaster. With Trump acquiescing to Schumer and Pelosi, Congress voted to raise the debt ceiling and fund the government until December as part of the hurricane relief bill. The Senate vote on September 7 was 80 to 17, and the House vote the next day was 316 to 90, with all of the "no" votes in both chambers coming from Republicans. "The nation can breathe a sigh of relief," said Schumer, who had more reason to be satisfied with the outcome than his Republican counterparts. "Deals are my art form," Trump once had tweeted, "preferably big deals. That's how I get my kicks." He ended September with a small deal whose artists were Democrats and, he later realized, himself "looking like the chump in the deal."[47] And because the president would need their votes again in December to avert a looming shutdown, Democratic congressional leaders would be in a strong position to exact additional concessions.

Meanwhile Congress still had not passed the budget resolution for the fiscal year that began on October 1, which among other things was a necessary precondition for folding tax reform legislation into the reconciliation process, thereby allowing a simple majority of Senate Republicans to pass a tax bill without having to overcome a Democratic filibuster. On October 5, surmounting both united Democratic opposition and considerable difficulty forging a consensus within the GOP, the House passed a budget resolution calling for about $4 trillion in tax cuts over the next ten years and an equal amount of spending reductions and loophole closings to offset them. Hours later, the Senate Budget Committee sent its own budget measure to the full Senate, which on October 19 passed it (as had the House) on a straight party-line vote. It allowed for $1.5 trillion more in tax cuts than in reduced spending and increased revenue. Because the lateness of the Senate committee action left little time for a conference committee to smooth out the differences between the two versions, on October 26 House Republicans, urged on by Speaker Ryan and President Trump, had little choice but to pass the Senate version as written.[48]

Specifics about the cuts in spending and taxes and the rest of the Republican plan were lacking in both chambers' budget resolutions, but after wasting the first four weeks of August, the month in which he had planned to sell tax reform to the country, on controversies such as the Arpaio pardon, the border wall, the Charlottesville protests, and other distractions, Trump presented at least the glimmerings of a plan in a speech in Missouri on August 30. Offering few details, he promised a tax cut that was "the biggest ever," including a steep reduction in the corporate tax rate that would be partially offset by "eliminating loopholes and complexity that primarily benefit the wealthiest Americans and special interests."[49]

By the end of September, working closely with Republican (but not Democratic) members of Congress in the hope of avoiding some of the miscommunications that hindered the health care reform effort, Treasury Secretary Stephen Mnuchin and National Economic Council director Gary Cohn developed a proposal to collapse the seven individual tax brackets into three (12 percent, 25 percent, and 35 percent); preserve the deductibility of mortgage interest and charitable donations for those who itemize and, for those who do not, nearly double the standard deduction to $12,000 for individuals and $24,000 for couples; increase the child tax credit; eliminate the estate tax and alternative minimum tax; and reduce the corporate tax rate from 35 percent to 20 percent. For months Trump had insisted that he wanted the corporate rate to be cut to 15 percent. "I was actually saying 15 for the purpose of getting to 20," he bragged, a peculiar claim because he got to 20 percent by negotiating the increase with himself, not as a concession to reluctant members of Congress.[50]

Unspecified in both the administration plan and the congressional budget resolution passed in October was how to offset most or all of the cost of the tax cuts during the next ten years, except for directing the Senate Energy and Natural Resources Committee to come up with $1 billion in savings—a thinly disguised way of allowing committee chair Lisa Murkowski of Alaska to authorize oil drilling in the Arctic National Wildlife Refuge, a long-standing goal of hers and of Republican presidents since the 1980s.[51] Both chambers eased the challenge of deficit forecasting by making optimistic assumptions about how fast the economy would grow through the late 2020s, but even so some existing tax deductions would have to be eliminated. The biggest target in the eyes of many Republicans was the deductibility of state and local taxes, which cost the federal government more than $100 billion in revenue each year. Most high-tax states were also blue states politically, with California, New York, New Jersey, and Illinois residents alone claiming about half the total value of the deduction. But thirty-five Republican House members were from these four high-tax states, and few of their votes could be spared. Twenty of them joined all 192 Democrats in opposition when the House finally adopted the Senate reconciliation resolution on October 26, enabling it pass by just four votes. Trump further roiled the waters by tweeting, "There will be NO changes to your 401(k)," a popular retirement savings plan but also one that shrank federal revenues by allowing people to forgo taxes on income they pay into an individual retirement account.[52]

Although it was called the Tax Cuts and Jobs Act, not the "Cut Cut Cut Act," as proposed by Trump, on November 2 the president's commitment to leave 401(k) plans untouched made it into the detailed proposal unveiled by the House Ways and Means Committee, which the full House passed two weeks later by a 227–205 vote. (This time thirteen Republicans from high-tax states voted with the unanimously opposed Democrats.) So did the 20 percent corporate tax rate, the end of the deductibility of state and local income (but not property) taxes, the increase in the standard deduction, the elimination of the alternative minimum tax and, over time, of the estate tax, the child tax credit increase, and the three new tax brackets for households earning $1 million or less. In another blow to people living in the wealthier and more expensive blue states of the Northeast and Pacific West, a fourth bracket, 39.6 percent, was added for those making more than $1 million per year, and the deduction for mortgage interest, previously available for loans as high as $1 million, was capped at $500,000 for future home purchases.

Senate Republicans soon offered their own plan, which because of the chamber's distinctive "Byrd rule," needed to project not only deficits that remained at or below $1.5 trillion over the next ten years but also a balanced budget in the years after that in order to be filibuster-proof.[53] They accepted the House's 20 percent corporate tax rate while delaying its implementation for a year; preserved the seven tax brackets in existing law while reducing the top one to 38.5 percent; left the existing $1 million ceiling on the mortgage deduction alone; reduced but did not eliminate the estate tax; and tinkered slightly with the House's proposed increases in the standard deduction and child tax credit, now up to $1,650 per child. With no Republicans representing the high-tax blue states in the Senate, the Senate GOP plan proposed to end the deductibility of state and local property taxes as well as income taxes.

The road to enactment of tax reform was still bumpy. Congressional Democrats strongly opposed both Republican plans. Adversely affected interest groups such as the National Association of Realtors, National Association of Home Builders, and AARP mobilized in opposition.[54] The differences in the two proposed bills, some of them rooted in the presence of blue-state Republicans in the House but not the Senate, were substantial. Staying under the $1.5 trillion cap while negotiating these differences was an intrinsically difficult challenge, not to mention avoiding projected deficits after ten years.

On November 13, three days before the scheduled vote on the House plan, Trump complicated matters further by abandoning his earlier support for a higher tax rate for the wealthy and instead tweeted that Congress should repeal the "Indiv mandate in Ocare," thereby saving enough money (more than $300 billion that the federal government would otherwise have spent) to "Cut top rate to 35% w/all of the rest going to middle income cuts?"[55] Republican senators quickly embraced the idea, whose original advocate was Senator Tom Cotton of Arkansas, in combination with parallel passage of the Alexander–Murray bill. The Senate Finance Committee added the new provision to its version of the tax measure even though the CBO estimated that it would cause insurance premiums to rise by about 10 percent and 13 million more people eventually would be uninsured; indeed, it was the reduced number who would receive supplements to pay for their insurance that would generate the additional $300 billion.

The Finance Committee also proposed to reduce the other rates on individual taxpayers slightly more; boost the child tax credit to $2,000; and, in order to keep the national debt from rising after ten years, provide that the individual tax cuts would expire in 2025. Republicans counted on future congresses feeling politically bound to renew those cuts when the time came.[56] Several studies, agreeing that the 2025 expiration date was phony, placed the true cost of the committee's proposed tax cuts at about $2 trillion. Several other studies of both chambers' tax bills projected that wealthier people would enjoy most of the benefits and that some poor and middle-class households' taxes actually would rise.[57]

Once again, as with health care reform, spending measures for the coming fiscal year, and the debt ceiling, the challenge for House and Senate Republicans was to agree on a bill that would keep the party's moderates and conservatives together. For some Senate Republicans, passing Alexander-Murray was essential to their supporting a tax bill that repealed the individual mandate. But House conservatives disliked spending the money that Alexander-Murray would cost. In any event, as a separate measure outside the reconciliation process, the bill would require sixty votes to pass the Senate, and Senate Democrats, including Murray, said they would not vote for it if the individual mandate were eliminated. Deficit hawks like Corker, McCain, and Flake intensely disliked the tax bill's planned $1.5 trillion addition to the national debt, not to mention the more realistic projection of $2 trillion. Wisconsin senator Ron Johnson said he could not vote for a bill that treated corporations better than small businesses. And once again, Trump did little to help matters, even gratuitously tweeting that Flake "will be a NO on tax cuts because his political career anyway is 'toast.'"[58] Only the Republicans' passion for cutting taxes and fear of having no accomplishments at all heading into the 2018 midterm election augured favorably for a tax bill.

IMMIGRATION

As discussed in chapter 4, Trump did not rely chiefly on legislation in pursuing his twin goals of deporting most undocumented immigrants already in the country and keeping additional immigrants out. But he did turn to Congress on two important immigration-related matters. The first was to secure funding to fulfill his campaign promise to build a wall along the nation's southern border, an approximately 1,900-mile-long structure that would span four states: California, Arizona, New Mexico, and Texas. The second, which was not foreshadowed during the campaign, was to embed in law the nation's policy toward immigrants who had been brought into the country illegally as children—the so-called "Dreamers." (DREAM stands for Development, Relief, and Education for Alien Minors.) The wall starkly divided the two parties in Congress. The Dreamers seemed to offer a possibility for bipartisan cooperation—until, that is, Trump decided to make building the wall a condition for helping the Dreamers.

Trump alternated between demanding that Congress appropriate funds to build a border wall and backing down when other matters became more urgent. In May he included $1.6 billion for the wall in a proposed omnibus appropriations bill to fund the government through the end of the fiscal year in September. Because some ardently conservative Republican members were determined to vote against any spending measure, the president needed Democratic votes to pass it. When congressional Democrats insisted that wall funding be eliminated as a condition of their support, Trump caved in, blustering on Twitter: "Our country needs a good 'shutdown' in September to fix mess!"[59] Soon afterward, he backed down again for the sake of securing Democratic support for the resolution to continue funding the government into December.

September also saw a series of events related to the Dreamers, whose legal status in the United States rested on the thin legal reed of an executive order of uncertain constitutionality that President Obama issued in 2012. On September 4, after Attorney General Jeff Sessions told the president that he would not defend the Obama order's legality in a lawsuit about to be filed the next day by several Republican state attorneys general, Trump authorized him to announce that he would repeal the order in six months. On September 13, however, Trump had dinner at the White House with Pelosi and Schumer, and the two Democratic congressional leaders came away convinced that they had persuaded the president to support the DREAM Act, a 2013 proposal to legalize the Dreamers' presence in the United States and create a path to citizenship for them.

Trump further agreed, Pelosi and Schumer said, to put aside his proposal for a wall in favor of other border security measures.[60] When they announced this right after dinner, conservative Republicans in Congress and on talk radio and social media exploded in protest. Breitbart, Trump's staunchest media supporter, labeled the president "Amnesty Don."[61] "No, we're not looking at citizenship," Trump said the next day, denying that any deal had been struck; "We're not looking at amnesty. We're looking at allowing people to stay here."[62] Simultaneously, the Congressional Hispanic Caucus blistered Schumer and Pelosi for offering to support enhanced border security of any kind, and other liberal Democrats criticized their leaders for "normalizing" Trump by dealing with him at all. "We get alarmed at the speculation that this might be a new day dawning," said Democratic representative Gerry Connolly of Virginia.[63]

Congressional Republicans who wanted to see the status of at least some of the Dreamers legalized offered measures such as the Succeed Act, which created a fifteen-year path to citizenship, and the Border Security and Deferred Action Recipient Relief Act, which paired a similar provision with enhanced border security. But on October 9, Trump issued a list of hard-line demands that he said "must be included" in any new legislation to protect the Dreamers. These included the hiring of new immigration agents, judges, and lawyers; rapid deportation of unaccompanied children crossing the border; the denial of federal grant money to "sanctuary cities" and of citizenship to the Dreamers; and, most of all, funding for the wall. "The administration can't be serious," said Schumer, despairing of the agreement he and Pelosi thought they had secured with the president four weeks earlier.[64] They joined a long list of Republican legislators who had come to realize that Trump viewed deal-making in highly fluid real estate terms rather than fixed political terms, in which standing by one's word is essential to being trusted in the future.

Trump went after Schumer again on November 1 after a terrorist inspired by ISIS drove a truck through a New York City bike path, killing eight people. The accused killer had been admitted to the United States from Uzbekistan through a bill Schumer sponsored in 1990, when he was a member of the House. The bill created a "diversity visa lottery," which granted permanent residency status to fifty thousand people per year from countries with few immigrants. Trump tweeted that the program was "a Chuck Schumer beauty" and called for its immediate repeal by Congress.[65]

OTHER MEASURES

For a newly elected president whose party controlled both houses of Congress even narrowly, Trump's first-year record of legislative futility was remarkable. Weeks beyond the anniversary of his election, Obamacare remained legally intact and the border wall remained unfunded. The short-term burst of regulatory rollbacks under the Congressional Review Act had ended in early May, and for months afterward little was enacted other than billions of dollars being earmarked for hurricane relief. Administration planning for a major infrastructure bill grounded in the president's original desire to emphasize public-private partnerships in building roads, air traffic control systems, and other networks was derailed in September when Trump suddenly decided that he wanted state governments, not the private sector, to foot most of the bill.[66] In any event, Republican legislators were unenthusiastic about launching an expensive new federal program.

One exception to this pattern of congressional inaction, discussed in chapter 8, was a bipartisan measure to impose sanctions on Russia over the president's strong objection. Another was a Senate measure to prevent the president making recess appointments during the chamber's summer recess in order to discourage Trump from firing Attorney General Sessions. In addition, various House and Senate committees, led by Republican chairs, launched investigations of Russian meddling on behalf of Trump's candidacy in 2016.

7 ★ COMMUNICATIONS

Donald Trump's public communications during the 2016 presidential campaign were as effective as they were unorthodox. Most candidates for president, including Hillary Clinton and Trump's rivals for the Republican nomination, followed the standard campaign playbook: raise massive amounts of money for paid media—that is, television, radio, and web-based advertising—and thereby control their message to the voters. In unscripted events, especially televised debates, the textbook strategy was to be as script-like as possible, delivering well-rehearsed sound bites regardless of the questions that were asked.

In sharp contrast, the Trump campaign downplayed paid media, partly because he, rather than political donors, was paying many of the bills with his own fortune and partly because it was so easy for him to make the sort of news that attracted extensive coverage—so-called earned media. News coverage during the year before an election usually is dominated by the candidate who does best in the polls and raises the most money.[1] For most of 2015 that was former Florida governor Jeb Bush. But cable news networks repeatedly televised Trump's speeches live, responding to the ratings surge that occurred whenever they showed or discussed him. Trump was "the new, the unusual, the sensational."[2] In addition to being a businessman, he was a celebrity. Before entering politics in 2015 Trump built a large audience as a best-selling author, a frequent talk-show guest, a guest battler in pro wrestling spectacles, and the star of two popular NBC television series. By mid-March 2016, he had already enjoyed an estimated $1.9 billion of earned media coverage of his campaign, compared with the $0.7 billion received by Hillary Clinton.[3]

Trump's reliance on the news media to advance his reputation went back a long way. In pursuit of his ambition to expand his family's Long Island–centered real estate business into the cutthroat Manhattan market, Trump began cultivating contacts in the New York press in the early 1970s—and never stopped. The city's famously competitive gossip columnists and tabloid newspapers—the *New York Daily News* and the *New York Post*— were only too happy to cooperate. Trump's eye-catching appearance, serial marriages and affairs, provocative pronouncements on controversial issues, ownership of a United States Football League team (and leadership of a much-publicized lawsuit against the National Football League), and flirtations with running for president as early as 1988 provided good fodder for blaring front-page headlines. So did his branding of prominent buildings and businesses (some of which later became defunct) with the Trump name: Trump Tower in midtown Manhattan, the Trump Taj Mahal casino in Atlantic City, a dozen Trump National Golf Clubs, various Trump International Hotel and Towers, the Trump Shuttle (a short-lived airline), Trump University (another flop), and so on. The television and radio networks' growing emphasis on nationally broadcast talk shows starting in the 1980s was tailor-made for the flamboyant, provocative Trump. He spent hours on the phone with reporters, gossip columnists, and talk-show hosts, sometimes even posing as someone else calling to pass along a hot tip about the celebrity known as "The Donald."[4] What Trump concluded from this experience was that being in the news was more important than what the news was. His prominence in the media fostered a public image of Trump as the embodiment of success, even as several of his companies underwent bankruptcies, lawsuits from unpaid contractors, and other failures.

In contrast to most of his rivals for the Republican presidential nomination in 2016, nothing about being in the bright media spotlight was new to Trump. His debate appearances during the campaign, like his speeches and interviews, were freewheeling and largely spontaneous. Bush, his main early rival for the Republican nomination, practically wilted when Trump branded him "low-energy" in one debate. When Ted Cruz replaced Bush as Trump's major rival for the nomination after winning the Iowa caucuses, Trump renamed him "Lyin' Ted." The label stuck even though Cruz's only offense was that his campaign circulated an errant CNN story that another candidate, Ben Carson, was dropping out of the race.

Knowing that Republican voters are especially distrustful of the news media, Trump made attacks on CNN, the *New York Times*, the *Washington Post*, and other mainstream outlets as "totally dishonest" and "scum" a standard feature of his rallies, thereby inoculating himself against their reports about his factually inaccurate statements and spotted business record. The rallies themselves bore some resemblance to rock concerts, the political scientist Bruce Miroff has argued: "the star performer in the spotlight, the fans garbed in Make America Great Again hats and tee shirts, the crowds aggressively chanting favorite lines, especially 'Build the Wall' and 'Lock Her Up.' "[5] Corey Lewandowski offered a different stadium-based comparison: "People weren't coming to a Trump rally so he could read off a teleprompter. . . . It's like going to a sporting event. You don't know what the outcome is going to be so you want to go and see it in person."[6]

In addition to free television, Trump made masterful and unprecedented use of a relatively new social medium: Twitter. Within the constraints of the 140-character tweet format, he could send messages directly to millions of voters, who in turn forwarded them to millions more. Trump used tweets to proclaim ("MAKE AMERICA GREAT AGAIN!"), to attack ("Hillary Clinton should have been prosecuted and should be in jail"), and to defend ("For those few people knocking me for tweeting at three o'clock in the morning, at least you know I will be there, awake, to answer the call!").[7] "Without the tweets I wouldn't be here," Trump said after taking office.[8]

As a candidate, Trump acknowledged that being president would be different than running for president. Concerning Twitter, he said: "I'll give it up after I'm president. We won't tweet any more. I don't know. Not presidential."[9] For the moment, at least, Trump seemed to grasp the distinction between campaigning and governing. Campaigns are won by defeating a series of opponents. The words spoken by a candidate, however specific, have no direct effect on the conduct of government. In contrast, governing is about securing cooperation from other constitutional actors in a government of "separated institutions sharing powers."[10] And words, spoken no longer by a presidential candidate but by a president, often have important consequences.

By inauguration eve, Trump had forgotten the difference and changed his mind about tweeting. "I think I'll keep it. . . . It's working," he said.[11] He did keep it, averaging about five tweets per day. As the journalist Michael Kruse has pointed out, Trump's tweets assumed a distinctive, almost genre-like form: "a one-sentence declaration . . . followed usually by a one-word assertion of emotion: 'Weak!' 'Strong!' "WIN!' 'Terrible!' 'Sad! 'BAD!'"[12] Sometimes these messages, however visceral, involved presidential-level public policy—for example, the Affordable Care Act is "horrible," "imploding," "dead." More often, however, Trump's tweets were impulsive, petty, aimed at small targets, and distinctly unpresidential—not just undignified but at times ineffective. His tweets tore down much more effectively than they built up.

"Crooked Hillary" and "Fake News" took root in a way that "great healthcare" and "a great plan" did not.[13] By the end of September 2017, Trump had tweeted the word "loser" 234 times, "incompetent" 92 times, and "pathetic" 72 times.[14] Nonetheless, on July 1 he tweeted, "My use of social media is not Presidential—it's MODERN DAY PRESIDENTIAL."[15] By December, Trump had more than 43 million followers on Twitter, exceeding the total number of daily subscribers (including online subscribers) to all the newspapers in the United States. Combining his various personal and White Houses social media accounts, Trump approached 120 million followers. "I wouldn't be here if it wasn't for social media," he said.[16] No one disputed the point.

For Trump, Twitter was a direct pipeline to his supporters, unfiltered by the news media. A July 2017 poll found that 91 percent of Republicans trusted him more than CNN. To keep his base mobilized, Trump left few criticisms unanswered during long stretches of watching four to eight hours of cable news programs per day.[17] He often reacted in the moment. "When somebody says something about me, I am able to go bing, bing, bing and I take care of it," Trump said.[18] At 9:00 a.m. on June 28, for example, apparently while viewing *Morning Joe* on MSNBC, the president tweeted an attack on cohosts "low I.Q. Crazy Mika" Brzezinski and "Psycho Joe" Scarborough, adding that in a recent meeting Brzezinski "was bleeding badly from a face lift."[19] A few days later he retweeted a 2007 video of himself body-slamming WWE owner Vince McMahon at a WrestleMania event, with McMahon's head replaced by a CNN logo. These tweets were posted during the administration's planned "Energy Week," seven days in which Trump was urged by aides to direct the nation's attention to his policies promoting oil, gas, and nuclear production. He then spent much of "Made in America" week tweeting attacks on his own attorney general, Jeff Sessions, for recusing himself from the Justice Department's investigation into Russian interference in the election.

Other targets of Trump's tweets included Arnold Schwarzenegger, comedian Kathy Griffin, *Saturday Night Live*, Germany, Sweden, Chicago, Nordstrom, federal judges, Senate Majority Leader Mitch McConnell and other Republican legislators, "Cryin' Chuck Schumer," the mayor of London, the mayor of San Juan, the Emmy awards, liberal filmmaker Michael Moore, and, repeatedly, "Fake News CNN, . . . NBC, CBS & NBC, . . . the failing @nytimes & @washingtonpost. They are all Fake News." In late November Trump singled out *Time* magazine for allegedly telling him "that I was PROBABLY going to be named Man (Person) of the Year. . . . I said probably is no good and took a pass."[20] No critic of the president was immune from Trump's retaliatory Twitter finger, but, along with the media, African Americans seemed to rouse his special ire: Obama, NBA start Stephen Curry, *SportsCenter* host Jemele Hill, protesting NFL players, Representatives John Lewis and Frederica Wilson—even LaVar Ball, the father of one of the three UCLA basketball players Trump criticized for not immediately thanking him when they were released from a Chinese jail on shoplifting charges. "IT WAS ME! . . . I should have left them in jail!" he tweeted on November 19, then branded Ball an "Ungrateful fool!" three days later for saying that if he was going to thank anybody, he would "probably thank President Xi" of China.[21] The president's attack on Senator Al Franken (labeled but misspelled as "Frankenstien") for admitting to sexually violating two women, even as Trump was exonerating accused Alabama Republican Senate candidate Roy Moore ("He says it didn't happen. You have to listen to him also") revived memories of the complaints that more than a dozen women lodged against Trump himself during the 2016 campaign.[22] As far as Trump was concerned, he and Moore were the true victims of "horrible, horrible liars."[23]

Trump's style as president mirrored his style as a candidate: he "repeated his claims incessantly and projected his own vices onto his opponents."[24] As a candidate, for example, Trump answered

Hillary Clinton's charge in their third debate that he was "Putin's puppet" playground style: "No puppet, no puppet. You're the puppet." As president, when news reports surfaced on October 29, 2017, that special counsel Robert Mueller was about to announce the first indictments in his investigation of possible collusion between Russia and the Trump campaign, Trump issued a flurry of tweets on the theme: "There is so much GUILT by Democrats/ Clinton, and now the facts are pouring out. . . . Instead they look at phony Trump/Russia 'collusion,' which doesn't exist."[25]

"Please just stop," an exasperated Republican senator Ben Sasse of Nebraska tweeted to the president; "This isn't normal and it's beneath the dignity of your office."[26] More than that, some of Trump's tweets provided fodder for judges ruling against the anti-Muslim bias of his travel bans and investigators looking into Russia's role in his election and his motives for firing FBI director James Comey. Upholding a lower court's decision that the travel ban on visitors from majority-Muslim countries was discriminatory, for example, on July 12, 2017, the Ninth Circuit Court of Appeals cited his tweet of a week earlier that "we need a TRAVEL BAN for certain DANGEROUS COUNTRIES, not some politically correct term that won't help us protect our people!"[27] At the October 30 sentencing hearing for Sergeant Bowe Bergdahl, who pleaded guilty to desertion in Afghanistan, the military judge said he would consider as "mitigation evidence" Trump's inflammatory statements during the campaign that Bergdahl was "a dirty, rotten traitor" who should be shot or dropped out of an airplane.[28] When the judge handed down a sentence that did not include further imprisonment, Trump tweeted, "The decision on Sergeant Bergdahl is a complete and total disgrace to our Country and to our Military."[29] On November 21 federal district court judge Marvin Garbis cited the president's "capricious, arbitrary, and unqualified tweet of new policy" to overturn a Trump order that the military not pay for gender-reassignment surgery for transgender service members.[30]

Trump's tweets sometimes had the effect of undermining his own administration. Some argued that his recurring anti-CNN tweets weakened the Justice Department's legal argument that AT&T should not be allowed to merge with Time-Warner, which owns the news network.[31] As discussed in chapter 8, Trump undercut even his own secretary of state, Rex Tillerson, with tweets on matters that Tillerson was in the midst of negotiating with foreign governments. "I wake up the next morning, the president's got a tweet out there," he said; "I wasn't expecting that."[32] A former CIA analyst described Trump's tweets as "a gold mine for every foreign intelligence agency" because they provided direct evidence of his "stress level and state of mind" as well as his "preoccupations, personality quirks, and habits."[33]

To the extent that a strategy governed Trump's broader range of public communications, it was the same as for his use of Twitter: to solidify his base and to change the subject when unfavorable developments dominated the news. Trump's inaugural address, for example, painted a dystopian portrait of "American carnage" marked by "the crime and the gangs and the drugs," "the ravages of other countries," and closed factories "like tombstones"—similar to his campaign speeches, but in sharp contrast to all fifty-seven previous inaugural addresses, each of which invoked widely shared American values and appealed for national unity.[34] Further uprooting long-established traditions, Trump bragged to the National Scout Jamboree about various states he carried in the election and urged naval personnel to contact Congress in support of his health care legislation. He was chastised by the Boy Scouts of America's chief executive for the first speech and by various military officers for the second.[35] Most of Trump's public speeches as president were stream-of-consciousness orations at campaign-style rallies held in states he carried in the election. In contrast, not once did Trump deliver an address to the nation explaining and defending his major legislative priority, repealing and replacing Obamacare.

In late September, in the face of headlines about the latest failure to repeal Obamacare and a looming defeat for the Trump-endorsed Senator Luther Strange in the Alabama Republican primary, Trump unleashed an extended series of feisty remarks and tweets attacking NFL players who refused to stand for the national anthem and the liberals and team owners who supported them. Striking a chord with some voters by transforming a protest against excessive police violence in minority neighborhoods into an unpatriotic gesture of disrespect toward the flag and the military, he kept it up in the months that followed, even as the number of defiant players went down. NFL commissioner Roger Goodell's concession that "we believe that everyone should stand for the National Anthem" was not enough for Trump, who tweeted: "The NFL has decided that it will not force players to stand for the playing of our National Anthem. Total disrespect for our great country!"[36] Television ratings for NFL games fell by about 7.5 percent from the previous year, and Dallas Cowboys owner Jerry Jones said, "There is no question the league is suffering negative effects from these protests."[37] "If Trump wins [in 2020]," wrote the conservative columnist Rich Lowry, "it will surely have something to with a dynamic like the one that played out with the NFL. Trump will cause an unthinking overreaction by Democrats on a culture issue or issues, and the party will be wrong-footed by the insularity of its own political and media ecosystem."[38] "Why cede the flag to Trump?" asked the *Atlantic* writer David Frum.[39]

A recurring theme of Trump's communications was that he was surrounded by enemies. Journalists are the "enemy of the American People"—"sick people" who "don't like our country," he tweeted in February and told an August rally in Phoenix.[40] "The president's enemies don't want him to succeed," said a television

ad aired by his reelection committee more than three years before
the 2020 election.[41] In the reality television programs on which
Trump thrived before entering politics, audiences much prefer
to see conflicts spiral out of control than to see them resolved.[42]
"You're fired!" was the popular catchphrase of *The Apprentice,* not
"you've got the job." Trump seemed determined to hang on to
the roughly one in five voters who supported him in the election
even though they viewed him negatively by keeping the focus on
those—Hillary Clinton then, the media, the Democrats, and out-
spoken black athletes now—whom they liked even less. Actually,
Clinton now as well—in an October 16 news conference, Trump
said, "Hillary, please run again!"[43]

Trump's recurring attacks on the "MSM" (mainstream media)
as the enemy of the people also were designed to keep those outlets on the defensive.[44] In this effort he was building on a foundation laid by Republicans a half century ago, when Richard Nixon
and his supporters waged a systematic campaign to discredit the
"liberal news media," especially the three broadcast networks
(ABC, CBS, and NBC) that dominated the airwaves at the time
and the leading eastern newspapers (especially the *New York Times*
and *Washington Post*) that shaped national news coverage. In the
1980s, after the Federal Communications Commission abolished
the fairness doctrine, talk radio emerged as an alternative source
of news and opinion for conservative voters, followed in the 1990s
by cable television's Fox News and in the 2000s by various online
outlets, including the Drudge Report and Breitbart. Vice President
Mike Pence hosted a talk radio program from 1995 to 1999 before
running successfully for Congress in 2000. In addition to rhetori-
cally discrediting the MSM, Trump steered his supporters to these
sympathetic outlets as well as to conservative social media groups.
But the ratings for all three cable news networks, not just Fox, rose
substantially during the president's first year with prime-time pro-
gramming that was essentially all Trump, all the time.[45]

As with the unilateral executive actions discussed in chapter 4, unilateral communications by a president are most effective when shaped and amplified by other members of the president's team. But Trump's White House communications office was in constant turmoil. At the eight-month mark of his presidency, Trump was already on his third communications director. Mike Dubke, who was first, left in early June after less than three months on the job. His replacement, Anthony Scaramucci, spent his eleven days in the position making profanity-laced phone calls to reporters and stirring strife within the White House staff, only to be succeeded in September by Hope Hicks, whose relationship with Trump extended back to the beginning of his campaign. Trump's first press secretary, Sean Spicer, became a laughingstock on *Saturday Night Live* and other comedy shows in his first week. Adding to Spicer's woes was Trump's displeasure with everything from the cut of his suits to his inability to defend the indefensible, such as the president's easily refuted assertion that the crowd at his inauguration was larger than the crowd at Obama's first inauguration. Senior Trump advisor Kellyanne Conway did not help matters when she defended Spicer as having offered "alternative facts."[46] Sarah Huckabee Sanders, who replaced Spicer in July, was a far more confident but no more persuasive defender of the president.

Leaks also plagued the Trump administration. During the campaign, when e-mails from Clinton and the Democratic Party were published online, Trump read from them to a campaign rally and said, "I love WikiLeaks."[47] His perspective changed after he became president, especially when members of the White House staff talked freely but anonymously to reporters in an effort either to undermine each other or to influence decisions they thought were going the wrong way. Other leaks came from dissident bureaucrats and were designed to embarrass their nominal bosses, the president and his cabinet members. An infuriated Trump pressured the attorney general to crack down on leakers. In an effort to get back in the president's good graces, on August 4 Sessions announced that the Justice Department was pursuing three times as many leak investigations as were open at the end of the Obama administration. He also reported that the FBI had created a new counterintelligence unit to pursue leaks of classified information from inside the government.[48]

Appointed as White House chief of staff to replace the hapless Reince Priebus in late July, General John Kelly brought some discipline to the staff. But Kelly despaired of changing the ways of the leading offender: the president himself. With a grim-faced Kelly looking on, Trump spent August 15, the first day of "Infrastructure Week," responding to reporters' questions about the previous weekend's events in Charlottesville, where racist demonstrators clashed with counterprotesters, one of whom was killed and more than a dozen injured. After having read a formal statement the day before denouncing "white supremacists" for the violence, Trump now defended his initial public reaction on the day of the riot, which was to "condemn hatred, bigotry and violence on many sides, on many sides."[49] "Not all of those people were neo-Nazis, believe me," Trump now said of the protestors, some of whom he described as "very fine people. . . . You had a group on the other side that came charging in without a permit, and they were very, very violent."[50]

Kelly's frustration with "Unplugged Trump" (as compared with the less rarely seen "Teleprompter Trump," who stuck to his script) extended to the president's continuing reliance on Twitter.[51] On one unusually (but not unprecedentedly) busy Sunday morning in September, Trump began tweeting at 7:50 a.m. One tweet taunted the young but nuclear-armed North Korean dictator Kim Jong-un as "Rocket Man." Another retweeted a user called @fuctupmind's doctored video of Trump driving a golf ball into Hillary Clinton's back. Yet another retweet showed an electoral map of the United States with every state colored red and the headline "keep it up

Libs. This will be 2020." The following weekend Trump tweeted a request to NFL fans to "refuse to go to the games until players stop disrespecting our Flag & Country." These player should be told: "YOU'RE FIRED."[52] Short stretches of disciplined communication invariably were followed by tweet storms. After remaining on script for much of his twelve-day trip to Asia in November, for example, Trump erupted on Twitter on the ninth day, attacking Obama, the "Fake News Media," "Crooked Hillary Clinton," and "the haters and fools" who opposed his Russia policy. Responding to a North Korean government statement that he was "an old lunatic," Trump took offense not at the lunacy charge but rather at the reference to his age. "Why would Kim Jong-un insult me by calling me 'old,' when I would NEVER call him 'short and fat'?" he tweeted.[53]

8 ★ FOREIGN POLICY

In matters of foreign policy, Donald Trump took office with no experience, little knowledge, and hardly any connections with people who did have experience or knowledge. During the campaign he offered a series of bold statements whose theme was that although recent presidents had been inept and weak in their dealings with the rest of the world, he would put "America First," winning back jobs that had gone overseas, securing the nation's borders, avoiding feckless wars, and, by drawing on his self-proclaimed deal-making prowess, forging agreements with foreign leaders from a position of economic and military strength. After the election Trump disdained the daily intelligence briefings that could have brought him up to speed on the issues for which he would be responsible as president. "I don't have to be told the same things in the same words every single day for the next eight years," he explained.[1] Trump dismissed the widely respected director of national intelligence, James Clapper, and CIA director John Brennan as "political hacks."[2]

AN OSCILLATING FOREIGN POLICY

Like most presidents, Trump enjoyed foreign policy, in which he got to play the statesman and commander in chief, more than domestic policy, with its tangled web of other constitutional actors and vocal grassroots demands. Comparing foreign to domestic policy in October 2017, Trump said: "I want to focus on North Korea, I want to focus on Iran. . . . I don't want to focus on fixing somebody's back or their knee or something. Let the states do that."[3] During the campaign he spoke with real relish about applying his deal-making skills as a real estate developer to negotiations with other heads of government. In his first hundred days in office, he hosted sixteen meetings with foreign leaders and talked on the phone with forty-three, often placing or returning calls without being briefed by foreign policy specialists in his administration.[4]

In several cases, these meetings and conversations led the president to change his mind. Chinese president Xi Jinping easily convinced Trump that his country was no longer, as Trump often had declared during the election, a "currency manipulator" that was artificially keeping down the value of the yuan in order to make its goods cheaper on world markets. King Abdullah II of Jordan readily persuaded Trump not to rush his campaign promise to move the American embassy in Israel to Jerusalem, which he had vowed to do on "Day One."[5] Yet in an early phone conversation in which Australian prime minister Malcolm Turnbull pressed him to honor an agreement to accept as many as 1,250 economic refugees from Iran, Pakistan, and Afghanistan, Trump bridled: "Who made the deal? Obama? This is a stupid deal. This deal will make me look terrible." "There is nothing more important in business or in politics than a deal is a deal," said Turnbull.[6]

Trump quickly forsook some additional rashly made campaign promises. As a candidate he proclaimed that he was "psyched" to terminate NAFTA, "the worst trade deal maybe ever signed anywhere"; that "Islam hates us"; that NATO is "obsolete"; that it was "time to get out of Afghanistan"; and that the war in Iraq was "one of the great mistakes in the history of our country."[7] Yet early in his first year as president Trump decided to try to renegotiate rather than repeal NAFTA; described Islam as "one of the world's great religions"; declared that the United States would "strongly support

NATO" ("It's no longer obsolete," he recanted); authorized the secretary of defense and the CIA director to intensify the war in Afghanistan; and expanded the American military presence in Iraq.[8] He did, however, keep certain campaign promises that were consistent with his America First theme, such as withdrawing the United States from the Trans-Pacific Partnership and initiating the three-year process required to leave the Paris climate accord.

Trump's oscillations in foreign policy reflected in part his lack of considered opinions ("I like to think of myself as a very flexible person") and, more importantly, the strong divisions among his advisors.[9] The new president's foreign policy team consisted largely of generals and business leaders whom he admired for their success in war and commerce, domains that (in contrast to civilian government service) he regarded highly. Secretary of State Rex Tillerson, Secretary of the Treasury Steve Mnuchin, and National Economic Council director Gary Cohn came from the world of business. Secretary of Defense James Mattis and National Security Advisor Michael Flynn were high-ranking generals in the U.S. Marine Corps and Army, respectively. All but Flynn were internationalists who wanted to steer Trump away from unilateralism and isolation. When Flynn was replaced just weeks into the administration by H. R. McMaster, another army general, the team became uniformly internationalist. In addition to his high regard for these individuals and openness to most of their views, Trump also delegated many military decisions to Mattis and, through the defense secretary, to the officer corps. Early resolves to drop the largest conventional bomb in history on an ISIS bunker complex and to arm the Syrian Kurds were made by Mattis, who in turn empowered theater commanders in Yemen and Somalia to launch strikes against terrorists on their own authority.

In contrast, the nationalists in Trump's administration were civilians concentrated mostly in the White House, notably the political strategist Steve Bannon and policy advisor and speechwriter Stephen Miller. Their influence was based less on the offices they occupied and Trump's respect for their expertise or pre-governmental accomplishments than on the loyalty they displayed during the campaign and their fidelity to his America First theme. Presidential speeches often became battlegrounds between them and the internationalists. Trump's May 25, 2017, address to NATO, for example, originally included a statement pledging his country's "unwavering . . . commitment to the NATO alliance," which the internationalists wanted. But it was excised by the nationalists from the version Trump actually delivered.[10] In July, a major foreign policy speech in Warsaw became a pastiche of nationalist and internationalist themes, embracing NATO but speaking darkly about the decline of the West and asking: "Do we have enough respect for our citizens to respect our borders? Do we have the desire and courage to preserve our civilization in the face of those who would subvert and destroy it?"[11] "Hey, I'm a nationalist and a globalist," said Trump, embracing the contradiction with postmodern zeal; "I'm both."[12]

Changes within the administration affected the relationship between nationalists and internationalists during the course of its first year. On one side, McMaster's removal of Bannon from the National Security Council's Principals Committee in February and Bannon's departure from the administration in August left the nationalists without their loudest voice in the White House. So did McMaster's firing of some nationalist members of the NSC staff, notably Ezra Cohen-Watnick, Sebastian Gorka, Rich Higgins, and Derek Harvey, as well as the reduction in status of trade hard-liner Peter Navarro, who was told in September to start reporting to Cohn instead of to the president.

On the other side, Trump's and several White House aides' growing disregard for Tillerson, who focused on studying ways to "redesign" the admittedly bloated, top-heavy State Department rather than on filling its most important policy-making and diplomatic positions, weakened his influence as well.[13] By late November, for example, with tensions flaring on the Korean peninsula, Tillerson had yet to choose an assistant secretary for East Asian and Pacific Affairs or an ambassador to South Korea.[14] On more than one occasion, the president publicly undermined the secretary. On June 9, when Tillerson called on Saudi Arabia and an allied bloc of Arab nations to end their air, sea, and land blockade of neighboring Qatar and begin "a calm and thoughtful dialogue," Trump immediately condemned Qatar as "a funder of terror at a very high level," claiming to have learned that on his recent trip to Saudi Arabia.[15] On October 1, one day after the secretary said while in China that "We ask [North Korea], 'Would you like to talk?' We have lines of communication to Pyongyang," Trump tweeted that Tillerson "is wasting his time trying to negotiate with Little Rocket Man," his epithet for North Korean dictator Kim Jong-un.[16] Senator Bob Corker charged that Trump was trying to "publicly castrate [his] own secretary of state."[17] When NBC News reported in October that Tillerson had referred to the president in July as a "f—ing moron" after he said in an Oval Office meeting that the United States should have 32,000 nuclear weapons instead of its current force of 4,000, Trump responded, "If he did that, I guess we'll have to compare I.Q. tests. And I can tell you who is going to win."[18]

Some foreign policy issues were less matters of nationalist-internationalist conflict within the administration than of the president's own confusion. During the campaign, Trump wondered, "If we could get along with Russia, wouldn't that be a good thing?"[19] Of Russian leader Vladimir Putin, he said: "I've always had a good instinct about Putin. . . . He's running his country and at least he's a leader, unlike what we have in this country."[20] What infuriated Trump was the great mass of evidence gathered by American intelligence agencies proving that Putin's government had covertly worked to help him win the election by undermining Hillary

Clinton, who had locked horns with the Russians several times as secretary of state. His reaction once in office was to oscillate between efforts to reach out to Putin and contradictory attempts to prove his independence by, for example, launching a cruise missile attack on April 6 against the Syrian government, Russia's ally, when it used chemical weapons in its civil war. Nor did Trump ever let go of his anger at news stories and Justice Department and congressional investigations probing Putin's support for his election, which in Trump's mind were designed to devalue his victory. The day after his son Donald Trump Jr. released e-mails showing that the Russian government wanted Trump to win, the president strangely claimed that Putin "would like Hillary [because] she wants to have windmills" and "wouldn't have spent the money on military" that Trump was spending.[21]

In the face of administration opposition Senate Republicans, long antagonistic toward Russia, and Senate Democrats, deeply antagonistic to Trump, put aside their differences and voted 98 to 2 in June for a bill to impose new sanctions on Russia and, in an act of uncommon disrespect, require the president to seek congressional approval before easing or lifting them. The House passed the bill in July by an equally lopsided 419–3 majority. With no prospect that a presidential veto would be upheld in either chamber, Trump reluctantly signed the measure. Putin, frustrated by his failed gamble that a Trump presidency would be consistently good for his government and, in particular, would provide relief from existing American and European sanctions imposed when he annexed Crimea in 2014, retaliated by ordering U.S. diplomatic missions in Russia to reduce their staffs by 775 people. But he was pleased once again by Trump's ready embrace when they met informally at the Asia-Pacific Economic Cooperation summit in Danang, Vietnam, in November. Trump is "very professional, very friendly, and behaves very appropriately," Putin said after Trump told the press that Putin "said he absolutely did not meddle in our election. . . .

I really believe that, when he tells me that, he means it."[22] "There are two approaches to the Kremlin inside this administration," wrote the journalist Susan Glasser in an article called "Trump's Russian Schizophrenia": "the president's and everyone else's."[23]

Aggravating Trump's lack of knowledge and experience concerning foreign policy was his impatience with others' efforts to educate him about the world. "It would take an hour and a half to learn everything there is to know about missiles," he once said when asked about forging a nuclear arms agreement; "I think I know most of it anyway."[24] McMaster found it difficult to hold Trump's attention when, based on the rigorous process he instituted to integrate the perspectives of relevant departments and agencies, he tried to brief the president on complex foreign policy issues. "I call the president the two-minute man," said one presidential confidant; "The president has patience for a half-page."[25] At one point in July, McMaster, Mattis, and Tillerson grew so concerned about Trump's lack of appreciation for the importance of a robust American diplomatic, military, and intelligence presence around the world that they forced an uninterruptible briefing on him in the secure Pentagon meeting room known as the Tank. Their strategy was to appeal to his long-standing habits as a real estate developer by using charts and maps to illustrate their points, as well as by focusing on the value that military officers, diplomats, and intelligence agents provide in securing foreign markets for the kinds of American-based businesses that Trump himself had invested in abroad.[26] Concerning Afghanistan and the Middle East, they were able to make some headway with him. Their efforts in regard to North Korea and Latin America were less successful.

THE WAR IN AFGHANISTAN

Nothing tested the ability of the determined internationalists on Trump's foreign policy team to influence the president more strenuously than the issue of what to do about the war in Afghani-stan. The war, which was in its sixteenth year when Trump took office, was launched one month after the September 11, 2001, attacks on the World Trade Center and the Pentagon. Its purpose was to topple and replace the radical Islamist Taliban regime that provided a safe haven for al Qaeda, the terrorist network that planned the attacks and trained the attackers. Initially successful in imposing a new regime in Kabul, the war soon deteriorated into a seemingly endless slog between a corrupt, ineffectual Afghan government, propped up by American and allied soldiers and money, and a resurgent Taliban. In December 2009, President Obama agreed to deploy additional troops to Afghanistan, raising the number above one hundred thousand, but he simultaneously declared that the "surge" would end and the troops withdraw in eighteen months. Military leaders, including Mattis and McMaster, both of whom had been stationed in Afghanistan, fumed at the time that Obama had undermined his own effort by telling the enemy exactly how long it had to wait before safely resuming its efforts to take over the country. When they entered the Trump administration they were determined to steer the new president onto a course different from those that Obama had pursued and Trump had promised during the campaign.

The challenge Mattis and McMaster faced was not easy. Trump repeatedly pressed them to explain why the United States was still in Afghanistan. He reluctantly authorized the secretary of defense to send an additional 3,900 troops there, which would raise the force to about 17,000 American and allied soldiers, but Mattis was shrewd enough not to do so until Trump was persuaded that the move made sense. The generals had to overcome opposition from Bannon, who reminded Trump that as early as 2012 he had tweeted: "Afghanistan is a complete waste! Time to come home."[27] Bannon proposed hiring a private military contractor or infiltrating covert intelligence agents instead of sending additional American troops but was marginalized when his close allies at Breitbart and other conservative publications began publicly attacking McMaster. By the time the president and his national security team gathered at Camp David to make a decision on the weekend of August 18, Bannon had been fired.

Mattis and McMaster, augmented by General John Kelly, the president's chief of staff, and Vice President Mike Pence, convinced the president to embrace a heightened military presence in Afghanistan by stressing the failures of the Obama administration—exactly the sort of argument at which Trump's ears perked up. By shrinking the American force in both Afghanistan and Iraq, they said, Obama had opened the door to the Taliban in the former and to ISIS—the even more nightmarishly radical Islamic State of Iraq and Syria—in the latter. Without the additional American troops they were recommending, Afghanistan would once again become a spawning ground for terrorist attacks against the United States. Equally to the point, they explained that the additional troops would not just be doing more of the same but would be training the Afghan army in the field instead of only at headquarters.

"My original instinct was to pull out," Trump told the nation in a televised prime-time speech on August 21, "and historically I like following my instincts." But he had been persuaded that "a hasty withdrawal would create a vacuum for terrorists, including ISIS and al Qaeda." "In the end, we will win," Trump said, without defining what victory would look like.[28] Tillerson, perhaps thinking that turnabout is fair play, undermined the president's claim by tweeting the next day: "We may not win."[29] Later Trump told a small gathering of financial supporters that the United States had no choice but to "knock the shit out of [the Taliban]." "The World Trade Center people were trained in Afghanistan," he added; "It's like the Wharton School of Finance for terrorism."[30]

NORTH KOREA

Trump's approach to Afghanistan resembled that of other presidents to important foreign policy issues: authorize the national security advisor to gather and synthesize information and advice from all the affected departments and agencies, assemble the secretaries of state and defense and other foreign policy principals in the administration, ask probing questions, and open one's mind to the possibility that matters that seemed clear during the campaign might look different after one was in office. "All my life, I've heard that decisions are much different when you sit behind the desk in the Oval Office," the president said in his August 21 speech.[31] He acted accordingly.

Trump's approach to North Korea's testing and launching of nuclear weapons and ballistic missiles could not have resembled his approach to Afghanistan less. To be sure, he inherited a long record of frustration and failure. Trump's three predecessors—Bill Clinton, George W. Bush, and Obama—had all tried to persuade the North Korean government to abandon its nuclear program, using a combination of economic incentives, economic sanctions, and diplomatic pressures. All three had been unsuccessful. By the time Trump took office, North Korea had as many as sixty nuclear weapons. During his administration's first few months, it tested missiles that conceivably could reach the western third of the United States, as well as nearby Japan and other Asian countries. The North Koreans still had to learn how to make their nuclear bombs small enough to fit on the missiles. But few doubted that they were well on their way to doing so.

Some of the Trump administration's responses to these provocations were in keeping with previous efforts. In January, Trump declined to declare China a currency manipulator when Xi promised to use his country's leverage as North Korea's most powerful neighbor and main supplier of energy, electrical equipment, and

machinery to back down the Kim Jong-un regime's nuclear program. "Why would I call China a currency manipulator when they
are working with us on the North Korean problem?" said Trump.[32]
He signed a directive launching a series of measures to weaken
North Korea, ranging from cyber warfare by the U.S. Cyber Command to sanctions by the Treasury Department against foreigners
who dealt with the Pyongyang regime. In August, one month after
North Korea fired a series of provocative missiles, the U.S. ambassador to the United Nations, Nikki Haley, persuaded the Security
Council to impose its eighth round of sanctions against the North
Korean economy. Three months later, Trump restored North
Korea to the short list of state sponsors of terrorism, a designation
removed by Bush in 2008 that triggered even more sanctions.[33]

Unprecedentedly, however, Trump engaged in an extended
and escalating exchange of taunts with Kim that, in the journalist Steve Coll's vivid phrase, "evoked a professional wrestling
match."[34] Issuing over-the-top insults was nothing new for North
Korea's despised and impoverished government, but no American president had ever stooped to reply in kind.[35] Yet on August 8,
Trump told reporters that "any more threats to the United States"
by North Korea "will be met with fire and fury like the world has
never seen."[36] Asked about this statement two days later, he said,
"Maybe it wasn't tough enough."[37] In September, after North
Korea successfully tested its largest-ever bomb, Trump used tweets
to brand Kim "Rocket Man" and then "Little Rocket Man."[38] In
the president's first formal address to the UN General Assembly
on September 19, he threatened that if the United States "is forced
to defend itself or its allies, we will have no choice but to totally
destroy North Korea. Rocket Man is on a suicide mission for himself and for his regime."[39] Two days later Kim replied, "I will surely
and definitely tame the mentally deranged U.S. dotard with fire."
(*Dotard* is the English version of the Korean word *neukdari*, meaning a lazy, useless, and demented old person.)[40] North Korea then

threatened to conduct an above-ground test of its newest nuclear device, which would be the first exploded anywhere on the planet's surface since 1980. When Trump visited South Korea as part of a twelve-day trip to Asia in November, fog denied him the chance to gaze balefully for the cameras into North Korea from the southern side of the demilitarized zone. The North Korean government called him "an old lunatic" anyway, prompting him to taunt Kim in a tweet for being "short and fat." "I try so hard to be his friend," Trump oddly added.[41]

Other than rattling the cage of the young, insecure, and dangerous Kim, what was the Trump administration's strategy toward North Korea? As previous presidents had found, no amount of suffering by the North Korean people, even from a total ban on exports, imports, and foreign aid, had ever moved the totalitarian regime to abandon its nuclear program. A bombing campaign aimed at destroying North Korea's nuclear weapons was unlikely to succeed because they were both hidden and scattered. The fallout from a nuclear attack on the "Hermit Kingdom" might cripple it but also would poison the atmosphere in the entire region, evoke a massive international outcry against the United States, and perhaps be answered with a nuclear attack against South Korea. In fact, any military attack on North Korea was all but certain to prompt it to overrun the most densely populated part of South Korea, which lies just south of the North Korean border, with artillery, rocket launchers, and special operations forces. As their mutual antagonism grew, the United States and North Korea risked what scholars call a "security dilemma," in which two nations drift into war not intentionally but out of fear of what the other might do.[42]

Visiting China in November, Trump was greeted with elaborate ceremony and listened to with utmost politeness as he pleaded with Xi for heightened Chinese pressure on North Korea and raised a long list of concerns about China's trade practices—and then saw his requests ignored. In general Trump overvalued his personal relations with foreign leaders, underestimating their commitment to act in their national interest, which in China's case meant preserving North Korea as a buffer between itself and staunchly pro-American South Korea. By abandoning the Trans-Pacific Partnership, Trump also unwittingly conferred on China a newfound status as the most important economic power in the region.

Trump publicly disdained Tillerson's efforts to open a line of communication with North Korea, and every member of the national security team did their best to reassure foreign governments that the president's rhetorical excesses should not be taken too seriously. "Diplomacy is our preferred means" of achieving the administration's major goal, Mattis and Tillerson wrote in the *Wall Street Journal*: "the complete, verifiable, and irreversible denuclearization of the Korean peninsula and a dismantling of the [North Korean] regime's ballistic missile programs."[43] "Clinton failed, Bush failed, and Obama failed," Trump tweeted on October 1; "I won't fail." Less than a week later, disdaining those presidents' "agreements violated before the ink was dry, making fools of U.S. negotiators," Trump tweeted: "Sorry, but only one thing will work!"[44] He left the meaning of "one thing" to the imagination.

With no acceptable means of forcing North Korea to accede to the administration's demands, it is hard to imagine Kim acquiescing to them. Fresh in the minds of Kim and other North Korean officials is the example of the former Libyan dictator Muammar Qaddafi. In 2003 Qaddafi surrendered his nation's weapons of mass destruction in return for a Bush administration promise of better relations. Eight years later the Obama administration helped to overthrow Qaddafi, leading to his capture, humiliation, and slaying by Libyan rebels. The "grave lesson," the North Korean government said at the time, was that any American effort to persuade a country to surrender its most potent weapons was "an invasion tactic."[45] Trump added to the uncertainty the North Koreans and others felt about American reliability by withdrawing (or threatening to withdraw) from the Paris climate accord, the Trans-Pacific Partnership, NAFTA, the Iran nuclear accord, UNESCO, and other agreements that previous presidents had negotiated. Walking away from a deal may sometimes make sense in the world of real estate that Trump inhabited before taking office, but if one president can so easily undo a deal made by a previous president, how could other countries enter into agreements with the United States confident that those agreements would last?[46]

THE MIDDLE EAST

Despite this troubled record, in one area of the world, Trump gave early signs of perhaps exceeding expectations. Unlike his recent predecessors in the White House, he took a purely transactional approach to the Middle East, putting aside concerns about democracy and human rights in the region that they had pursued with good intentions but negligible results. Trump strengthened the American commitment to Israel, expressing indifference toward "two-state and one-state" solutions to the Palestinian question. "I can live with either one," he said.[47] At the same time Trump forged a much stronger connection with Saudi Arabia and its allies than Obama had by focusing narrowly on their shared goals of reining in Iran and defeating ISIS, which suffered serious military setbacks throughout 2017 in part because Trump, while preserving most elements of the strategy he inherited from Obama, gave American commanders in the field more autonomy.[48]

The Saudi connection sometimes put the president at odds with his secretaries of state and defense, who were hoping to mediate a conflict between Qatar and the Saudi-led alliance of Egypt, Bahrain, and the United Arab Emirates when Trump intervened with a tweet condemning Qatar.[49] Reminding the president that the tiny nation is also the site of the largest American air base in the Middle

East and the center of military operations against ISIS, his advisors eventually persuaded him to adopt a more balanced approach. "I think you'd have a deal worked out pretty quickly," Trump said on September 9, after arranging a phone call between the Qatari and Saudi leaders.[50] But his early pro-Saudi bias made him an ineffective mediator, the phone call was unproductive, and the stalemate continued. Meanwhile, the uneasy anti-ISIS alliance that temporarily placed the United States and its Kurdish allies on the same side as Iran, Russia, the Syrian government, and pro-Iranian Shiite militia left many difficult questions hanging about what would happen in Iraq and Syria in the aftermath of victory against ISIS.

Trump assigned his son-in-law and White House aide Jared Kushner responsibility for seeking a peace agreement between Israel and the Palestinians. Kushner's efforts were the latest in a long series of attempts by previous administrations dating back nearly a half century to the Nixon era. Working in Kushner's favor was his close family connection with the president, which in the Middle East is widely regarded as evidence of a leader's seriousness and respect.[51] Working against him was his inexperience in the region (and in diplomacy more generally), his multiple responsibilities in the White House, and the confusion caused about how his efforts related to those traditionally undertaken by the State Department and the national security advisor. In addition, visiting the Middle East in August, Kushner found that he was dealing with two leaders who, for different reasons, were politically weak: Prime Minister Benjamin Netanyahu of Israel and Palestinian Authority president Mahmoud Abbas. Netanyahu was unable to risk embracing a two-state solution, and Abbas was in no position to abandon it. The only agreement Kushner was able to salvage was to keep the negotiations going.

The Saudi-Qatar conflict was contained, and the Israeli-Palestinian situation was ongoing. Neither approached the status of a crisis. But Iran did. In 2015 the Obama administration, the other permanent members of the UN Security Council (Great Britain, France, Russia, and China), and Germany—the so-called P5+1—negotiated an agreement with Iran that removed economic sanctions in return for an Iranian commitment to end its nuclear weapons program for at least ten years. For as long as the agreement was in effect, the International Atomic Energy Agency (IAEA) would monitor and recertify Iran's compliance on a regular basis. In addition, Congress mandated in the Iran Nuclear Agreement Review Act of 2015—better known as the Corker-Cardin bill—that the president would have to review it every ninety days to ascertain whether Iran was still complying and the agreement remained in the national security interest of the United States.

During the campaign Trump had excoriated the Iran agreement as a "catastrophe" and (yet another) "worst deal ever," in part because it did not keep Iran from advancing its missile technology or funding terrorist groups in other Middle Eastern nations.[52] But as president he unhappily renewed it in April and July while signaling that he would not do so much longer.[53] "If it was up to me, I would have had them noncompliant 180 days ago," he said when he signed the recertification document in July.[54] In September Trump told the General Assembly that the Iran deal was an "embarrassment to the United States."[55] All of the other parties to the agreement and the IAEA made clear that they thought it was working and would not join the United States if Trump refused to recertify and Congress voted to reimpose sanctions on Iran.

Fortunately for Trump, a thorough policy review overseen by McMaster found him a way out—that is, a way to not recertify Iranian compliance in October without provoking open conflict with Iran and the other signatories. McMaster showed the president that a decision not to recertify would trigger American sanctions only if Congress voted within sixty days to reimpose them.[56] The administration's new approach would be to refuse recertification (which was important to Trump), refuse to reimpose sanctions (which would keep Iran from resuming its nuclear program), and instead urge Congress to separately target Iran's ballistic missile program and support for terrorist groups such as Hezbollah (which would help mollify congressional Republicans). Tillerson and Mattis, who would have preferred that Trump simply continue recertifying Iranian compliance, went along with this recommendation as a way of keeping the agreement alive.[57] On October 12, the ninety-day mark for the president to decide whether to recertify, Trump announced the new policy.

LATIN AMERICA

No foreign country was the object of more animus during Trump's election campaign than Mexico. Starting on the day of his announcement as a candidate on June 16, 2015, Trump launched a two-pronged attack against the United States' southern neighbor. One prong was aimed at immigrants crossing the border into the country illegally. "When Mexico sends its people, they're not sending their best," Trump said; "They're bringing drugs. They're bringing crime. They're rapists." His solution: "I will build a great, great wall on our southern border. And I will have Mexico pay for that wall." The other prong was directed at the unfair economic advantages Mexico supposedly gained from NAFTA, which Trump attacked regularly. Mexico "is laughing at us, at our stupidity," he declared; "And now they are beating us economically. They are not our friend, believe me."[58]

In a phone call shortly after he took office, Trump berated Mexican president Enrique Peña Nieto, threatening to "put a very substantial tax on the border" and cancel a scheduled meeting of the two presidents "if you are going to say that Mexico is not going to pay for the wall."[59] When Peña Nieto made clear that he would say exactly that, the meeting was canceled. Mexican officials, instead of knuckling under to Trump's threats, felt they had no choice but to defy him. In response to strong advice from NEC director Gary Cohn and other members of the president's economic and national security teams, Trump allowed renegotiations of NAFTA with Mexico and Canada to go forward but told an August rally in Phoenix, "I think we'll probably end up terminating NAFTA."[60] The administration's negotiating strategy seemed to be to push for changes—such as adding a sunset clause to the agreement and increasing the share of each product that must be manufactured in the United States—that the Mexicans and Canadians would find unacceptable.[61]

As with Mexico's leaders, those in other Latin American countries had no particular desire to lock horns with the president of the United States. Nor did they have any fondness for Venezuelan president Nicolas Maduro and his incompetent leftist government. But in August, when Trump offhandedly remarked, "We have many options for Venezuela, including a possible military option," the continent's other leaders felt bound to object.[62] With Vice President Pence by his side in Bogotá, for example, Colombian president Miguel Santos said: "The possibility of a military intervention shouldn't even be considered. . . . America is a continent of peace."[63] Trump's animus toward Maduro found other outlets, including an attack on his "disastrous rule" in the president's speech to the General Assembly and the inclusion of Venezuelan government officials in the third version of his travel ban. In November, Trump also instructed Haley, his UN ambassador, to vote against a resolution to condemn the United States trade embargo imposed on Cuba by Congress more than a half century ago. With all of Latin America, Europe, Africa, and Asia voting for the resolution and only Israel joining the United States in opposition, it passed by 191 to 2.[64]

9 ★ PROSPECTS FOR REMOVAL

Challenges to Donald Trump's constitutional legitimacy as president were an ongoing part of his first year, starting the day after the election when protesters in several cities chanted, "Not my president!" For weeks afterward, college administrators and faculty treated the election results as a traumatic event for their students. On the eve of Trump's inauguration, the respected civil rights leader and sixteen-term Democratic congressman John Lewis of Georgia said that he did not regard Trump as a "legitimate president."[1] Nearly seventy Democratic members of Congress boycotted the inaugural ceremony after Trump tweeted that Lewis was "all talk, talk, talk—no action or results."[2] Grassroots party activists regarded Trump as a sexist, racist, unqualified bully who had both gamed the system by winning the Electoral College while losing the national popular vote and cheated it by colluding with, or at least benefiting from, the covert Russian campaign to defeat Hillary Clinton.

Efforts to find a way to remove Trump from office began almost immediately after he took the oath. Constitutionally, two mechanisms exist that allow a president's tenure to be ended against his will before the expiration of the four-year term. The first, impeachment, has been in the Constitution from the beginning. If a majority of the House of Representatives and, after a Senate-conducted trial, two-thirds of that body decide that the president is guilty of "Treason, Bribery, or other high Crimes and Misdemeanors," he is removed from office. The second mechanism, which took effect with the enactment of the Twenty-Fifth Amendment in 1967, concerns presidential disability. If the vice president and a majority of the heads of the fifteen cabinet departments decide that for reasons of mental or physical incapacity "the President is unable to discharge the powers and duties of his office," the vice president shall "immediately" become "Acting President" until such time as the president declares that "no inability exists." If the vice president and cabinet disagree with the president's claim to be able, Congress has twenty-one days to decide who is right, with a two-thirds vote of both houses needed to unseat the president. Anticipating that an "unable" president might fire the cabinet to keep it from meeting, the amendment also permits Congress to authorize some "other body" to act in the cabinet's place.

No president has been forced out by the vice president and cabinet on grounds of disability, nor has a vice president and cabinet ever tried to do so. Only two presidents have been impeached by the House, Andrew Johnson in 1868 and Bill Clinton in 1998. Both were charged with having committed various acts that violated their constitutional duty to "take care that the Laws be faithfully executed." Both survived the Senate trial, Johnson barely and Clinton handily. The one president who was driven from office through the impeachment process was Richard Nixon, who resigned in 1974 in the face of certain removal.

IMPEACHMENT

What accounts for the varying ways Congress dealt with the Johnson, Nixon, and Clinton impeachment controversies?[3] As might be expected from a constitutional process that entrusts impeachment and removal to elected officials, partisan politics was one important element. An overwhelmingly Republican Congress (191–46 in the House and 42–11 in the Senate) impeached and came within one vote of removing the Democrat Johnson. A solidly Democratic Congress (242–191 in the House and 56–42 in the Senate) forced the Republican Nixon to resign in the face of certain impeachment and removal. A Republican House impeached Clinton, a Democrat.

A Congress controlled by the opposition party may be a necessary condition for impeaching and removing the president, but clearly it is not a sufficient one. Most recent presidents have faced such a Congress for at least some of their time in office without being impeached. A second part of the explanation is the president's standing with the voters. Even without polls to measure how unpopular Johnson was, the results of the 1866 midterm election made clear that he had little public support. Nixon's job approval rating in the Gallup Poll sank below 30 percent in late 1973 and stayed there. Clinton's case is more complicated. His party actually gained five House seats in the 1998 midterm election, the first time this happened during a president's second term since 1822. His job approval rating remained above 60 percent during the entire controversy, soaring to 73 percent in December 1998 when the House was voting to impeach him. House Republicans, however, were motivated by fear of their chamber's party leaders, who were determined to force out the president, and by their knowledge that the greatest possible threat to their reelection would come from the equally anti-Clinton Republican primary voters in their districts. Representing more politically competitive states and enjoying longer terms of office, a significant number of Republican senators broke ranks and supported Clinton on the final votes.

A third element in explaining impeachment politics is the immediate practical consequence of removal. To remove one president is to install another. Enough moderate Republicans dreaded the prospect of the radical Senate president pro tempore Benjamin Wade becoming president that they held their noses and stood by Johnson. In contrast, Vice President Gerald Ford, well known on

Capitol Hill and widely admired for his integrity, was a more than acceptable replacement for Nixon among both Democrats and Republicans. Clinton's case is again less clear. Congressional Democrats would have been happy and Republican legislators unhappy to see Vice President Al Gore succeed to the presidency, and for the same reason: it would give him the advantages of incumbency in the 2000 presidential election. But the fervency of both parties' primary electorates prevented them from acting on this basis.

Finally, public attitudes toward impeachment in general color the likelihood that a president may be impeached. During the 184-year period from 1789 to 1973, only one president, Johnson, underwent the process, and that failed effort seemed to discredit impeachment for decades to come as a "vengefully political act," such that in the judgment of the political scientist Clinton Rossiter, "I do not think we are likely ever again to see such a trial."[4] Rossiter, who published these words in 1960, was proven wrong just fourteen years later. In the twenty-five years from 1974 to 1999, two presidents were in effect impeached. More to the point, every president since Clinton has been the object of a grassroots campaign to impeach him by opposition party activists. In the contemporary climate of bitter partisan polarization, impeachment strikes many as just another form of "politics by other means."[5]

In Trump's case, impeachment talk moved from left-wing social media to mainstream telecasts and publications and the halls of Congress less than four months into his term, after he fired FBI director James Comey on May 9 for continuing to investigate possible criminal links between Russia and the Trump election campaign. As Trump publicly explained the firing: "I said to myself, I said, 'You know, this Russia thing with Trump and Russia is a made-up story. It's an excuse by the Democrats for having lost an election that they should have won.'"[6] Of Comey, he told the Russian ambassador and defense minister, "He was crazy, a real nut job."[7] According to Comey, in a private meeting on February 14, the day after General Michael Flynn resigned as national security advisor, Trump told him: "I hope you can see your way clear to letting this go, to letting Flynn go. He is a good guy." Comey said he took the request "as a direction," greeted it with a noncommittal, "he is a good guy," and continued the investigation.[8] Frustrated, Trump reportedly tried, again without success, to persuade national intelligence director Dan Coats and National Security Agency director Mike Rogers to deny publicly that there had been any collusion between his campaign and Russia and to ask Comey to back off the Flynn investigation.[9]

Democratic leaders who had harshly attacked Comey during the election for criticizing Hillary Clinton's mishandling of classified e-mails when she was secretary of state now lionized him for standing up to Trump. On May 13 a prominent Democratic constitutional scholar, Laurence Tribe, argued in the *Washington Post* that Trump's expression of "hope" that Comey would drop the Flynn investigation and his subsequent firing of the director constituted obstruction of justice. This, Tribe argued, was an even worse "high Crime and Misdemeanor" than the ones that drove Nixon from office because it "involv[ed] national security matters vastly more serious than the 'third-rate burglary' that Nixon tried to cover up in Watergate."[10] On May 24, Representative Al Green, a Texas Democrat, announced that he was drafting articles of impeachment based on Trump's conduct toward Comey, and on June 12 Democratic representative Brad Sherman of California actually did so. An August poll showed that although about 70 percent of Democrats said that Trump deserved to be impeached, only 40 percent of all Americans agreed.[11]

Taking a different tack, in September and October President Obama's White House counsel, Bob Bauer, maintained that "a president who is a demagogue, whose demagoguery defines his style of political leadership, is subject for that reason to impeachment." Trump's rhetoric, Bauer argued, "is extremely and consistently

loose with truth, often outrightly false, and contemptuous of institutions, including courts of law." One series of lies, Bauer argued,
involved Trump "actively deceiving the public by denying Russian
interference in the 2016 election," an impeachable offense because
"Nixon's lies to the public about Watergate were the subject of
one article of impeachment approved by the House" (or, rather,
its Judiciary Committee, since Nixon resigned before the House
ever acted).[12] Even less plausibly, Representative Steve Cohen of
Tennessee argued on August 16 that because a high crime and misdemeanor is anything Congress says it is, a president could theo-
retically be impeached "for jaywalking." Cohen said that Trump
should be impeached for equating racist demonstrators with those
who protested against them in Charlottesville on August 12.[13] In
October, Representative Green read an impeachment resolution to
the House of Representatives, this time accusing Trump of, among
other things, "inciting white supremacy, sexism, bigotry, hatred,
xenophobia, race-baiting and racism by demeaning, defaming,
disrespecting, and disparaging women and certain minorities."[14]
Under House rules, Green could have forced an immediate vote
on his resolution but was pressured not to do so by Democratic
leaders, who thought such an action was premature.[15] On November 15, Cohen, Green, and four other Democrats introduced an
impeachment resolution charging Trump with obstruction of justice, violating the Constitution's emoluments clauses, and undermining the federal judiciary and freedom of the press.[16]

The billionaire investor Tom Steyer, who donated more money
to Democratic candidates in 2014 and 2016 than any other individual, applied pressure of a different kind when he wrote to every
Democrat in Congress demanding that they pledge to impeach
Trump if their party won a majority of the House in the 2018 midterm election.[17] Larry Flynt, best known as the publisher of *Hustler*
magazine, placed an ad in the October 15 edition of the *Washington Post*, offering "$10 Million for Information Leading to the

Impeachment and Removal from Office of Donald J. Trump," preferably a "smoking gun" that proved, perhaps, that Trump had made "some financial quid pro quo with the Russians."[18] Meanwhile, most Republicans either defended Trump or remained silent, but Arizona senator John McCain said that the Comey controversy was of "Watergate size and scale," and Representative Justin Amash of Michigan declared that Comey's allegations, if true, were grounds for impeachment.[19]

A more serious threat to Trump lay outside Congress, whose investigations of Russian interference in the 2016 election by the House Intelligence Committee and the Senate Judiciary and Intelligence Committees were mired in sloth and partisanship.[20] On May 17, eight days after Comey was fired, Deputy Attorney General Rod Rosenstein appointed former FBI director Robert Mueller as special counsel to investigate the various allegations about Russia and the Trump campaign. Rosenstein made the decision because Attorney General Jeff Sessions had recused himself from the matter on March 2 after it was revealed that during his Senate confirmation hearing he failed to mention two meetings with the Russian ambassador. Then and later Trump was furious at Sessions for ceding control of the investigation. On July 19 he told the *New York Times* that if Sessions "was going to recuse himself he should have told me before he took the job and I would have picked somebody else."[21] For weeks afterward, Trump belittled Sessions in a series of tweets and interviews.

Mueller made clear that he would turn over any evidence that Trump had obstructed justice or committed other offenses to Congress as part of a possible impeachment proceeding. Information far outstripped speculation about the investigation during most of Trump's first year, but the special counsel's requests to the White House for e-mails and documents made clear that he was looking into possible obstruction in Trump's firing of Comey, as well as the president's decision to remove General Flynn as national security advisor and his role in drafting a misleading statement about a meeting between his son Donald Trump Jr., son-in-law Jared Kushner, and Russian-born visitors during the election campaign.[22] Trump's insistent unwillingness to admit that Russia had worked on his behalf gave the July 2017 revelation about the meeting the previous June the appearance of a cover-up, even though it produced nothing and did not include the candidate himself. Trump Jr. and Kushner took the meeting because they had been promised "official documents" that would "incriminate Hillary" as part of "Russia and its government's support for Mr. Trump."[23] When the meeting became public a year later, the president apparently helped his son draft a statement claiming that it concerned Russian adoptions, a falsehood that was easily disproven by Trump Jr.'s e-mails and that the special counsel regarded as suspicious.[24]

On October 30 Mueller issued his first indictments. None connected Trump with any crime or misbehavior, but clearly not every prosecutorial shoe had yet been dropped. Not just Trump Jr. and Kushner, who were not charged, but also junior campaign aide George Papadopoulos, who pleaded guilty to lying to the FBI, were found to have reached out to Russian officials for dirt on Hillary Clinton.[25] Depending on the results of Mueller's investigation, as well as on continuing congressional and media revelations of other troubling presidential conduct, public opinion may turn so strongly against Trump as to persuade some Republican members of Congress that it is politically safe to abandon him.

Fervent though Republican voters' support for Trump was, a measurable number of them—as many as one in five—began leaving the party because they disapproved of his conduct as president.[26] Some rank-and-file Republicans and many Republican members of Congress would be much happier with President Pence than President Trump. Pence remained unwaveringly loyal to Trump's policies but consistently distanced himself from controversial "stories about the time before he joined the ticket" in July 2016.[27] He even created a political action committee—the Great America Committee—to fund his political travel and contributions to candidates, something no previous vice president had done. "At this point, who DOESN'T want Trump impeached?" asked the conservative polemicist Ann Coulter after Trump briefly cozied up to Democratic congressional leaders Charles Schumer and Nancy Pelosi in September 2017. "If we're not getting a [border] wall," Coulter said, "I'd prefer President Pence."[28] Personal loyalty to Trump among Republican legislators, never great to begin with, was shredded by his disrespectful treatment of Sessions, as well as by his threats to senators such as Dean Heller and Lisa Murkowski and harshly disparaging tweets about John McCain, Bob Corker, Jeff Flake, Lindsey Graham, and Senate Republican leader Mitch McConnell.[29]

A year in advance of the 2018 midterm election, signs were good that the Democratic Party might take control of the House. Twenty-nine Republican incumbents, but only eleven Democrats, announced that they were retiring, and Democrats led Republicans by about 10 percentage points in the so-called generic congressional ballot.[30] In special and scheduled elections held throughout 2017, Democratic candidates exceeded their party's normal strength and made tangible gains in state and local legislative contests. By September, 162 Democratic candidates in Republican-held districts had raised more than $100,000 in campaign funds, four times as many as in other recent midterm elections.[31] Depending on the extent of Trump's unpopularity, the Democrats conceivably could even buck the odds and win the Senate in 2018. Such an outcome would shock the political community because Democrats are defending three times as many Senate seats as Republicans. It not only would make impeachment by a majority of the Democrat-controlled House more likely, it might even alarm enough Republican senators so that a two-thirds majority for removal could be forged in that chamber.

Perhaps anticipating the latter possibility, Trump kept his grassroots support fertilized and watered with a constant supply of rally-style oratory and provocative tweets, most of them aimed at reinforcing his followers' loathing of the president's foes. These ranged from the "fake news" mainstream media to professional athletes who refused to stand for the national anthem to potential Republican critics in Congress, many of whom worried that if they turned against him he would support a primary challenger in the next election.[32] And even as the mainstream and liberal media focused on Trump's myriad Russia problems, Fox News and other conservative outlets deflected their audiences' attention to other Russia-related matters more favorable to the president, such as the purchase of the Canadian mining company Uranium One by the Russian government while Hillary Clinton was secretary of state.[33]

DISABILITY

Finding the impeachment process too difficult to navigate, some critics who wanted Trump forced from office offered the Twenty-Fifth Amendment as an alternate route. Historically, two presidents, Ronald Reagan and George W. Bush, had voluntarily invoked the amendment for very brief periods while undergoing minor surgery. But on no occasion had the vice president and a majority of the cabinet even considered exercising their authority to transfer the powers and duties of the presidency to the vice president on the grounds that the president was "unable to discharge" them.[34] To invoke the amendment against Trump would mean entering uncharted constitutional territory. Nevertheless, public discussions of doing so began early in the president's first year.

By the time Democratic representative Jamie Raskin of Maryland introduced a bill in June 2017 to remove the Trump-appointed cabinet from disability determinations and replace it with a

"Commission on Presidential Capacity" consisting mostly of physicians and psychiatrists, a few conservative columnists, including Ross Douthat and George F. Will, had already argued that Trump was unfit by reason of temperament, character, and mental health to be president.[35] On July 6 the American Psychoanalytic Association broke with past practice and said that its members are "free to comment about political figures as individuals."[36] By the end of the month nearly sixty thousand self-identified "mental health professionals" had signed a petition declaring that "Trump manifests a serious mental illness" and "should be removed from office" under the terms of the amendment.[37] In July, Democratic senator Jack Reed of Rhode Island confided to a colleague, "I think he's crazy."[38]

In August, Republican senator Bob Corker said that Trump "has not yet been able to demonstrate the stability, nor some of the competence, that he needs."[39] He later accused Trump of "volatility," of "heading towards World War III," and of needing to be contained by aides "every single day at the White House" in a kind of "adult day care center."[40] In October, Yale psychiatry professor Bandy Lee and more than two dozen colleagues published *The Dangerous Case of Donald Trump.* Lee had already warned that Trump's "severe emotional impediments" pose "a grave threat to international security."[41] Other contributors to the book assessed Trump as being pathologically hedonistic, narcissistic, or sociopathic, among other diagnoses.[42] Law professor Eric Posner argued that legislators should not confine themselves to medical diagnoses in assessing Trump's fitness. Although the authors of the Twenty-Fifth Amendment had illness in mind, "they deliberately used broad language that goes beyond psychological or physical disability." Trump should be removed because he was "politically incompetent," Posner suggested, "having lost the confidence of the public because of a failure of temperament, ideology, or ability."[43]

While still on the White House staff, Steve Bannon reportedly estimated that Trump had only a 30 percent chance of completing his term and told the president that the biggest threat he faced was the Twenty-Fifth Amendment, of which Trump apparently had never heard.[44] In truth, to the extent that its proponents based the disability approach on ease of accomplishment compared with impeachment, they probably were misguided. Even if Congress replaced the cabinet with a medical board or a Presidential Oversight Council composed of "senior elected officials of both parties" (Posner's idea), the amendment cannot be used against an unwilling president without the vice president's agreement. And if the president were to appeal an adverse decision to Congress, as Trump certainly would, a two-thirds majority of both chambers, not just of the Senate, would have to vote against him. Even if they did, he could start the process all over again (and again) by claiming that his disability was ended. The premise of the amendment is that the president retains the office even when shorn of its powers and duties, and that these should be restored to him as soon as he is well.

OTHER CONTINGENCIES

The Constitution mentions two other contingencies that may create a premature vacancy in the presidency: not just impeachment and disability, but also death and resignation. In February a historian at California State University, Fresno, tweeted, "Has anyone started soliciting money and design drafts for a monument honoring the Trump assassin?"[45] In August a Democratic state legislator from Missouri posted on Facebook, "I hope he is assassinated!" Both drew sharp reprimands from across the political spectrum.[46] Others noted that Trump's age, eating habits, and lack of exercise, joined with the stresses of being president, placed him in actuarial danger of death by natural causes.

Resignation was another possibility, albeit just as unlikely. A columnist for the *Washington Post* suggested that because "the more he sees of the job, the less he wants to do it," Trump should ask himself, "at his age and station, what's the point of staying in a job he doesn't want?"[47] Tony Schwartz, coauthor of *Trump: The Art of the Deal*, predicted that Trump would resign, and former vice president Al Gore urged him to do so.[48] In the aftermath of a series of resignations from Congress in response to allegations of sexual misconduct, so did several Democratic senators.

Not relying on removal, nearly a hundred Democratic members of Congress introduced a resolution to censure Trump for his "repulsive defense of white supremacists" in the wake of the Charlottesville riot, as well as for having "surrounded himself with, and cultivated the influence of, senior advisors and spokespeople who have long histories of promoting white nationalist, racist, and anti-Semitic principles and policies."[49] During the Clinton impeachment controversy, congressional Democrats offered to support a censure resolution but Republicans, dead set on trying to remove the president from office, refused to let one come to a vote. The prospects for censuring Trump, like the prospects for removal by impeachment or disability, will depend heavily on the results of both the 2018 election and the special counsel's investigation, as well as on which course the Democrats choose to pursue.

CONCLUSION

During the seventeen months of Donald Trump's presidential campaign, the nearly three months of his transition from president-elect to president, and his first eleven months in office, he displayed virtually no knowledge of history, no awareness of the depth of fierce partisan opposition that all of his recent predecessors had faced during the previous quarter century, and no comprehension of how narrow his victory was. Trump actually thought that he had won the "biggest" electoral vote victory since Ronald Reagan (not even close), that he had outpolled Hillary Clinton in the national popular vote (false to an extent unsurpassed in American political history), and that the Russian government had tried to help get her elected president rather than, as was actually the case, helping him.[1]

As Paul Light has shown, a president's political influence usually declines over the course of the first year—but seldom, as Trump's did, during its first days. To be sure, one reason Trump's political standing in Congress and the country was low from the start was the relentless hostility of Democratic officeholders and voters, spurred on by the party's grassroots activists. Another was that both he and the Republican Congress had been elected by attacking the federal government, not by advancing a positive agenda that could readily translate into legislative accomplishments. But the most important reason was Trump's own insensitivity toward anyone, in government or out, who disagreed with him about

anything and his unwillingness to reach out, as most presidents do
at least symbolically, to the unconverted. Trump's dark, campaign-
style inaugural address, for example, violated all the traditions of
unifying rhetoric that have marked inaugurations since George
Washington first took the oath in 1789. So did his wild charge that
President Barack Obama "had my 'wires tapped' in Trump Tower
just before the victory" and daily tweets in which, by one count, he
attacked 382 individuals, news organizations, countries, and other
targets by mid-October 2017.[2]

Presidential effectiveness usually grows during the first year
even as presidential influence declines. Presidents become more
surefooted in the job by doing it. They get better because they
cram during the transition period, surround themselves (sometimes sooner, but always later) with advisors experienced in government, and learn from their mistakes. Trump was arguably the
first exception to all of these rules in the history of the presidency.
Claiming that he makes great decisions "with very little knowledge
other than the knowledge I [already] had, plus the words 'common sense' because I have a lot of common sense and I have a lot of
business ability," Trump added: "I could actually run my business
and run the government at the same time." "I'm president. Hey, I'm
president," he marveled. "Can you believe it?"[3] "The president's
new at this," said Speaker of the House Paul Ryan. "I think President Trump is learning the job," added Senate Republican leader
Mitch McConnell, with (unintended?) condescension. Idaho congressman Mike Simpson was more blunt: "At first it was 'Well, this
is the guy we elected. He'll learn, he'll learn.' And you just don't see
that happening."[4]

"We need a truly great leader," Trump said during the campaign.
"We need a leader that wrote *The Art of the Deal*."[5] Trump's confidence about his deal-making prowess was overweening. "I deal
with Steve Wynn. I deal with Carl Icahn," he boasted, referring to
two well-known businessmen; "I deal with killers that blow these

[politicians] away. It's not even the same category. This [politics] is a category that's like nineteen levels lower."[6]

Trump was surely right to think that striking deals—also known as forging compromises, reaching agreements, and finding common ground—is an important part of being president. The Constitution assigns the presidency few powers that are not shared with Congress or the states and reviewable by the courts. "The Constitution boils down to one thing," former president Bill Clinton has long been fond of saying: "Let's have an argument and then let's make a deal."[7]

"Deals are my art form," Trump once bragged. Yet overconfidence blinded him to the reality that unlike the desire to maximize profits that animates the private economy, the motivations of legislators, judges, lobbyists, journalists, state and local officials, and foreign heads of government are varied, complex, and subtle. In politics, unlike the cutthroat world of real estate development in which deal-making is extremely fluid and abandoning a bargain is tolerable, a reputation for standing by one's word when reaching agreements is the coin of the realm, and thereby essential to being trusted in the future.[8] Similarly, in the international arena, forsaking an agreement made by a previous president is likely to dissuade foreign governments from thinking that any deal they reach with the United States can be relied on to last.

Nor, never having dealt in the business world with shareholders or an independent board of directors, did Trump seem to fully realize that, as president, other constitutional actors had to be reckoned with. The president cannot, for example, plausibly threaten to walk away when negotiations break down with Congress and find another legislature to deal with. He cannot fire and replace the several million civil servants on whom he must rely to implement his decisions. Trump "never seems to recognize how much leverage he has or doesn't have, or what his negotiating partners might need," the journalist Michael Grunwald observed;

"He just blurts out what he thinks should happen and then dis-
tributes the blame when it doesn't."[9] For nearly all of Trump's first
year—with him having blown any chance for even a short honeymoon and failed to take advantage of a unified party government,
relative global peace, and rising prosperity—not a single important piece of legislation that he supported was enacted. A tax-cut
bill, the near-inevitable consequence of electing a Republican
Congress, was the only accomplishment that loomed on the hori-
zon at year's end.

Trump's presidential candidacy came less than a quarter century after the independent campaigns launched in the 1990s by
another celebrity business leader, Ross Perot. Perot, like Trump,
led in the polls for a period of time. Like Trump, Perot caught fire
with his appealing performances on talk shows and in debates. But
like Trump, too, once Perot's snappy one-liners were exhausted,
the shallowness of his understanding of the challenges a president
faces and his unwillingness to learn more about them became all
too apparent. Yet by 2017 Perot's unusual success as an independent candidate and Trump's election as the Republican nominee
already had made at least three billionaires—hedge fund virtuoso
Tom Steyer, Dallas Mavericks owner Mark Cuban, and Facebook
founder Mark Zuckerberg—begin to consider candidacies of their
own in 2020.[10]

President of the United States, the most powerful office in the
world, is not an entry-level government job. Appeals such as "I'm
not part of that mess" or "My success in business (or academe or
the media or some other realm) proves that I can lead the government" may sound good in an election campaign, but a candidacy
built on them is ungrounded in reality. Presidents need certain
distinctive leadership skills if they are to govern the nation effectively.[11] Skills of political rhetoric and bargaining suitable for governing seem to be developed best by running for and serving in
office for a period of years. The same can be said of the subtle but

vital capacity to sense the public's willingness to be led in different directions at different paces at different times. The challenges of administrative management are different in government than in the business world, especially the sort of personal operation that Trump was able to micromanage with a handful of family members and loyal retainers. Success in the private sector speaks well of a person and usually requires some of these skills, although Trump's lack of prepresidential accountability to directors and shareholders made his business experience even less relevant to governing than that developed by the heads of publicly traded corporations. But only politics requires all of the skills and knowledge necessary to be an effective president.[12]

As Trump's first year drew to a close, serious questions remained that only the passage of time can answer. Will his ongoing breaches of long-standing presidential norms—his mendacity, divisiveness, and vengefulness—set a precedent for future presidents or serve as a cautionary tale about how not to succeed in the office? Will his authoritarian tendencies—threatening the press, intervening in the normal processes of law enforcement, intimating the legitimacy of violence—be emulated in an ever more bitterly polarized political environment, or will it induce American voters and political leaders to pull back from the brink? Is Trump an aberration, whose presidency was only possible because of Hillary Clinton's flaws as a candidate, or does he portend a new and harsher style of presidential leadership?

"The Trump presidency has called into sharp question the integrity and resilience of the American regime and the future of liberal democracy in the United States," wrote a team of accomplished political scientists in August 2017, taking the pessimistic view. "Is American democracy under threat?" they asked; "The answer is yes. . . . Once unthinkable scenarios now seem plausible: an unconstitutional third term in office, for example, or emergency government in the wake of a terrorist attack."[13]

Fortunately for the country, flawed as Trump is by aberrant personality defects—overweening self-centeredness, an inadequate attention span, and an inability to deal with criticism except in the angriest terms—not everything hinges on the president, even if, at age seventy-eight, assuming he had won a second term, he did somehow decide he wanted a third. The Constitution created a system of "separated institutions sharing powers" both among the three branches of the federal government and between the federal government and the states. It safeguarded the right of the people to speak, publish, petition, and assemble. From the resistance to Trump that emerged in Congress, the courts, the bureaucracy, the states and localities, the media, and the opposition party, he has been taught the hard way what most of the country has rejoiced in for more than two centuries: that the American constitutional system is well designed "to counteract ambition" when ambition aspires to roam directionless and unrestrained.[14]

EPILOGUE
December 1

The events of a single day, December 1, 2017, represented both the best and worst of times for Donald Trump during his first year as president.

On the best-of-times side of the ledger, the Senate passed an administration-endorsed tax reform bill, with the final vote coming at two o'clock the following morning. Cutting taxes in ways that chiefly benefit corporations and well-to-do individuals has been at the heart of Republican orthodoxy since the Reagan era. "All my members, from [Maine senator Susan] Collins to [Texas senator Ted] Cruz, were just more comfortable with this issue," said Senate Republican leader Mitch McConnell. Tax cutting "is who they are," echoed House Democratic leader Nancy Pelosi.[1] Indeed, for a Republican Congress not to pass a tax bill during a Republican president's first year would be extraordinary. The bill approved by the Senate in December was substantially written by congressional Republicans but included several items that President Trump explicitly emphasized: a substantial reduction in the corporate tax rate, preservation of the tax advantages of 401(k) retirement accounts, and a repeal of the individual mandate to purchase health insurance.

Ironically, McConnell—long the target of disdainful presidential tweets—played the crucial role in bringing about what by year's end was the chamber's only major legislative victory for Trump. As late as the afternoon of December 1, with all forty-eight Senate Democrats united in opposition, the tax bill was still several Republican votes shy of a majority. McConnell and other party leaders, including Vice President Mike Pence, engineered a congeries of amendments to bring their recalcitrant colleagues aboard. These included a larger tax reduction for small (and not-so-small) "pass-through" businesses to please Senators Ron Johnson of Wisconsin and Steve Daines of Montana; a $10,000 property tax deduction and a commitment to the Alexander-Murray bill to shore up Obamacare insurers financially for the next two years, both of which Senator Collins badly wanted; and a promise to provide "fair and permanent protections" for the undocumented childhood immigrants—the Dreamers—about whom Arizona senator Jeff Flake was especially concerned.[2] Only one of the Republican holdouts, Senator Bob Corker of Tennessee, could not be won over—and even Corker was prepared to vote for the measure after McConnell agreed to add a provision that would trigger a tax increase if the economy slowed. The Senate parliamentarian ruled the provision out of order on procedural grounds, however. With Corker the only Republican voting against the bill, it passed the Senate on an otherwise straight party-line vote of 51–49.

Challenges still awaited final enactment of tax legislation. Polls consistently showed that the bill was unpopular with Democratic and independent voters.[3] Time was of the essence: in January the winner of the Alabama special Senate election, Democrat Doug Jones, would replace Republican Luther Strange, reducing the GOP's ranks in the chamber from fifty-two to fifty-one, the barest of majorities. Differences between the Senate version and the one passed by the House on November 16 needed to be ironed out well before the new year began. Among these differences, the House reduced the number of individual tax brackets to four while the Senate left it at seven, the House capped the mortgage interest deduction at $500,000 while the Senate left it at $1 million, the Senate reduced certain small business taxes more than the House did, the Senate delayed the corporate tax cut for a year while the House had it take effect immediately, the Senate's child tax credit was more generous than the House's, and, most important, the Senate repealed the individual mandate, a matter on which the House was silent.

None of these differences was insurmountable, although the concessions on Obamacare and the Dreamers that McConnell made to win the votes of Collins and Flake were unpopular and perhaps unenforceable among House conservatives. House and Senate Republican leaders quickly appointed a conference committee to write a common version of the bill, which would then be voted on without amendment by each chamber before going to the president. Trump instantly complicated matters. After negotiating himself up from a 15 percent to a 20 percent corporate tax rate, he now said "it could be 22," a higher rate than in either the House or Senate bills and one for which McConnell and House Freedom Caucus members expressed an immediate dislike.[4] Overall, however, the president played a more constructive role in selling the bill among congressional Republicans than in previous efforts.[5]

On December 13 the conference committee settled on a corporate rate of 21 percent. Committee members used the additional revenue that the 1 percent increase would generate to have the cut take effect immediately, as in the House version, and to reduce the top rate on individuals and households to 37 percent. They split the difference on other matters, such as a $750,000 mortgage interest deduction (halfway between the House and Senate versions) and a $10,000 maximum deduction for all state and local taxes, not just property taxes. House Republican conferees, still frustrated over Congress's failure to repeal the Affordable Care Act, were only too happy to accept the Senate's decision to abolish the individual mandate for health insurance.[6] With little choice but to accept or reject the conference committee bill as written, and unwilling to end the year without tax legislation, the Republican majorities in both chambers moved rapidly toward passage in time for Christmas. All knew that even if three Republican senators were to join the forty-eight Democrats in rejecting the conference bill, the House could simply pass the Senate's original version and it would become law. But even Corker came around to support final passage.

December 1 was a difficult as well as a triumphant day in the life of the Trump presidency. That morning, former general Michael Flynn pleaded guilty to lying to the FBI about his conversations with Russian ambassador Sergey Kislvak in late December 2016, weeks after President-elect Trump announced that Flynn would be his national security advisor but weeks before either one of them took office. On December 22 Flynn requested that Russia not support a UN resolution to condemn Israeli West Bank settlements, and on December 29 he asked that Russia not retaliate against sanctions imposed by the Obama administration as punishment for Russian interference in the election. Before making the first call Flynn consulted with, among others, Trump's son-in-law, Jared Kushner, and before making the second he talked with deputy foreign policy aide K. T. McFarland. Although it is not unusual for incoming administrations to communicate with foreign governments, Flynn was both asking Russia to act in conflict with the incumbent president's preferences and strongly implying that better relations awaited when Trump took office. On January 24, four days after he officially became national security advisor, Flynn then lied about the matter to the FBI as well as to Vice President Pence. Trump fired him on February 13.[7]

Flynn was the first high-ranking administration official to be indicted by special counsel Robert Mueller and the highest-ranking staff member in any administration to be convicted of a crime in nearly thirty years. During the campaign Flynn had decried Hillary

Clinton's alleged criminality, leading crowds in chants of "Lock her up!" and saying, "If I did a tenth of what she did, I would be in jail today!"[8] Now, as part of his plea bargain with Mueller, he promised to cooperate with the investigation into possibly illegal conduct by others in the Trump campaign and administration. Some congressional Democrats had argued for months that the president should be impeached for firing FBI director James Comey when Comey refused Trump's expressed desire that he "let Flynn go." After Flynn's guilty plea they argued even more forcefully that the president had obstructed justice, a felony in federal criminal law and, by most reckonings, a "high Crime and Misdemeanor."

Democrats saw the Flynn indictment as the thin edge of a wedge that eventually might open the gate to impeachment—although not yet in early December, when Representative Al Green insisted on offering an impeachment resolution, which under House rules had privileged status requiring an immediate vote. Despite Pelosi's objection that "now is not the time," fifty-eight Democrats voted against a motion to table the resolution, and four others voted present. Although the motion to table was approved 364–58, Congressional Black Caucus members voted 23–16 to proceed with an impeachment debate.[9] Most other Democrats counseled patience. Flynn, they predicted, would provide Mueller with evidence that eventually would confirm their suspicions about the president.

Trump personally responded to Flynn's guilty plea with a series of tweeted attacks on the FBI ("its reputation is in Tatters—worst in History!"), the Justice Department (for not going after "totally Crooked Hillary . . . No justice!"), and Comey ("I never asked Comey to stop investigating Flynn . . . another Comey lie!").[10] In one tweet Trump claimed that he "had to fire General Flynn because he lied to the Vice President and the FBI."[11] In truth, if the president knew about Flynn's lies to the FBI before he asked Comey to let Flynn go and then fired the FBI director, that almost certainly would constitute obstruction of justice. Realizing this,

John Dowd, one of Trump's lawyers, claimed that he, not the president, had been the author of the tweet.[12]

The common thread running through Trump's best and worst day and its aftermath was his dependence on his Republican base, which he spent much of December working to solidify. In an appeal to evangelical Christians and some Orthodox Jews, including Republican megadonor Sheldon Adelson, Trump reversed earlier decisions—his own and previous presidents'—and announced that the United States now recognized Jerusalem as the capital of Israel while launching the long process of moving the U.S. embassy there. Protests of the decision in Arab capitals and condemnations by most foreign governments and international organizations quickly followed.[13] In another gesture to his core supporters, Trump campaigned for the controversial conservative Christian Roy Moore in the December 12 Alabama Senate election, despite multiple accusations of sexual misconduct by the candidate toward teenage girls. Moore's loss to Jones was a double defeat for the president, who had endorsed Moore's Republican primary opponent, Senator Strange, before endorsing Moore in the general election. Convinced that his supporters shared his belief that African American critics of his presidency treat him unfairly, Trump attended the opening of the Mississippi Civil Rights Museum. Predictably, this provoked the local NAACP president to denounce Trump's presence as "an affront to the veterans of the civil rights movement," while Representative John Lewis and other dignitaries withdrew from the event.[14] The day before a scheduled Oval Office meeting that included Pelosi and Senate Democratic leader Charles Schumer, Trump tweeted that Pelosi and Schumer "want illegal immigrants flooding into our Country unchecked, are weak on Crime and want to substantially RAISE taxes." Pelosi and Schumer canceled the meeting.[15] Then, in a nod to congressional Republicans, the president embraced their idea of reducing spending on entitlement programs such as Medicare in 2018, which he had pledged not to do during his presidential campaign.[16]

Trump continued to lean heavily on his favorite means of communicating directly with supporters: Twitter, offhand comments to the media, and free-flowing speeches at rallies. Despite previously acknowledging its authenticity, he cast doubt—"I don't talk like that"—on the *Access Hollywood* tape that captured him lewdly bragging to Billy Bush about his sexually aggressive approach to women. "He said it. Grab 'em by the pussy," retorted Bush on behalf of himself and seven other witnesses.[17] In a move condemned by the British prime minister for disseminating a "hateful narrative," Trump retweeted three inflammatory anti-Muslim videos posted by the Britain First extremist group, including one headlined "Muslim Migrant Beats Up Dutch Boy on Crutches!" whose villain turned out to be neither Muslim nor a migrant.[18] When an illegal immigrant accused of murder was acquitted in a California trial, Trump tweeted that the verdict was "disgraceful" and "a complete travesty of justice. BUILD THE WALL!"[19] As part of his relentless assault on so-called "fake news" ("one of the greatest of all terms I've come up with is 'fake,'" he bragged), the president implied baselessly in a tweet that MSNBC host Joe Scarborough might somehow be implicated in the "unsolved mystery" of an aide's death when Scarborough was in Congress.[20] At a ceremony honoring Navajo heroes of World War II, he digressed to disparage Senator Elizabeth Warren, a frequent critic, as "Pocahontas."[21] "This is a rigged system," Trump later told a rally in Florida, dusting off his election-year complaint that he would be cheated out of victory and applying it to the Justice Department's decision to indict Flynn but not Hillary Clinton. "This is a sick system from the inside."[22] When Senator Kirsten Gillibrand became the fifth Democratic senator to call for Trump's resignation, he lewdly labeled her as "someone who would come to my office 'begging' for campaign contributions not so long ago (and would do anything for them)."[23]

More substantively, Trump relied on the pro-business tax bill and, as he had from the beginning, executive actions to shore up support among business and other mainstream Republican constituencies, who found relief in his administration's relaxed regulatory standards. He ordered that about 2 million acres in two national monuments in Utah, Bears Ears and Grand Staircase-Escalante, be stripped of monument status and made available for mining and other commercial activities, a goal sought by western conservatives. A rigorous *New York Times* study of the Environmental Protection Agency under director Scott Pruitt found that during the first nine months of the Trump administration, the number of civil cases the EPA filed against polluters not only was down one-third from the comparable period in the Obama administration, but down one-fourth from the first nine months of the George W. Bush administration. The civil penalties sought by the EPA were only about 70 percent of those sought under Bush, Trump's most recent Republican predecessor, and less than 40 percent of those sought under Obama. Demands by the EPA to retrofit factories to reduce pollution were less than half of those sought under Bush and barely 10 percent of those sought under Obama. Trump linked his deregulatory policies to his party's first president by declaring, "Honest Abe Lincoln was a regulation guy. . . . a regulation cutter," new information for the nation's many Lincoln scholars.[24]

In the end, because the legislative and impeachment processes have become so partisan in recent decades, a trend accelerated during Trump's first year, the 2018 midterm elections promised to be among the most consequential in history. Relying on his Republican base may not be enough to sustain the president: GOP partisans still support him strongly, but their number has shrunk to about 25 percent since he took office.[25] "Early on, his supporters gravitated to the prospect of a leader who could translate the principles of business to government," wrote the journalist Jelani Cobb, "but they overlooked a crucial pitfall. Trump has governed like the president of a company that is hesitant to expand beyond its target demographic, for fear of diluting its brand."[26] Not just the president but all of the nation's constitutional actors—the House, the Senate, the states and cities, the executive departments, and ultimately the courts—will be strongly affected by the results of the November elections.[27] So will Vice President Pence, who has longstanding presidential ambitions of his own.[28] And so, of course, will Donald Trump.

NOTES

INTRODUCTION

1. This and the subsequent examples of first-year crises are taken from various essays in *Crucible: The President's First Year*, ed. Michael Nelson, Stefanie Georgakis Abbott, and Jeffrey L. Chidester (Charlottesville: University of Virginia Press, 2018).

2. Frank Newport, "Middle-Class Identification in U.S. at Pre-Recession Levels," Gallup News, June 7–11, 2017, http://www.gallup.com/poll/212660/middle-class-identification-pre-recession-levels.aspx.

1. TRUMP IS ELECTED

1. "Clown Runs for Prez," *New York Daily News*, June 17, 2017.

2. Ryan Grim and Danny Shea, "A Note about Our Coverage of Donald Trump's 'Campaign,'" Huffington Post, July 17, 2015, http://www.huffingtonpost.com/entry/a-note-about-our-coverage-of-donald-trumps-campaign_us_55a8fc9ce4b0896514d0fd66.

3. Hillary Rodham Clinton, *What Happened* (New York: Simon and Schuster, 2017), 7.

4. Natalie Jackson, "HuffPost Forecast Hillary Clinton Will Win with 323 Electoral Votes," Huffington Post, November 7, 2016, http://www.huffingtonpost.com/entry/polls-hillary-clinton-win_us_5821074ce4b0e80b02cc2a94; Sam Wang, "Is 99% a Reasonable Probability?," Princeton Electoral Consortium, November 6, 2016, http://election.princeton.edu/2016/11/06/is-99-a-reasonable-probability/; Peter Baker, *Obama: The Call of History* (New York: Callaway, 2017), 290. Even FiveThirtyEight gave Trump only a 28 percent chance of winning ("Who Will Win the Presidency?" FiveThirtyEight, November 8, 2016, https://projects.fivethirtyeight.com/2016-election-forecast/).

5. "The Untold Stories of Election Day 2016," *Esquire*, November 5, 2017.

The article he posted instead was "An American Tragedy," https://www
.newyorker.com/news/news-desk/an-american-tragedy-2.

6. Alan I. Abramowitz, "Forecasting the 2016 Presidential Election: Will
Time for Change Mean Time for Trump?," *Sabato's Crystal Ball*, August 11,
2016, http://www.centerforpolitics.org/crystalball/articles/forecasting
-the-2016-presidential-election-will-time-for-change-mean-time-for
-trump/. For a long list of errant predictions about Trump's prospects, see
Joel B. Pollak and Larry Schweikart, *How Trump Won: The Inside Story of a
Revolution* (Washington, DC: Regnery, 2017), 2–3.

7. George C. Edwards III, "No Deal: Donald Trump's Leadership of
Congress," *Forum* 15 (October 2017): 465–66, 468.

8. Louis Jacobson, "Donald Trump's Electoral College Victory Was
Not a 'Massive Landslide,'" PolitiFact, December 12, 2016, http://www
.politifact.com/truth-o-meter/statements/2016/dec/12/donald-trump/
donald-trumps-electoral-college-victory-was-not-ma/; Rebecca Savransky,
"Trump Falsely Claims He Got Biggest Electoral College Win since Reagan," *The Hill*, February 16, 2017, http://thehill.com/business-a-lobbying/
donald-trump-falsely-claims-biggest-electoral-win-since-reagan.

9. Two Trump-pledged electors defected, one to Ohio governor John
Kasich and the other to former Texas congressman Ron Paul. Four Clin-
ton-pledged electors in Washington and one in Hawaii cast three votes for
former general Colin Powell, one for Vermont senator Bernie Sanders, and
one for Yankton Sioux Nation leader Faith Spotted Eagle.

10. Aaron Blake, "Trump Claims None of Those 3 to 5 Million Illegal
Votes Were Cast for Him. None," *Washington Post*, January 26, 2017.

11. Andrew J. Clarke and Jeffery A. Jenkins, "Who Are President
Trump's Allies in the House of Representatives?," *Forum* 15 (October
2017): 419–20.

12. "Trump Reversal on Obama Birthplace Conspiracy Stokes More
Controversy," *Chicago Tribune*, September 16, 2016.

13. "Transcript: Donald Trump's Taped Comments about Women,"
New York Times, October 8, 2016.

14. Ashley Parker, "'You Have to Brand People,' Donald Trump Says,"
New York Times, March 13, 2016.

15. Ben Schreckinger, "Trump Attacks McCain: 'I Like People Who
Weren't Captured,'" Politico, July 18, 2015, http://www.politico.com/
story/2015/07/trump-attacks-mccain-i-like-people-who-werent-captured
-120317.

16. Institute for Politics, *Campaign for President: The Managers Look at
2016* (Lanham, MD: Rowman and Littlefield, 2017), 140.

17. Mark K. Updegrove, *The Last Republicans: Inside the Extraordinary Relationship between George H. W. Bush and George W. Bush* (New York: Harper, 2017).

18. Paul J. Quirk, "The Presidency: Donald Trump and the Question of Fitness," in *The Elections of 2016*, ed. Michael Nelson (Washington, DC: CQ Press, 2018), 189–216; "Full Transcript: Mitt Romney's Remarks on Donald Trump and the 2016 Race," Politico, March 3, 2016, http://www.politico .com/story/2016/03/full-transcript-mitt-romneys-remarks-on-donald -trump-and-the-2016-race-220176.

19. For example, *National Review* devoted its January 21, 2016, issue to the theme "Against Trump."

20. David A. Farenthold, "Trump Recorded Having Extremely Lewd Conversation about Women in 2005," *Washington Post*, October 8, 2016.

21. Meg Kelly, "President Trump and Accusations of Sexual Misconduct: A Complete List," *Washington Post*, November 22, 2017; Jenna Johnson, "Trump Often Condemns Democrats, Defends Republicans on Harassment Allegations," *Washington Post*, November 17, 2017.

22. Nick Gass, "Trump Promises to Create 25 Million Jobs with Economic Plan," Politico, September 15, 2015, http://www.politico.com/ story/2016/09/donald-trump-jobs-economic-plan-228218; Caitlin Yilek, "Trump: I Will Eliminate U.S. Debt in 8 Years," *The Hill*, April 2, 2016, http://thehill.com/blogs/ballot-box/presidential-races/275003-trump-i -will-eliminate-us-debt-in-8-years; "Here's Donald Trump's Presidential Announcement Speech," *Time*, June 16, 2015.

23. Ronald J. Rapoport and Walter J. Stone, "The Sources of Trump's Support," in *Trumped: The 2016 Election That Broke All the Rules*, ed. Larry J. Sabato, Kyle Kondik, and Geoffrey Skelley (Lanham, MD: Rowman and Littlefield, 2017), 138.

24. "Here's Donald Trump's Presidential Announcement Speech."

25. "The CNN-Telemundo Debate Transcript, Annotated," *Washington Post*, February 25, 2016.

26. Rob Crilly, "Donald Trump Finding Out That Winning as President Does Not Come Easy, as Dealmaker-in-Chief Comes Up Short on Healthcare," *Telegraph*, March 24, 2017.

27. James W. Ceaser, Andrew E. Busch, and John J. Pitney Jr., *Defying the Odds: The 2016 Election and American Politics* (Lanham, MD: Rowman and Littlefield, 2017), 167, 170.

28. John Sides, Michael Tesler, and Lynn Vavreck, *Identity Crisis: The 2016 Presidential Campaign and the Battle for the Meaning of America* (Princeton, NJ: Princeton University Press, forthcoming 2018).

29. Rebecca Kaplan, "Trump's Immigration Comments Open Rift in GOP," CBS News, July 5, 2015, http://www.cbsnews.com/news/trump-immigration-comments-open-rift-gop/.

30. Miriam Valverde, "How Trump Plans to Build, and Pay for, a Wall along the U.S.-Mexico Border," PolitiFact, July 26, 2016, http://www.politifact.com/truth-o-meter/article/2016/jul/26/how-trump-plans-build-wall-along-us-mexico-border/; Jenna Johnson, "Trump Calls for 'Total and Complete Shutdown of Muslims Entering the United States,'" *Washington Post*, December 7, 2015.

31. Eugene Kiely, "Yes, Trump Said Bush 'Lied,'" FactCheck, March 17, 2016, http://www.factcheck.org/2016/03/yes-trump-said-bush-lied/; Robert Costa, "Donald Trump and a GOP Primary Race Like No Other," in *Trumped*, ed. Sabato, Kondik, and Skelley, 105.

32. Ali Vitali, "Donald Trump: 'Torture Works,'" NBC News, February 17, 2016, http://www.nbcnews.com/politics/2016-election/donald-trump-torture-works-n520086.

33. M. J. Lee, "Donald Trump's Pledge: 'We're Gonna Be Saying Merry Christmas,'" CNN, October 22, 2015, http://www.cnn.com/2015/10/21/politics/donald-trump-iowa-rally/index.html.

34. "Rise of the Anti-Establishment Presidential Candidates," *Washington Post*, September 14, 2015.

35. Trevor Hughes, "Trump Calls to 'Drain the Swamp' of Washington," *USA Today*, October 18, 2016.

36. Joshua Green, *Devil's Bargain: Steve Bannon, Donald Trump, and the Storming of the Presidency* (New York: Penguin, 2017), 117.

37. Michael Kranish and Marc Fisher, *Trump Revealed: An American Journey of Ambition, Ego, Money, and Power* (New York: Scribner, 2016), 289.

38. Sides, Tesler, and Vavreck, *Identity Crisis*.

39. Michael Nelson, "Did Donald Trump Kill the United States Football League?" *Cook Political Report*, March 21, 2016.

40. Kranish and Fisher, *Trump Revealed*, 110.

41. Liz Smith, *Natural Blonde: A Memoir* (New York: Hachette, 2000).

42. Kranish and Fisher, *Trump Revealed*, 21.

43. Ibid., 202.

44. Thomas B. Edsall, "Hurricane Trump," *New York Times*, September 23, 2015; "Here's Donald Trump's Presidential Announcement Speech."

45. Maureen Dowd, "Liberties; Trump Shrugged," *New York Times*, November 28, 1999.

46. Institute for Politics, *Campaign for President: The Managers Look at 2016*, 28.

47. "The Definitive Net Worth of Donald Trump," *Forbes*, May 4, 2017.

48. Institute for Politics, *Campaign for President: The Managers Look at 2016*, 30.

49. The front page of the *New York Daily News* featured the break-up between Trump and his first wife, Ivana, for twelve consecutive days; it was covered on the *New York Post*'s front page for eight consecutive days (Marc Fisher, "How Liz Smith Invented Donald Trump," *Washington Post*, November 13, 2017).

50. Kranish and Fisher, *Trump Revealed*, 261.

51. Michael Kruse, "The True Story of Donald Trump's First Campaign Speech—in 1987," *Politico Magazine*, February 5, 2016, http://www.politico.com/magazine/story/2016/02/donald-trump-first-campaign-speech-new-hampshire-1987-213595.

52. Kranish and Fisher, *Trump Revealed*, 276.

53. Ibid., 284.

54. Zeke Miller, "When Donald Trump Praised Hillary Clinton," *Time*, July 17, 2015.

55. Michael D'Antonio, *Never Enough: Donald Trump and the Pursuit of Success* (New York: Thomas Dunne, 2015), 247.

56. Ronald Reagan used a similar phrase when he successfully ran for president in 1980: "Let's make America Great Again" (Shirley Anne Warshaw, "The Struggle to Govern in the Trump White House: Competing Power Centers, Personalities, and World Visions," *Forum* 15 [October 2017]: 574).

57. "Exit Polls," CNN, http://edition.cnn.com/election/results/exit-polls/national/president.

58. Gary C. Jacobson, "Donald Trump, the Public, and Congress: The First Seven Months," *Forum* 15 (October 2017): 537.

59. Donna Brazile, *Hacks: The Inside Story of the Break-ins and Breakdowns That Put Donald Trump in the White House* (New York: Hachette, 2017), chap. 11. Biden had seriously considered seeking the Democratic nomination before deciding not to in fall 2015. "If [my son] Beau had not gotten sick, we would already have been running," he later wrote (Joe Biden, *Promise Me Dad: A Year of Hope, Hardship, and Purpose* [New York: Flatiron, 2017], 223).

60. Thomas B. Edsall, "The Struggle between Clinton and Sanders Is Not Over," *New York Times*, September 7, 2017.

61. Clinton, *What Happened*, 229.

62. Sides, Tesler, and Vavreck *Identity Crisis*, chap. 7. See also Nate Silver, "The Comey Letter Probably Cost Clinton the Election," FiveThirtyEight,

May 3, 2017, https://fivethirtyeight.com/features/the-comey-letter
-probably-cost-clinton-the-election/; and Nate Cohn, "A 2016 Review:
There's Reason to Be Skeptical of a Comey Effect," *New York Times*, May 8,
2017. To a one, Clinton's leading campaign advisors blamed the Comey letter
(see their comments in *Campaign for President: The Managers Look at 2016*).

63. Lisa Mascaro, "Trump Welcomes FBI Probe: 'Clinton's Corruption
Is on a Scale We Have Never Seen,'" *Los Angeles Times*, October 28, 2016.

64. Mark Murray, "12 Days That Stunned a Nation: How Hillary Clinton
Lost," NBC News, August 23, 2017, https://www.nbcnews.com/politics/
elections/12-days-stunned-nation-how-hillary-clinton-lost-n794131.

65. Clinton, *What Happened*, passim.

66. Craig Timberg, Elizabeth Dwoskin, Adam Entous, and Karoun
Demirgian, "Russian Ads, Now Publicly Released, Show Sophistication of
Influence Campaign," *Washington Post*, November 1, 2017; Rosalind S. Hel-
derman, Tom Hamburger, and Carol D. Leonnig, "At Least Nine People in
Trump's Orbit Had Contact with Russians during Campaign and Transi-
tion," *Washington Post*, November 5, 2017.

67. Harry Litman, "Why George Papadopoulos Is More Dangerous
Than Paul Manafort," *New York Times*, October 30, 2017.

68. Steven E. Schier and Todd E. Eberly, *The Trump Presidency: Outsider
in the Oval Office* (Lanham, MD: Rowman and Littlefield, 2017), 5.

69. Russell Berman, "What Hillary Clinton Says She Learned from Her
Defeat," *Atlantic*, September 12, 2017; Robert Griffin, Ruy Texeira, "Trump
Supporters Are 'Deplorables,'" CNNPolitics, September 12, 2016, http://
www.cnn.com/2016/09/09/politics/hillary-clinton-donald-trump-basket
-of-deplorables/index.html.

70. David Remnick, "Hillary Clinton Looks Back in Anger," *New Yorker*,
September 25, 2017.

71. Robert Griffin, John Halpin, and Ruy Teixeira, "Democrats Need
to Be the Party of and for Working People—Of All Races," *American
Prospect* (Summer 2017), http://prospect.org/article/democrats-need-be
-party-and-working-people%E2%80%94-all-races.

72. John Sides, "New Poll: Obama-Trump Voters Are Starting to Sour
on Trump," *Washington Post*, September 6, 2017.

73. Robert Costa and Jenna Johnson, "Evangelical Leader Jerry Falwell
Jr. Endorses Trump," *Washington Post*, January 26, 2016.

74. E. J. Dionne, Norman J. Ornstein, and Thomas E. Mann, *One Nation
after Trump: A Guide for the Perplexed, the Disillusioned, the Desperate, and
the Not-Yet-Deported* (New York: St. Martin's, 2017), 164–65.

75. Ibid., 24–25; Sides, Tesler, and Vavreck *Identity Politics*; Michael

Nelson, *Resilient America: Electing Nixon in 1968, Channeling Dissent, and Dividing Government* (Lawrence: University Press of Kansas, 2014).

76. William Safire, *Before the Fall: An Inside View of the Pre-Watergate White House* (Garden City, NY: Doubleday, 1975), 116.

77. Stephen Skowronek, "What Time Is It? Tracking Trump in Secular and Political Time," in *Crucible: The President's First Year,* ed. Michael Nelson, Jeffrey L. Chidester, and Stefanie Georgakis Abbott (Charlottesville: University of Virginia Press, 2018), 11–15.

2. A CYCLE OF DECREASING INFLUENCE AND DECREASING EFFECTIVENESS

1. Paul C. Light, *The President's Agenda: Domestic Policy Choice from Kennedy to Reagan* (Baltimore: Johns Hopkins University Press, 1991), 37.

2. Sidney M. Milkis and Michael Nelson, *The American Presidency: Origins and Development: 1776–2014* (Washington, DC: CQ Press, 2015), chap. 3.

3. See the relevant essays in *Crucible: The President's First Year,* ed. Michael Nelson, Jeffrey L. Chidester, and Stefanie Georgakis Abbott (Charlottesville: University of Virginia Press, 2018).

4. Ibid..

5. Michael Nelson, "A Short, Ironic History of American National Bureaucracy," *Journal of Politics* 44 (August 1982): 747–78.

6. Paul Brace and Barbara Hinckley, *Follow the Leader: Opinion Polls and the Modern Presidency* (New York: Basic, 1993), chap. 2.

7. Erwin C. Hargrove and Michael Nelson, *Presidents, Politics, and Policy* (Baltimore: Johns Hopkins University Press, 1984), 20–24.

8. Michael Nelson, "Evaluating the Presidency," in *The Presidency and the Political System,* ed. Nelson, 8th ed. (Washington, DC: CQ Press, 2006), 1–27.

9. Light, *The President's Agenda,* 42.

10. Ibid., 52.

11. Mike DeBonis and Ed O'Keefe, "Republicans Increasingly Uncertain of a Legislative Victory before August," *Washington Post,* July 8, 2017.

12. Marc J. Hetherington, "The Election: The Allure of the Outsider," in *The Elections of 2016,* ed. Michael Nelson (Washington: CQ Press, 2018), 63–86.

13. "Presidential Approval Ratings—Gallup Historical Statistics and Trends," Gallup News, http://news.gallup.com/poll/116677/presidential -approval-ratings-gallup-historical-statistics-trends.aspx.

14. Daniel Brazenoff, "Electoral College: Make Hillary Clinton President," change.org, December 19, 2016, https://www.change.org/p/electoral-college-make-hillary-clinton-president-on-december-19-4a78160a-023c-4ff0-9069-53cee2a095a8?recruiter=627835418&utm_source=share_petition&utm_medium=email&utm_campaign=share_email_responsive.

15. "Presidential Approval Ratings—Gallup Historical Data and Trends," Gallup News, http://www.gallup.com/poll/116677/presidential-approval-ratings-gallup-historical-statistics-trends.aspx; Frank Newport, "Trump Approval Nudges Down to New Monthly Low," Gallup News, June 5–11, 2017, http://www.gallup.com/poll/212120/trump-approval-edges-down-new-weekly-low.aspx.

16. Gary C. Jacobson, "Donald Trump, the Public, and Congress: The First Seven Months," *Forum* 15 (October 2017): 525–45.

17. George C. Edwards III, "No Deal: Donald Trump's Leadership of Congress," *Forum* 15 (October 2017): 473.

18. This is essentially what happened in September 2017 when Senate Democratic leader Charles Schumer and House Democratic leader Nancy Pelosi persuaded Trump to raise the ceiling on the national debt only through December without agreeing to vote for funds to build a wall along the nation's southern border with Mexico (Damian Paletta and Ashley Parker, "Trump, Schumer Agree to Pursue Plan to Repeal the Debt Ceiling," *Washington Post*, September 7, 2017).

19. Louis Nelson, "Clinton Won't Rule Out Challenging Legitimacy of 2016 Election," Politico, September 18, 2017, http://www.politico.com/story/2017/09/18/hillary-clinton-trump-challenge-2016-election-legitimacy-242848.

20. Scott Cacciola, "Stephen Curry, on a 'Surreal' Day, Confronts a Presidential Snub," *New York Times*, September 23, 2017.

21. Michael Powell, "As Trump Takes on Athletes, Watch Them Rise," *New York Times*, September 23, 2017.

22. The first use of the term I can find was in 2009 (see John Blake, "Obama Takes on Role as Consoler in Chief," *CNN Politics*, December 9, 2009: http://edition.cnn.com/2009/POLITICS/12/03/obama.console/).

23. Barbara A. Perry, "7 Moments That Shaped the President's Role as Comforter-in-Chief," *Time*, October 10, 2017.

24. Jenna Johnson, "The Past Week Showed Trump Is Struggling to Be the President He Promised," *Washington Post*, September 30, 2017; Jenna Johnson and Ashley Parker, "Trump Hails 'Incredible' Response

in 'Lovely' Trip to Storm-Torn Puerto Rico" *Washington Post*, October 3, 2017.

25. Mark Landler, "Trump Lobs Praise, and Paper Towels, to Puerto Rico Storm Victims," *New York Times*, October 3, 2017; David Jackson, "Trump Praises Puerto Rico Recovery, but Critics Assail Comments on Budget and Death Toll," *USA Today*, October 3, 2017.

26. Johnson and Parker, "Trump Hails 'Incredible' Response in 'Lovely' Trip to Storm-Torn Puerto Rico."

27. Philip Rucker, "Trump Warns Puerto Rico: 'We Can't Keep FEMA, the Military and the First Responders . . . Forever!'" *Washington Post*, October 12, 2017.

28. "Remarks by President Trump to Civilian Heroes and Law Enforcement Officials," White House, October 4, 2017, https://www.whitehouse .gov/the-press-office/2017/10/04/remarks-president-trump-civilian -heroes-and-law-enforcement-officials.

29. Louis Nelson and Marc Caputo, "Trump: Dem Congresswoman 'Totally Fabricated What I Said' to Soldier's Widow," Politico, October 18, 2017, http://www.politico.com/story/2017/10/18/trump-fallen-soldier -widow-frederica-wilson-243899.

30. Ibid.

31. Eugene Scott, "Accusations of Racism and Grandstanding Fly between Wilson and Kelly, Overtaking Big Questions about Niger Attack," *Washington Post*, October 20, 2017.

32. Ibid.; Akela Lacy, "Trump: Wilson 'Killing' the Democratic Party amid Gold Star Family Feud," Politico, October 21, 2017, http://www .politico.com/story/2017/10/21/trump-frederica-wilson-democratic -party-244017; Michael D. Shear, "Political Guardrails Gone, a President's Somber Duty Skids into Spectacle," *New York Times*, October 21, 2017; Louis Nelson, Trump Spars with Widow of Slain Soldier about Condolence Call," Politico, October 23, 2017, http://www.politico.com/ story/2017/10/23/la-david-johnson-widow-myeshia-interview-trump -244060. Trump also bungled a consoling message to the victims of a school shooting in California, tweeting instead that "the FBI and Law Enforcement has arrived [*sic*]" to "the people of Sutherland Springs, Texas," whose own mass shooting had occurred more than a week earlier. Eileen Sullivan and Michael D. Shear, "Trump Offers Condolences, for the Wrong Mass Shooting, *New York Times*, November 15, 2017.

33. Peter Baker, "A Divider, Not a Unifier, Trump Widens the Breach," *New York Times*, September 24, 2017.

34. Peter Baker, "Trump Takes on All Comers, Believing Himself the Victor," *New York Times*, October 1, 2017.

35. Amita Kelly and Barbara Sprunt, "Here Is What Donald Trump Wants to Do in His First 100 Days," NPR, November 9, 2017, http://www.npr.org/2016/11/09/501451368/here-is-what-donald-trump-wants-to-do-in-his-first-100-days; "Trump's 100-Day Plan, Annotated: Where His Promises Stand," NPR, April 24, 2017, https://www.npr.org/2017/04/24/520159167/trumps-100-day-action-plan-annotated.

36. Wilson Andrews, Linda Qiu, and Kevin Quealy, "'Soon,' 'Very Soon,' 'Eventually': A Detailed List of Things Trump Said Would Happen," *New York Times*, September 27, 2017.

37. Dan Balz and Scott Clement, "Poll: Trump's Performance Lags behind Even Tepid Public Expectations," *Washington Post*, November 5, 2017.

38. Calculated from data in Harry Enten, "Six Months In, Trump Is Historically Unpopular," FiveThirtyEight, July 17, 2017, https://fivethirtyeight.com/features/six-months-in-trump-is-historically-unpopular/.

39. Harry Entman, "Trump Is Far Less Popular Than the Economy Suggests He Should Be," FiveThirtyEight, October 13, 2017, https://fivethirtyeight.com/features/trump-is-far-less-popular-than-the-economy-suggests-he-should-be/.

40. See, for example, David A. Graham, "Trump's Shrinking, Energized Base," *Atlantic*, September 8, 2017; and Brendan Nyhan, "Why Trump's Base of Support May Be Smaller Than It Seems," *New York Times*, July 19, 2017.

41. Gallup News, "Party Affiliation," Gallup Poll, news.gallup.com.

42. Scott Detrow, "Show's Over? Trump Pledges to Be So Presidential You Will Be So Bored," NPR, April 21, 2016, http://www.npr.org/2016/04/21/475126907/shows-over-trump-pledges-to-be-so-presidential-you-will-be-so-bored.

43. Mike Allen, "Playbook," Politico, March 10, 2016, http://www.politico.com/playbook/2016/03/trump-at-the-right-time-i-will-be-so-presidential-that-youll-call-me-and-youll-say-donald-you-have-to-stop-that-rubios-schoolyard-attacks-backfire-213129.

44. John Wagner and Jenna Johnson, "At an Ohio Campaign Rally, Trump Offers an 'Unfiltered' View of His Presidency," *Washington Post*, July 25, 2017.

45. Chris Cillizza, "Donald Trump Is a 'Smart Person,' in Case You Forgot," *Washington Post*, December 12, 2017.

46. Aaron Blake, "Trump's Hypocritical Quote on Taking Blame Just About Says It All," *Washington Post*, October 16, 2017.

3. FORMING (AND RE-FORMING) THE ADMINISTRATION

1. Randall Lane, "Inside Trump's Head: An Exclusive Interview with the President, and the Single Theory That Explains Everything," *Forbes,* November 14, 2017. The board of directors for Trump Hotels and Resort Casinos, the only public company Trump ever ran, had only three outside members, all of whom "were widely seen as bowing to his wishes" (Ross Buettner and Charles V. Bagli, "How Donald Trump Bankrupted His Atlantic City Casinos, but Still Earned Millions," *New York Times,* June 11, 2016). According to *Fortune* magazine, "No amount of spin will make Trump's dozen years at the helm of Trump Hotels . . . look like anything but a flop that damaged thousands of shareholders, bondholders, and workers" (Shawn Tully, "How Donald Trump Made Millions Off His Biggest Business Failure," *Fortune,* March 10, 2016).

2. Donald Trump with Charles Leerhsen, *Trump: Surviving at the Top* (New York: Random House, 1990).

3. James P. Pfiffner, "Organizing the Trump Presidency," paper prepared for presentation at the annual meeting of the American Political Science Association, San Francisco, August 31–September 3, 2017.

4. Katy Tur, *Unbelievable: My Front-Row Seat to the Craziest Campaign in American History* (New York: Dey St., 2017), 159.

5. Donald J. Trump with Tony Schwartz, *Trump: The Art of the Deal* (New York: Random House, 1987), 1.

6. Alex Isenstedt, "Inside Chris Christie's Fall from Grace," Politico, November 19, 2016, http://www.politico.com/story/2016/11/chris-christie -fall-grace-trump-231659.

7. Jane Mayer, "The Danger of President Pence," *New Yorker,* October 23, 2017.

8. John P. Burke, "The Institutional Presidency," in *The Presidency and the Political System,* ed. Michael Nelson, 11th ed. (Washington, DC: forthcoming, CQ Press, 2019).

9. John P. Burke, *The Institutional Presidency: Organizing and Managing the White House from FDR to Clinton* (Baltimore: Johns Hopkins University Press, 2000).

10. Shirley Anne Warshaw, "The Struggle to Govern in the Trump White House: Competing Power Centers, Personalities, and World Visions," *Forum* 15 (October 2017): 569.

11. Andrew Restuccia, Nahal Toosi, and Tar Palmeri, "Kelly Folds Navarro's Trade Shop into National Economic Council," Politico, September 27, 2017, http://www.politico.com/story/2017/09/27/peter-navarro

-trade-office-national-economic-council-243217; Ana Swanson, "Trump's America First Trade Agenda Roiled by Internal Divisions," *New York Times,* October 20, 2017.

12. Sidney M. Milkis and Michael Nelson, *The American Presidency: Origins and Development, 1776–2014* (Washington, DC: CQ Press, 2015), chap. 16; Joel K. Goldstein, *The White House Vice Presidency: The Path to Significance, Mondale to Biden* (Lawrence: University Press of Kansas, 2016).

13. Eliana Johnson and Andrew Restuccia, "Pence's Power Play," Politico, December 4, 2016, http://www.politico.com/story/2016/12/mike -pence-power-play-trump-transition-232151.

14. Mayer, "The Danger of President Pence."

15. Paul C. Quirk, "Presidential Competence," in *The Presidency and the Political System,* ed. Nelson. See also David A. Graham, "Trump: Middle East Peace 'Is Not as Difficult as People Have Thought,'" *Atlantic,* May 3, 2017; and Avantika Chilkoti, "With World Bank Initiative, a Change in Tone for Trump Administration," *New York Times,* July 19, 2017.

16. Jim Acosta, "Trump Picks Priebus as White House Chief of Staff, Bannon as Top Advisor," CNN, November 14, 2016.

17. Ryan Lizza, "Anthony Scaramucci Called Me to Unload about White House Leavers, Reince Priebus, and Steve Bannon," *New Yorker,* July 27, 2017; Julie Bykowicz and Jonathan Lemire, "Scaramucci's Profanity-Laced Tirade Brings Smoldering White House Tensions into the Open," *Chicago Tribune,* July 27, 2017.

18. Robert Kuttner, "Steve Bannon—Unrepentant," *American Prospect,* August 16, 2017, http://prospect.org/article/steve-bannon-unrepentant.

19. Corey R. Lewandowski and David N. Bossie, *Let Trump Be Trump: The Inside Story of His Rise to the Presidency* (New York: Center Street, 2017), 256; Warshaw, "The Struggle to Govern in the Trump White House," 574.

20. Burke, "The Institutional Presidency."

21. Trump, *Trump: The Art of the Deal,* 1.

22. Josh Dawsey, "White House Aides Lean on Delays and Distractions to Manage Trump," Politico, October 9, 2017, http://www.politico.com/ story/2017/10/09/trump-aides-guard-rails-243608.

23. Sally Persons, "Trump Denies White House Chaos in a Tweet," *Washington Times,* July 31, 2017; "Trump: The Mood in the White House is 'Fantastic,'" Politico, July 13, 2017, http://www.politico.com/ story/2017/07/13/trump-white-house-mood-fantastic-240495.

24. Ashley Parker and Philip Rucker, "Enforcer of 'Choke Point'? Kelly

Seeks to Bring Order to Chaotic White House, *Washington Post,* September 22, 2017.

25. Michael D. Shear, "Trump's Chief of Staff, Speaking with Press, Walks a Verbal Tightrope," *New York Times,* October 12, 2017.

26. Eliana Johnson and Nancy Cook, "Kelly Moves to Control the Information Trump Sees," Politico, August 24, 2017, http://www.politico.com/story/2017/08/24/john-kelly-trump-control-241967.

27. Matt Flegenheimer, "Stephen Miller, the Powerful Survivor on the President's Right Flank," *New York Times,* October 9, 2017.

28. Jonathan Blitzer, "How Stephen Miller Single-Handedly Got the U.S. to Accept Fewer Refugees," *New Yorker,* October 13, 2017.

29. Sharon LaFraniere, Maggie Haberman, and Peter Bake, "Jared Kushner's Vast Duties, and Visibility in White House, Shrink," *New York Times,* November 25, 2017.

30. Glenn Thrush and Maggie Haberman, "Forceful Chief of Staff Grates on Trump, and the Feeling Is Mutual," *New York Times,* September 1, 2017.

31. Ashley Parker and Greg Jaffe, "Inside the 'Adult Day Care Center': How Aides Try to Control and Coerce Trump," *Washington Post,* October 16, 2017.

32. Mark Landler and Maggie Haberman, "Trump's Tweets about London Bombing Anger British Leaders," *New York Times,* September 15, 2017.

33. Annie Karnie, "Aides Give Up on Trying to Control Trump's Tweets," Politico, November 17, 2017, https://www.politico.com/story/2017/11/17/trump-al-franken-tweets-twitter-247662.

34. Peter Baker, and Choe Sang-Hun, "Trump Threatens 'Fire and Fury' against North Korea If It Endangers US," *New York Times,* August 8, 2017.

35. Max Bearack, "Trump's Attacks on Press 'Could Amount to Incitement,' UN Human Rights Chief Says," *Washington Post,* August 30, 2017.

36. Philip Rucker and Ashley Parker, "During a Summer of Crisis, Trump Chafes against Criticism and New Controls," *Washington Post,* August 31, 2017.

37. For Kelly's comment on Wilson, see chapter 2. In an October 31, 2017, interview, Kelly said "the lack of an ability to compromise led to the Civil War," a judgment disputed by nearly every scholar of the war (Jennifer Schuessler, "A Refusal to Compromise? Civil War Scholars Beg to Differ," *New York Times,* November 1, 2017).

38. Greg Jaffe and Anne Gearan, "Kelly Was Brought to the White House to Impose Order. Now He's Stirring Controversy," *Washington Post,* October 31, 2017.

39. Aaron Blake, "Trump's Top Economic Adviser Just Delivered an Extraordinary Rebuke of His Boss," *Washington Post,* August 25, 2017.

40. Leo Shane III, "Military Times Poll: What You Really Think about Trump," *Military Times,* October 23, 2017, https://www.militarytimes .com/news/pentagon-congress/2017/10/23/military-times-poll-what-you -really-think-about-trump/#.We617FI69Mt.twitter.

41. Jonathan Swan, "Government Workers Shun Trump, Give Big Money to Clinton," *The Hill,* October 26, 2017, http://thehill.com/ homenews/campaign/302817-government-workers-shun-trump-give-big -money-to-clinton-campaign.

42. Johnson and Restuccia, "Pence's Power Play"; Michael Grunwald, "How Trump Learned to Love the Swamp," *Politico,* November 9, 2017, https://www.politico.com/magazine/story/2017/11/09/donald-trump -drain-the-swamp-reversal-215808.

43. Ted Johnson, "Steve Bannon on '60 Minutes': Mainstream Media Trying to Destroy Donald Trump," *Variety,* September 10, 2017.

44. Katie Reilly, "Rick Perry Infamously Forgot about the Department of Energy. Now He Might Lead It," *Time,* December 13, 2016.

45. Michael Grunwald, "Mick the Knife," *Politico Magazine,* September/ October 2017, http://www.politico.com/magazine/story/2017/09/01/ mick-mulvaney-omb-trump-budget-profile-feature-215546.

46. Victoria Guida, "Trump Taps Mulvaney to Head CFPB, Sparking Confusion over Agency's Leadership," *Politico,* November 24, 2017.

47. Katie Rogers, "Tom Price's Spending Habits Catch Trump's Attention: 'I'm Not Happy about It,' " *New York Times,* September 27, 2017.

48. Pfiffner, "Organizing the Trump Presidency"; Grunwald, "Mick the Knife."

49. Michael S. Schmidt and Maggie Haberman, "Trump Humiliated Jeff Sessions after Mueller Appointment," *New York Times,* September 14, 2017.

50. Peter Baker, Jeremy W. Peters, and Rebecca R. Ruiz, "In Trump's Word, 'Very Weak' Sessions Twists in Wind," *New York Times,* July 25, 2017.

51. Julie Hirschfeld Davis, "Trump's Cabinet, with a Prod, Extols the 'Blessing' of Serving Him," *New York Times,* June 12, 2017.

52. Eric Bradner, "Keith Ellison Prods Bernie Sanders to Help Out DNC," *CNN,* January 18, 2017, http://www.cnn.com/2017/01/18/politics/ dnc-chair-debate-ellison-sanders/index.html.

53. Glenn Kessler, "President Trump's Claim His Nominees Faced 'Record-Setting Long' Delays," *Washington Post,* June 13, 2017; Carl Hulse, "Democrats Perfect Art of Delay While Republicans Fume over Trump Nominees," *New York Times,* July 17, 2017.

54. The five hundred–plus positions identified as especially important by the nonprofit Partnership for Public Service at the start of the Trump administration are only a fraction of the 3,653 political appointments available to the president. Of these, 1,054 require the consent of the Senate, 527 do not, 680 are classified as non-career Senior Executive Service appointments, and 1,392 are Schedule C appointments (Pfiffner, "Organizing the Trump Presidency").

55. Jason Zengerle, "Rex Tillerson and the Unraveling of the State Department," *New York Times Magazine,* October 17, 2017.

56. Matthew Rosenberg, Sharon LaFraniere, and Matt Apuzzo, "Ongoing Trump Migraine: His Initial Foreign Policy Team," *New York Times,* October 31, 2017.

57. "Tracking How Many Key Positions Trump Has Filled So Far," *Washington Post,* July 19, 2017, https://www.washingtonpost.com/graphics/politics/trump-administration-appointee-tracker/database/?hpid=hp_hp-top-table-main_6months-tracker-1125am%3Ahomepage%2Fstory; Michelle Cheng, "Trump Still Hasn't Filled Top Jobs, and He Has (Mostly) Himself to Blame," FiveThirtyEight, July 3, 2017, https://fivethirtyeight.com/features/trump-still-hasnt-filled-top-jobs-and-he-has-mostly-himself-to-blame/.

58. Having to deal as chief of staff with Elaine Duke, his interim successor at Homeland Security pending Nielsen's confirmation, Kelly grew frustrated when she extended Temporary Protected Status to fifty-seven thousand Hondurans who had left their country after a hurricane in 1998 and had been living in the United States ever since (Nick Miroff, "White House Chief of Staff Tried to Pressure Acting DHS Secretary to Expel Thousands of Hondurans," *Washington Post,* November 9, 2017).

59. Calculated from data in Josh Dawsey, "Trump Badly Lagging Obama, Bush, Clinton in Political Appointees," Politico, July 14, 2017, http://www.politico.com/story/2017/07/14/trump-political-appointees-compared-to-obama-bush-240573; and Karen Yourish and Gregor Aisch, "The Top Jobs in Trump's Administration Are Mostly Vacant: Who's to Blame?" *New York Times,* July 17, 2017.

60. Jan Diehm et al., "Tracking Trump's Nominations," CNN, October 6, 2017, http://www.cnn.com/interactive/2017/politics/trump-nominations/.

61. Robert Costa, Abby Phillips, and Karen DeYoung, "Bannon Removed from Security Council as McMaster Asserts Control," *Washington Post,* April 5, 2017.

62. Michael Grunwald, Andrew Restuccia, and Josh Dawsey, "Trump

Starts Dismantling His Shadow Cabinet," Politico, May 1, 2017, http://www.politico.com/story/2017/05/01/trump-starts-dismantling-his-shadow-cabinet-237819.

63. Cody Derespina, "Trump: No Plans to Fill 'Unnecessary' Appointed Positions," Fox News, February 28, 2017, http://www.foxnews.com/politics/2017/02/28/trump-no-plans-to-fill-unnecessary-appointed-positions.html.

64. Randall Lane, "Inside Trump's Head: An Exclusive Interview with the President, and the Single Theory That Explains Everything," *Forbes,* November 14, 2017.

65. Jesse Byrnes, "Trump on Lack of Nominees: 'I Am the Only One That Matters,'" *The Hill,* November 2, 2017, http://thehill.com/blogs/blog-briefing-room/news/358573-trump-on-lack-of-nominees-i-am-the-only-one-that-matters.

66. Brianna Ehley, Josh Dawsey, and Sarah Karlin-Smith, "Blindsided Trump Officials Scrambling to Develop Opioid Plan," Politico, October 20, 2017, http://www.politico.com/story/2017/10/20/trump-opioid-plan-blindsides-advisers-243974; Julie Hirschfeld-Davis, "Trump Declares Opioid Crisis a 'Health Emergency' but Requests No Funds," *New York Times,* October 26, 2017.

67. Nancy Cook, "Kelly Tries to Get Empty Administration Jobs Filled Fast," Politico, October 15, 2017, http://www.politico.com/story/2017/10/15/kelly-trump-administration-jobs-243768.

68. Madeline Conway, "Trump: 'Nobody Knew That Health Care Could Be So Complicated,'" Politico, February 27, 2017, http://www.politico.com/story/2017/02/trump-nobody-knew-that-health-care-could-be-so-complicated-235436; Dana Milbank, "Lincoln Was a Republican, Slavery Is Bad—and More Discoveries by President Obvious," *Washington Post,* March 22, 2017.

69. Jeremy Diamond, "Trump: Defense Secretary Mattis Can 'Override' Me on Torture," CNN, January 27, 2017, http://www.cnn.com/2017/01/27/politics/donald-trump-defense-secretary-override-on-torture/index.html.

70. Amanda Erickson, "Trump Thought China Could Get North Korea to Comply. It's Not That Easy," *Washington Post,* April 13, 2017. In a February 2016 Republican debate, Trump said that the Chinese "have total, absolute control, practically, of North Korea" (Steven E. Schier and Todd E. Eberly, *The Trump Presidency: Outsider in the Oval Office* [Lanham, MD: Rowman and Littlefield, 2017], 118).

71. Carol Morello, "Iran Nuclear Deal Could Collapse under Trump," *Washington Post,* November 9, 2017.

72. Ashley Parker et al., " 'I Was All Set to Terminate': Inside Trump's Sudden Shift on NAFTA," *Washington Post,* April 27, 2017.

73. Christopher Mele, "Trump on Being President: 'I Thought It Would Be Easier,' " *New York Times,* April 28, 2017.

4. EXECUTIVE ACTION

1. Andrew Rudalevige, "The Presidency and Unilateral Power: A Taxonomy," in *The Presidency and the Political System,* ed. Michael Nelson, 11th ed. (Washington, DC: CQ Press, forthcoming 2019); Andrew Rudalevige, "Candidate Trump Attacked Obama's Executive Orders. President Trump Loves Executive Orders," *Washington Post,* October 17, 2017.

2. Scott Clement and Dan Balz, "Poll Finds Trump's Standing Weakened since Springtime," *Washington Post,* July 16, 2017; "How Popular/ Unpopular Is Donald Trump?," FiveThirtyEight, https://projects.fivethirty eight.com/trump-approval-ratings/?ex_cid=rrpromo.

3. Lisa Rein, "Trump's Stark Priorities in Funding and Cutting Are Keenly Felt by the Federal Workforce," *Washington Post,* July 19, 2017.

4. Sidney M. Milkis, "The Presidency and the Party System," in *The Presidency and the Political System,* ed. Nelson.

5. Rudalevige, "The Presidency and Unilateral Power."

6. David H. Becker, "Changing Directions in Administrative Agency Rulemaking: 'Reasoned Analysis,' the Roadless Rule Repeal, and the 2006 National Park Service Management Policies," *Environs* 30 (December 2006), 66–99.

7. Brady Dennis, "Trump Administration Will Propose Repealing Obama's Key Effort to Combat Climate Change," *Washington Post,* October 5, 2017.

8. Lisa Friedman, "Court Blocks E.P.A. Effort to Suspend Obama-Era Methane Rule," *New York Times,* July 3, 2017.

9. Erin Seims, "Mueller, Sessions and Cuba: Trump News of the Week," *New York Times,* June 16, 2017.

10. Sidney M. Milkis and Nicholas Jacobs, " 'I Alone Can Fix It': Donald Trump, the Administrative Presidency, and the Hazards of Executive-Centered Partisanship," *Forum* 15 (October 2017): 600.

11. Daniel W. Drezner, "Why the Trump Administration's Accomplishments Are Driving the President Crazy," *Washington Post,* August 30, 2017.

See also Marc Landy and Sidney M. Milkis, "The Presidency in History: Leading from the Eye of a Storm," in *The Presidency and the Political System*, ed. Nelson.

12. Gardiner Harris, "Trump Tightens Cuba Embargo, Restricting Access to Hotels and Businesses," *New York Times*, November 8, 2017.

13. White House, "Statement by President Trump on the Paris Climate Accord," whitehouse.gov, June 1, 2017, https://www.whitehouse.gov/the-press-office/2017/06/01/statement-president-trump-paris-climate-accord.

14. Ronald Brownstein, "The Executive Branch's Sharp Turn to the Right," *Atlantic*, August 3, 2017. https://www.theatlantic.com/politics/archive/2017/08/trump-obama-regulations/535770/.

15. Tiffany Hsu, "Administration Scraps Local-Hiring Plan for Public Works," *New York Times*, August 24, 2017.

16. Abby Goodnough and Robert Pear, "Trump Administration Sharply Cuts Spending on Health Care Enrollment," *New York Times*, August 31, 2017; Audrey Carlson and Haeyoun Park, "The Same Agency That Runs Obamacare Is Using Taxpayer Money to Undermine It," *New York Times*, September 4, 2017.

17. Adam Cancryn, "How the Trump Administration Is Reshaping Health Care—without Congress," Politico, September 13, 2017, http://www.politico.com/story/2017/09/13/trump-obama-health-care-legacy-242683.

18. Robert Pear, Rebecca R. Ruiz, and Laurie Goodstein, "Trump Administration Rolls Back Birth Control Mandate," *New York Times*, October 6, 2017.

19. Amy Goldstein, "Trump Signs Order to Eliminate ACA Insurance Rules, Undermine Marketplaces," *Virginian-Pilot*, October 12, 2017.

20. Amy Goldstein and Julie Eilperin, "Trump to End Key ACA Subsidies, a Move That Will Threaten the Law's Marketplaces," *Washington Post*, October 13, 2017.

21. On October 17 Republican senator Lamar Alexander of Tennessee and Democratic senator Patty Murray of Washington introduced a bill they had been working on for months to provide a legal basis to continue making payments to the insurance companies for another two years, evoking contradictory responses from Trump.

22. Robert Pear and Reed Abelson, "Foiled in Congress, Trump Moves on His Own to Undermine Obamacare," *New York Times*, October 11, 2017.

23. Margot Sanger-Katz, "Trump's Attack on Insurer 'Gravy Train' Could Actually Help a Lot of Consumers," *New York Times*, October 18, 2017.

24. Noam Scheiber, "Trump Shifts Labor Policy Focus from Worker to Entrepreneur," *New York Times*, September 3, 2017.

25. Susan Svrluga and Nick Anderson, "DeVos Decries 'Failed System' on Campus Sexual Assault, Vows to Replace It," *Washington Post*, September 7, 2017.

26. Emma Green, "The Department of Justice Takes a Stand against Transgender Rights in the Workplace," *Atlantic*, October 5, 2017. https://www.theatlantic.com/politics/archive/2017/10/the-department-of-justice-takes-a-stand-against-transgender-rights-in-the-workplace/542154/.

27. Ben Protess, Danielle Ivory, and Steve Eder, "Where Trump's Hands-Off Approach to Governing Does Not Apply," *New York Times*, September 10, 2017; Adam Liptak, "Back at Full Strength, Supreme Court Faces a Momentous Term," *New York Times*, October 1, 2017.

28. Phillip Rucker and Matt Zapotosky, "Trump Breaches Boundaries by Saying DOJ Should Be 'Going After' Democrats," *Washington Post*, November 3, 2017.

29. Jeremy W. Peters, "Alternative Narrative Emerges in Conservative Media as Russia Inquiry Widens," *New York Times*, November 3, 2017.

30. Peter Baker, "Trump Shatters Longstanding Norms by Pressing for Clinton Investigation," *New York Times*, November 14, 2017.

31. Coral Davenport and Eric Lipton, "Scott Pruitt Is Carrying Out His E.P.A. Agenda in Secret, Critics Say," *New York Times*, August 11, 2017; Philip Bump, "What Trump Has Undone," *Washington Post*, August 24, 2017.

32. Julie Turkewitz and Lisa Friedman, "Interior Secretary Proposes Shrinking Four National Monuments," *New York Times*, August 24, 2017; Juliet Eilperin, "Shrink at Least 4 National Monuments and Modify a Half-Dozen Others, Zinke Tells Trump," *Washington Post*, September 17, 2017.

33. Lisa Friedman and Brad Plumer, "Coal Mining Health Study Is Halted by Interior Department," *New York Times*, August 21, 2017.

34. Nadja Popovich and Livia Albeck-Ripka, "52 Environmental Rules on the Way out under Trump," *New York Times*, October 6, 2017.

35. Eric Lipton, "Courts Thwart Administration Effort to Rescind Obama-Era Environmental Regulations," *New York Times*, October 6, 2017.

36. Julie Eilperin, Lisa Rein, and Marc Fisher, "Resistance from Within: Federal Workers Push Back against Trump," *Washington Post*, January 31, 2017.

37. Jack Goldsmith, "Will Donald Trump Destroy the Presidency?" *Atlantic*, October 2017.

38. Gabriel Debenedetti, "Clinton Urges Government Workers Not to

Quit Their Posts," Politico, September 18, 2017, http://www.politico.com/story/2017/09/18/hillary-clinton-government-workers-242865. For the views of four civil servants who quit their jobs rather than serve under Trump, see Lydia Polgreen, "Four Quitters Walk into a Bar," Huffington Post, October 25, 2017, http://highline.huffingtonpost.com/articles/en/trump-quitters/.

39. Greg Miller, Julie Vitkovskaya, and Reuben Fischer-Baum, "'This Deal Will Make Me Look Terrible': Full Transcripts of Trump's Calls with Mexico and Australia," Washington Post, August 3, 2017.

40. Darryl Fears and Julie Eilperin, "Zinke Says a Third of Interior's Staff Is Disloyal to Trump and Promises 'Huge' Changes," Washington Post, September 26, 2017; Eilperin, Rein, and Fisher, "Resistance from Within: Federal Workers Push Back against Trump."

41. Joe Davidson, "Interior's 'Unusual' Transfer of Senior Executives Spurs Official Probe," Washington Post, September 12, 2017.

42. Abby Phillip, Thomas Gibbons-Neff, and Mike DeBonis, "Trump Announces That He Will Ban Transgender People from Serving in the Military," Washington Post, July 25, 2017.

43. Shirley Anne Warshaw, "The Struggle to Govern in the Trump White House: Competing Power Centers, Personalities, and World Visions," Forum 15 (October 2017): 577.

44. Thomas Gibbons-Neff, "Despite Trump Announcement, Coast Guard Will Not 'Break Faith' with Transgender Troops," Washington Post, August 1, 2017.

45. Michael R. Gordon and Emily Cochrane, "Trump Gives Mattis Wide Discretion over Transgender Ban," New York Times, August 25, 2017.

46. Dave Phillips, "Judge Blocks Trump's Ban on Transgender Troops in Military," New York Times, October 30, 2017; Helene Cooper, "Pentagon Approves Gender-Reassignment Surgery for Service Members," New York Times, November 15, 2017.

47. Lisa Friedman, "Trump Signs Order Rolling Back Environmental Rules on Infrastructure," New York Times, August 15, 2017.

48. Juliet Eilperin, "After Harvey, the Trump Administration Reconsiders Flood Rules It Just Rolled Back," Washington Post, September 1, 2017.

49. U.S. vs. Garland, 71 U.S. 333 (1867), https://www.law.cornell.edu/supremecourt/text/71/333.

50. Noah Feldman, "Arpaio Pardon Would Show Contempt for Constitution," BloombergView, August 23, 2017, https://www.bloomberg.com/view/articles/2017-08-23/arpaio-pardon-would-show-contempt-for-constitution.

51. Kristen Bahler, "Here Are the 9 Attorneys General Who Led the Campaign to End DACA," *Money,* September 5, 2017.

52. Michael D. Shear and Julie Hirschfeld Davis, "Trump Moves to End DACA and Calls on Congress to Act," *New York Times,* September 5, 2017.

53. "Transcript of AP Interview with Trump," Associated Press, April 23, 2017, https://www.apnews.com/c810d7de280a47e88848b0ac74690c83.

54. Sophie Tatum, "Trump: I'll 'Revisit' DACA If Congress Can't fix in 6 Months," CNNPolitics, September 6, 2017, http://www.cnn.com/2017/09/05/politics/donald-trump-revisit-daca/index.html.

55. Adam Liptak, "Appeals Court Will Not Reinstate Trump's Revised Travel Ban, *New York Times,* May 25, 2017.

56. Caitlin Dickerson, "Immigration Arrests Rise Sharply as a Trump Mandate Is Carried Out," *New York Times,* May 17, 2017; Maria Sacchetti and Nick Miroff, "How Trump Is Building a Border Wall That No One Can See," *Washington Post,* November 21, 2017.

57. Farhana Khera and Johnathan J. Smith, "How Trump Is Stealthily Carrying Out His Muslim Ban," *New York Times,* July 18, 2017.

58. Mirian Jordan, "Trump Administration Ends Temporary Protection for Haitians," *New York Times,* November 20, 2017.

59. Sacchetti and Miroff, "How Trump Is Building a Border Wall That No One Can See."

60. Devlin Barrett, "White House Expands Travel Ban, Restricting Visitors from Eight Countries," *Washington Post,* September 24, 2017; Michael D. Shear, Ron Nixon, and Adam Liptak, "Supreme Court Cancels Hearing on Previous Trump Travel Ban," *New York Times,* September 25, 2017.

61. Shear, Nixon, and Liptak, "Supreme Court Cancels Hearing on Previous Trump Travel Ban."

62. Julie Hirschfeld Davis and Miriam Jordan, "Trump Plans 45,000 Limit on Refugees Admitted to U.S.," *New York Times,* September 25, 2017.

5. LOCI OF OPPOSITION

1. Paul Nolette, "State Attorneys General Have Taken Off as a Partisan Force in National Politics," *Washington Post,* October 23, 2017.

2. Brent Kendall, "Trump Says Judge's Mexican Heritage Presents 'Absolute Conflict,'" *Wall Street Journal,* June 3, 2016. See also Institute for Politics, *Campaign for President: The Managers Look at 2016* (Lanham, MD: Rowman and Littlefield, 2017), 184.

3. Ben Wolfgang and Stephen Dinan, "Trump Says His Justices Will Overturn *Roe v. Wade,*" *Washington Times,* October 19, 2016.

4. Michael D. Shear, "Trump Names Supreme Court Candidates for Nonexistent Vacancy," *New York Times,* November 17, 2017.

5. Harper Neidig, "McConnell: Don't Replace Scalia until after the Election," *The Hill,* February 13, 2017, http://thehill.com/homenews/senate/269389-mcconnell-dont-replace-scalia-until-after-election.

6. In the two years before Obama left office, the Senate confirmed only twenty-two judicial nominations, the fewest by any Congress since the Truman presidency.

7. Charlie Savage, "Trump Is Rapidly Reshaping the Judiciary. Here's How," *New York Times,* November 11, 2017.

8. Ronald A. Klain, "The One Area Where Trump Has Been Wildly Successful," *Washington Post,* July 19, 2017.

9. Editorial Board, "Trump's Excellent Judges," *Wall Street Journal,* October 1, 2017.

10. Seung Min Kim, "Trump's Judge Picks: 'Not Qualified,' Prolific Bloggers," Politico, October 17, 2017, http://www.politico.com/story/2017/10/17/trump-judges-nominees-court-picks-243834?jumpEdition=.

11. The American Bar Association said that Trump's nominee to the Eighth Circuit Court of Appeals, Leonard Steven Grasz, and three of his district court nominees were "not qualified," a judgment conservatives attacked as evidence of the ABA's liberal bias (see, for example, Alex Swoyer, "American Bar Association Refers to 'You People' When Rating Trump's Judicial Pick," *Washington Times,* November 1, 2017).

12. The other three early appeals court nominees from Trump's first two lists were Amul Thapar of Kentucky for a seat on the Sixth Circuit Court of Appeals, Allison Eid of Colorado for a seat on the Tenth Circuit Court, and Don Willett of Texas for a seat on the Fifth Circuit. All were from states represented by at least one Republican senator, who quickly returned their blue slips.

13. Burgess Everett and Seung Min Kim, "McConnell Ratchets up Judicial Wars," Politico, October 11, 2017, http://www.politico.com/story/2017/10/11/mitch-mcconnell-judicial-battles-243669.

14. Carl Hulse, "Trump and McConnell See a Way to Make Conservatives Happy," *New York Times,* October 17, 2017.

15. Amy B. Wang, "Trump Lashes Out at 'So-Called Judge" Who Temporarily Blocked Travel Ban," *Washington Post,* February 4, 2017.

16. Ibid.; David Jackson, "Trump Rips 'Disgraceful' Court Decision in Immigration Ban," *USA Today,* February 10, 2017.

17. Stephen E. Schier and Todd E. Eberly, *The Trump Presidency: Outsider in the Oval Office* (Lanham, MD: Rowman and Littlefield, 2017), 115.

18. Richard Perez-Pena, "2nd Federal Judge Strikes down Trump's New Travel Ban," *New York Times*, October 18, 2017.

19. Miriam Jordan, "Appeals Court Partly Reinstates Trump's New Travel Ban," *New York Times*, November 13, 2017.

20. Eli Rosenberg, "Federal Judge Blocks Trump's Executive Order on Denying Funding to Sanctuary Cities," *Washington Post*, November 21, 2017.

21. Dave Phillips, "Trump's Ban on Transgender Troops in Military," *New York Times*, October 30, 2017.

22. E. J. Dionne Jr., Norman J. Ornstein, and Thomas E. Mann, *One Nation after Trump: A Guide for the Disillusioned, the Desperate, and the Not-Yet-Deported* (New York; St. Martin's, 2017), 104.

23. Calculated from data in the monthly series tracking political protests by Erica Chenoweth and Jeremy Pressman's Crowd Counting Consortium, published on the *Washington Post's* Monkey Cage blog between April and December of 2017.

24. Dionne, Ornstein, and Mann, *One Nation after Trump*, 278–79; *Indivisible: A Practical Guide for Resisting the Trump Agenda*, https://www.indivisible.org/guide/. The four authors are Ezra Levin, Jeremy Haile, Leah Greenberg, and Angel Padilla.

25. Charles M. Blow, "The New Democratic Party," *New York Times*, November 5, 2017.

26. See, for example, Gideon Lewis-Kraus, "How the 'Resistance' Helped Democrats Dominate Virginia," *New York Times Magazine*, November 13, 2017.

27. Miriam Jordan, "Immigration Agents Arrest Hundreds in Sweep of Sanctuary Cities," *New York Times*, September 28, 2017.

28. Lizette Alvarez, "Mayors, Sidestepping Trump, Vow to Fill Void on Climate Change," *New York Times*, June 26, 2017.

29. Lisa Friedman and Brad Plumer, "U.S. Governors at U.N. General Assembly: 'You Have Allies' on Climate Change," *New York Times*, September 18, 2017.

30. Brad Plumer, "How Can U.S. States Fight Climate Change if Trump Quits the Paris Accord?" *New York Times*, September 20, 2017.

31. Lisa Friedman, "A Shadow Delegation Stalks the Official U.S. Team at Climate Talks," *New York Times*, November 11, 2017.

32. Hunter Walker, "Donald Trump Just Released an Epic Statement Raging against Mexican Immigrants and 'Disease,'" *Business Insider*, July 6, 2015, http://www.businessinsider.com/donald-trumps-epic-statement-on-mexico-2015-7.

33. Ariella Phillips, "Texas Judge Blocks State from Handing over Voter Info to Trump Commission," *Washington Examiner*, October 3, 2017.

34. Deborah Barfield Berry, "Trump Voter Fraud Commission Appears to Have Gone Dark," *USA Today*, November 6, 2017; John Wagner, "Trump Voter Fraud Commission Sued by One of Its Own Members, Alleging Democrats Are Being Kept in the Dark," *Washington Post*, November 9, 2017.

35. George C. Edwards III, "No Deal: Donald Trump's Leadership of Congress," *Forum* 15 (October 2017): 451.

36. Jonathan Lemire, "Trump Makes Puzzling Claim about Andrew Jackson, Civil War," *Chicago Tribune*, May 1, 2017.

37. John Wagner, "Trump: Most People Don't Know President Lincoln Was a Republican," *Washington Post*, March 22, 2017.

38. Noah Bierman, "Trump Says Frederick Douglass Did 'An Amazing Job,'" *Los Angeles Times*, February 1, 2017.

39. Adam Liptak, "Trump vs. the Constitution," *New York Times*, November 29, 2016.

40. Peter Baker, "'People Love You': For Trump, a Welcome Respite from the Capital," *New York Times*, July 25, 2017.

41. Aaron Blake, "Trump Botches Reference to 'President' of Virgin Islands a Day after Rick Perry Called Puerto Rico a 'Country,'" *Washington Post*, October 13, 2017.

6. CONGRESS AND DOMESTIC POLICY

1. Susan Davis, "'Dawn of a New Unified Republican Government' Coming in 2017," NPR, December 22, 2016, http://www.npr.org/2016/12/22/505618360/-dawn-of-a-new-unified-republican-government-coming-in-2017; Rachel Bade, "Ryan: GOP Will Replace Obamacare, Cut Taxes, and Fund Wall by August," Politico, January 25, 2017, http://www.politico.com/story/2017/01/republican-agenda-retreat-obamacare-wall-tax-cuts-234176.

2. Michael D. Shear and Cheryl Gay Stolberg, "Trump and McConnell Strive for Comity Amid Rising Tensions," *New York Times*, October 16, 2017.

3. As Allen Schick, who drafted the 1974 Budget and Impoundment Control Act that created the reconciliation process, wrote, "Reconciliation was intended to deal with legislative decisions made during the interval of the first budget resolution [in April] and consideration of [a] second resolution [in September.]" Starting in the 1990s, however, reconciliation instead became a device to pass money-related bills through the Senate without having to overcome a filibuster—that is, with fifty-one votes

instead of sixty (Jeff Davis, "The Rule That Broke the Senate," *Politico*, October 15, 2017, https://www.politico.com/magazine/story/2017/10/15/how-budget-reconciliation-broke-congress-215706).

4. The Republican nominee, Roy Moore, was disavowed by most national party leaders after accusations surfaced that he had sexually assaulted several teenage girls in the 1970s. Senate Majority Leader McConnell vowed that Moore would immediately face Ethics Committee proceedings if he were elected (Seung Min Kim and John Bresnahan, "McConnell Predicts Expulsion If Moore Wins," *Politico*, November 14, 2017, https://www.politico.com/story/2017/11/14/moore-senate-republicans-expulsion-244907).

5. Ibid. Twelve who did not support Trump were still in the Senate during his first year: Mike Crapo of Idaho, Cory Gardner of Colorado, Mike Lee of Utah, Rob Portman of Ohio, Ben Sasse of Nebraska, Dan Sullivan and Lisa Murkowski of Alaska, Susan Collins of Maine, John McCain and Jeff Flake of Arizona, Lindsey Graham of South Carolina, and Dean Heller of Nevada. During his first year, Trump locked horns with most of them, especially Collins, McCain, Murkowski, Heller, and Graham.

6. Perry Bacon Jr., "The Senate Seems More Willing to Push Back against Trump Than the House—Why?" FiveThirtyEight, August 4, 2017, https://fivethirtyeight.com/features/the-senate-seems-more-willing-to-push-back-against-trump-than-the-house-why/.

7. Theda Skocpol and Vanessa Williamson, *The Tea Party and the Remaking of Republican Conservatism* (New York: Oxford University Press, 2012), 56, 68–69.

8. Michael Grunwald, "Mick the Knife," *Politico Magazine*, September–October 2017, http://www.politico.com/magazine/story/2017/09/01/mick-mulvaney-omb-trump-budget-profile-feature-215546.

9. As measured by DW-Nominate scores (George C. Edwards, "No Deal: Donald Trump's Leadership of Congress," *Forum* 15 [October 2017]: 456–57).

10. Robert Draper, "Trump vs. Congress—Now What?," *New York Times Magazine*, March 26, 2017. Strangely, Trump claimed to have invented the phrase "prime the pump," which has been used frequently for more than a century (Max Ehrenfreund, "Behind Trump's 'Prime the Pump' Gaffe Is a Bunch of Real News," *Washington Post*, May 11, 2017).

11. Karen Tumulty, "Trump Learns That Dealmaking Is Not the Same as Leadership," *Washington Post*, March 24, 2017.

12. Mike DeBonis, "It's Almost July, and House Republicans Still Can't Pass a Budget," *Washington Post*, June 27, 2017.

13. One reading of the act that created the CFPB seemed to support English, but a different reading seemed to support Mulvaney, as did another piece of legislation, the Federal Vacancies Reform Act (Renae Merle, "The CFPB Now Has Two Directors. And Nobody Knows Which One Should Lead the Federal Agency," *Washington Post*, November 24, 2017; Victoria Guida, "Trump Says Mulvaney to Head CFPB, Sparking Confusion over Agency's Leadership," Politico, November 24, 2017, https://www.politico.com/story/2017/11/24/richard-cordray-successor-cfpb-leandra-english-259612).

14. Renae Merle, "Leandra English, the Woman at the Center of a White House Battle for Control of the CFPB, Files Lawsuit against Trump Pick to Head Watchdog Agency," *Washington Post*, November 26, 2017; Lorraine Woellert, "Consumer Bureau's Top Lawyer Sides with Trump in Leadership Clash," Politico, November 26, 2017: https://www.politico.com/story/2017/11/26/consumer-bureau-trump-english-cordray-260062?lo=ap_a1.

15. Michael D. Shear and Karen Yourish, "Trump Says He Has Signed More Bills Than Any President, Ever. No, He Hasn't," *New York Times*, July 17, 2017.

16. Randall Lane, "Inside Trump's Head: An Exclusive Interview with the President, and the Single Theory That Explains Everything," *Forbes*, November 14, 2017,

17. Edwards, "No Deal," 482.

18. George Tsebelis, "This Is Why Trump's 'Art of the Deal' Doesn't Work in Politics," *Washington Post*, March 29, 2017.

19. Donald J. Trump (realDonaldTrump), "The ABC/Washington Post Poll, even though almost 40% is not bad at this time, was just about the most inaccurate poll around election time!," July 16, 2017, 9:10 a.m., https://twitter.com/realDonaldTrump/status/886588838902206464.

20. Jonathan Martin and Mark Landler, "Bob Corker Says Trump's Recklessness Threatens 'World War III,'" *New York Times*, October 8, 2017.

21. Ryan Koronowski, "68 Times Trump Promised to Repeal Obamacare," ThinkProgress, March 24, 2017, https://thinkprogress.org/trump-promised-to-repeal-obamacare-many-times-ab9500dad31e.

22. Paul Kane, "One Reason the GOP Health Bill Is a Mess: No One Thought Trump Would Win," *Washington Post*, July 6, 2017.

23. Matthew J. Dickinson, "The President and Congress," in *The Presidency and the Political System*, ed. Michael Nelson, 11th ed. (Washington, DC: CQ Press, forthcoming 2018).

24. Adam Cancryn, "Pence's Healthcare Power Play," Politico, November 13, 2017, https://www.politico.com/story/2017/11/13/pence -health-care-azar-244859?lo=ap_a1.

25. Julie Hirschfeld Davis, Thomas Kaplan, and Maggie Haberman, "Trump Demands That Senators Find a Way to Replace Obamacare," New York Times, July 19, 2017.

26. David Weigel and Sean Sullivan, "McCain Considers a New Obama- care Repeal Bill, and Activists Scramble to Stop It," Washington Post, Sep- tember 6, 2017.

27. Mike DeBonis, Kelsey Snell, and Robert Costa, "Trump to GOP Critics of Health-Care Bill: 'I'm Gonna Come after You,' " Washington Post, March 21, 2017; Annie Karnie and Eliana Johnson, "Trump's Year of Anger, Disruption and Scandal," Politico, November 4, 2017, https://www .politico.com/story/2017/11/04/trump-first-year-office-244542.

28. Thomas Kaplan, Jennifer Steinhauer, and Robert Pear, "Trump, in Zigzag, Calls House Republicans' Bill 'Mean,' " New York Times, June 13, 2017.

29. Nolan D. McCaskill, "Trump: McCain 'the Only Reason We Don't Have' Obamacare Repealed," Politico, September 25, 2017, http://www .politico.com/story/2017/09/25/trump-blames-john-mccain-obamacare -243097.

30. Louis Nelson, "Trump Slams Flake as 'Toxic' ahead of Phoenix Rally," Politico, August 17, 2017, http://www.politico.com/story/2017/08/ 17/trump-criticize-jeff-flake-241728.

31. Eugene Scott and Miranda Green, "Trump, Graham Feud over President's Charlottesville Response," CNNPolitics, August 17, 2017, http://www.cnn.com/2017/08/16/politics/lindsey-graham-donald-trump -charlottesville/index.html.

32. Julia Manchester, "Trump Slams GOP Senator: Corker 'Didn't Have the Guts to Run,' " The Hill, October 8, 2017, http://thehill.com/ homenews/administration/354438-trump-corker-didnt-have-the-guts-to -run; Peter Baker, "Trump Mocks Bob Corker's Height, Escalating Feud with a Key Republican," New York Times, October 10, 2017.

33. Martin and Landler, "Bob Corker Says Trump's Recklessness Threat- ens 'World War III' "; Natalie Neysa Alund, "Bob Corker's #AlertThe DaycareStaff Tweet about President Trump Sets Twitter on Fire," USA Today, October 24, 2017.

34. "Read Excerpts from Senator Bob Corker's Interview with the Times," New York Times, October 9, 2017.

35. Jacqueline Thomsen, "Scaramucci: Some Trump Officials 'Think It Is Their Job to Save America from This President,'" *The Hill,* July 27, 2017, http://thehill.com/blogs/blog-briefing-room/news-other-administration/344077-scaramucci-some-trump-officials-think-its.

36. Dana Milbank, "The Trump Demogorgon Devours Paul Ryan," *Washington Post,* October 17, 2016; Don Gonyea, "Republicans Worry Trump Is Falling into the Arms of 'Chuck and Nancy,'" NPR, September 7, 2017, http://www.npr.org/2017/09/07/549184337/republicans-worry-trump-is-falling-into-the-arms-of-chuck-and-nancy.

37. Rebecca Savransky, "Trump: Can You Believe McConnell Couldn't Repeal, Replace Obamacare?," *The Hill,* October 10, 2017, http://thehill.com/homenews/administration/345999-trump-can-you-believe-mcconnell-couldnt-repeal-replace-obamacare.

38. Ryan Nobles, "McConnell Criticizes Trump's 'Excessive Expectations,'" CNNPolitics, August 8, 2017, http://www.cnn.com/2017/08/08/politics/mitch-mcconnell-excessive-expectations/index.html; Alan Fram, "'Why Not Done?': Trump Hits McConnell for Senate Crash of Obama Health Repeal," *Chicago Tribune,* August 9, 2017.

39. Rebecca Savransky, "Trump: GOP 'Wasting Time" if They Don't Get Rid of Filibuster," *The Hill,* August 23, 2017, http://thehill.com/homenews/administration/347620-trump-gop-wasting-time-if-they-dont-get-rid-of-filibuster.

40. Nolan D. McCaskill, "Trump on His Feuds with GOP Senators: 'Sometimes It Helps, to Be Honest with You,'" Politico, October 20, 2017, http://www.politico.com/story/2017/10/20/trump-feuds-senators-response-243993.

41. Sheryl Gay Stolberg, "Jeff Flake, a Fierce Trump Critic, Will Not Seek Re-Election for Senate," *New York Times,* October 24, 2017.

42. Mark Landler, "Schumer Says He Rebuffed Another Offer from Trump on Health Care," *New York Times,* October 7, 2017.

43. Lily Mahalik, "24 Hours in, Trump's Mixed Signals on Alexander-Murray," Politico, October 18, 2017, http://www.politico.com/interactives/2017/obamacare-trump-alexander-murray-mixed-signals/.

44. Paul Kane, "Paul Ryan Begins a Make-or-Break Push for Tax Legislation—and His Future," *Washington Post,* October 28, 2017.

45. Frances Lee, "This Is How Trump Turned the Politics of the Debt Ceiling Upside Down," *Washington Post,* September 10, 2017; Frances E. Lee, *Insecure Majorities: Congress and the Perpetual Campaign* (Chicago: University of Chicago Press, 2016).

46. Rachel Bade and Kyle Cheney, "House Republican Lash Mnuchin,

Mulvaney behind Closed Doors," Politico, September 8, 2017, http://
www.politico.com/story/2017/09/08/house-republicans-ciriticize-steven
-mnuchin-mick-mulvaney-242490.

47. Donald J. Trump, Twitter, December 29, 2014, https://twitter.com/
realdonaldtrump/status/549590421190770688?lang=en; and Josh Dawsey,
Sean Sullivan, and Ed O'Keefe, "Trump Tells Confidants That a Government Shutdown Might Be Good for Him," *Washington Post*, November 30,
2017.

48. John Wagner and Tory Newmyer, "Trump Joins House GOP Call to
Rally Support for Senate Budget Bill," *Washington Post*, October 22, 2017.

49. Julie Hirschfeld Davis and Binyamin Appelbaum, "Trump in Missouri Lays Groundwork for Tax Overhaul but Offers No Details," *New York
Times*, August 30, 2017.

50. Lane, "Inside Trump's Head."

51. Henry Fountain and Lisa Friedman, "G.O.P. Seizes Chance to Open
Drilling in Arctic Wildlife Refuge," *New York Times*, October 20, 2017.

52. Eileen Sullivan and Jim Tankersley, "Trump Promises 'No Change to
Your 401(k)' as Congress Considers a Contribution Cap," *New York Times*,
October 23, 2017.

53. The rule took its name from its sponsor, former Senate Democratic
leader Robert Byrd.

54. Max Greenwood, "Trump Pushed for Tax Plan to Be Called 'Cut
Cut Cut Act'": Report," *The Hill*, November 1, 2017, http://thehill.com/
homenews/house/358230-trump-gop-leaders-disagree-on-what-to-name
-tax-bill-report; Jim Tankersley and Alan Rappeport, "Republicans Release
Tax Plan, Cutting Corporate and Middle-Class Taxes," *New York Times*,
November 2, 2017; Damian Paletta, "Trump Throws Curveball in Tax
Talks, Says Bill Should Include Obamacare Changes," *Washington Post*,
November 1, 2017.

55. Alan Rappeport, "Trump Again Wades into Tax Debate, Suggesting
Repeal of Obamacare Mandate," *New York Times*, November 13, 2017.

56. Thomas Kaplan and Jim Tankersley, "Senate Plans to End Obamacare Mandate in Revised Tax Proposal," *New York Times*, November 14,
2017; Mike DeBois and Damian Paletta, "Senate GOP Changes Tax Bill to
Add Obamacare Mandate Repeal, Make Individual Income Cuts Expire,"
Washington Post, November 14, 2017.

57. Heather Long, "Senate GOP Tax Bill Hurts the Poor More Than
Originally Thought, CBO Finds," *Washington Post*, November 26, 2017.

58. Thomas Kaplan, "After House Vote on Taxes, Spotlight Shifts to
Undecided Senators," *New York Times*, November 20, 2017.

59. Rebecca Savransky and Jordan Fabian, "Trump: US 'Needs a Good Shutdown,'" *The Hill*, May 2, 2017, http://thehill.com/homenews/administration/331512-trump-us-needs-a-good-shutdown.

60. Maggie Haberman and Yamiche Alcindor, "Pelosi and Schumer Say They Have Deal with Trump to Replace DACA," *New York Times*, September 13, 2017.

61. John Binder, "Report: Trump Caves on DACA, Wants 'Quick' Amnesty for 800K Illegal Aliens," Breitbart, September 13, 2017, http://www.breitbart.com/big-government/2017/09/13/report-trump-caves-on-daca-wants-quick-amnesty-for-800k-illegal-aliens/.

62. Jordan Fabian, "Trump: We're Not Looking at Amnesty," *The Hill*, September 14, 2017, http://thehill.com/homenews/administration/350644-white-house-there-will-be-no-amnesty-under-trump.

63. Elana Schor and Heather Caygle, "Pelosi, Schumer Face Ire from the Left over Dreamer Talks," Politico, September 14, 2017, http://www.politico.com/story/2017/09/14/pelosi-schumer-democrats-backlash-trump-deal-daca-242741.

64. Michael D. Shear, "White House Makes Hard-Line Demands for any 'Dreamers' Deal," *New York Times*, October 8, 2017; David Nakamura, "Trump Administration Releases Hard-Line Immigration Principles, Threatening Deal on 'Dreamers,'" *Washington Post*, October 8, 2017.

65. Derek Hawkins, Samantha Schmidt, and J. Freedom du Lac, "'A Chuck Schumer Beauty': Trump Calls for End to Diversity Visa Program," *Washington Post*, November 1, 2017.

66. Tory Newmayer and Damian Paletta, "Trump Backs Off Vow That Private Sector Should Help Pay for Infrastructure Package," *Washington Post*, September 26, 2017.

7. COMMUNICATIONS

1. Steven E. Schier and Todd E. Eberly, *The Trump Presidency: Outsider in the Oval Office* (Lanham, MD: Rowman and Littlefield, 2017), 11.

2. Thomas E. Patterson, "Pre-Primary News Coverage of the 2016 Presidential Race: Trump's Rise, Sanders's Emergence, Clinton's Struggles," Shorenstein Center on Media, Politics and Public Policy, Harvard University, June 13, 2016.

3. E. J. Dionne, Norman J, Ornstein, and Thomas E. Mann, *One Nation after Trump: A Guide for the Perplexed, the Disillusioned, the Desperate, and the Not-Yet-Deported* (New York: St. Martin's, 2017), 40.

4. Michael D'Antonio, "Donald Trump's Long, Strange History of Using Fake Names," *Fortune,* May 18, 2016.

5. Bruce Miroff, "The Presidential Spectacle," in *The Presidency and the Political System,* ed. Michael Nelson, 11th ed. (Washington, DC: CQ Press, forthcoming 2018).

6. Institute for Politics, *Campaign for President: The Managers Look at 2016* (Lanham, MD: Rowman and Littlefield, 2017), 44.

7. "15 of Donald Trump's Most Popular Tweets," Twitter, November 7, 2016, https://twitter.com/i/moments/795695925566050304.

8. Michael Kruse, "I Found Trump's Diary—Hiding in Plain Sight," *Politico Magazine,* June 25, 2017, http://www.politico.com/magazine/story/2017/06/25/i-found-trumps-diaryhiding-in-plain-sight-215303.

9. Nick Gass, "Trump Says He Won't Tweet as President," Politico, April 25, 2016, http://www.politico.com/blogs/2016-gop-primary-live-updates-and-results/2016/04/trump-no-tweeting-president-222408.

10. The phrase is Richard E. Neustadt, *Presidential Power and the Modern Presidents: Presidential Leadership from Roosevelt to Reagan* (New York: Free Press, 1990).

11. Jennifer Calfas, "Trump to Continue Using @realDonaldTrump Account as President," *The Hill,* January 15, 2017, http://thehill.com/blogs/blog-briefing-room/news/314440-trump-to-use-personal-twitter-not-potus-account-as-president.

12. Kruse, "I Found Trump's Diary."

13. Emily Badger and Kevin Quealy, "Trump Seems Much Better at Branding Opponents Than Marketing Policies," *New York Times,* July 18, 2017.

14. Timothy Egan, "The Trump Fog Machine," *New York Times,* September 29, 2017.

15. Rebecca Morin, "Trump: My Social Media Use Is 'Modern Day Presidential,'" Politico, July 1, 2017, http://www.politico.com/story/2017/07/01/trump-tweets-modern-day-presidential-240170.

16. Nolan D. McCaskill, "Trump Credits Social Media for His Election," Politico, October 20, 2017, http://www.politico.com/story/2017/10/20/trump-social-media-election-244009.

17. Marjorie Randon Hershey, "The Presidency and the Media: The Case of Donald Trump," in *The Presidency and the Political System,* ed. Nelson; Maggie Haberman, Glenn Thrush, and Peter Baker, "Inside Trump's Hour-by-Hour Battle for Self-Preservation," *New York Times,* December 9, 2017.

18. John Wagner, "'Bing, Bing, Bing'": Trump Reveals His Thinking behind Firing off All Those Tweets," *Washington Post,* October 20, 2017.

19. Glenn Thrush and Maggie Haberman, "Trump Mocks Mika Brzezinski; Says She Was 'Bleeding Badly from a Facelift,'" *New York Times,* June 29, 2017.

20. Emily Cochrane, "Only 'Probably' Time's Person of the Year? No Thanks, Trump Tweets," *New York Times,* November 24, 2017.

21. Benjamin Hoffman, "Trump Blasts LaVar Ball: 'I Should Have Left Them in Jail!" *New York Times,* November 19, 2017; Louis Nelson, "Trump: 'Ungrateful Fool' LaVar Ball Is a Poor Man's Version of Don King," Politico, November 22, 2017: https://www.politico.com/story/2017/11/22/trump-lavar-ball-feud-258069?lo=ap_a1.

22. Michael D. Shear, "Trump Defends Roy Moore, Citing Candidate's Denial of Allegations," *New York Times,* November 21, 2017.

23. Jonathan Martin, Maggie Haberman, and Alexander Burns, "Why Trump Stands by Roy Moore, Even as It Fractures His Party," *New York Times,* November 25, 2017; "Donald Trump Says Sexual Misconduct Accusers Are 'Horrible, Horrible Liars,'" *Guardian,* October 13, 2016.

24. Jeffrey K. Tulis, "The Two Constitutional Presidencies," in *The Presidency and the Political System,* ed. Nelson.

25. Julie Hirschfeld Davis, "Trump Tries to Shift Focus as First Charges Loom in Russia Case," *New York Times,* October 29, 2017. As it turned out, the twelve-count indictment of former Trump campaign chairman Paul Manafort and business partner Rick Gates announced on October 30 did not involve Trump's presidential campaign, but a guilty plea by George Papadopoulos, revealed the same day, did.

26. Max Greenwood, "GOP Senators: Trump Attack on MSNBC Hosts 'Beneath the Dignity' of His Office," *The Hill,* June 29, 2017, http://thehill.com/homenews/senate/340037-gop-senators-trump-attack-on-morning-joe-hosts-beneath-the-dignity-of-his.

27. Alana Abramson, "A Judge Just Cited a Trump Tweet When Ruling against Him. Again," *Time,* June 12, 2017.

28. Associated Press, "Military Judge in Army Sgt. Bowe Bergdahl Desertion Case Worries about Trump Impact," *Los Angeles Times,* October 23, 2017.

29. Peter Baker, "'Very Frustrated' Trump Becomes Top Critic of Law Enforcement," *New York Times,* November 3, 2017.

30. Stephen Dinan, "Courts Use Trump's Pontificating to Rule Against His Policies," *Washington Times,* November 21, 2017.

31. Steven Overly, "Trump Tweets on CNN Could Muddy AT&T-Time Warner Lawsuit," Politico, November 20, 2017: https://www.politico.com/story/2017/11/20/trump-cnn-tweets-time-warner-lawsuit-182454.

32. Jason Zengerle, "Rex Tillerson and the Unraveling of the State Department," *New York Times,* October 17, 2017.

33. Mark Moore, "Trump Goes after 'Failing' New York Times Again," *New York Post,* June 28, 2017; Liz Stark, "Ben Sasse Blasts Trump's Twitter Behavior: 'This Isn't Normal,'" CNNPolitics, June 29, 2017, http://www.cnn.com/2017/06/29/politics/sasse-trump-twitter/index.html; Nada Bakos. "This Is What Foreign Spies See When They Read President Trump's Tweets," *Washington Post,* June 23, 2017.

34. Michael Nelson, "Speeches, Speechwriters, and the American Presidency," in *The President's Words: Speeches and Speechwriting in the Modern White House,* ed. Nelson and Russell L. Riley (Lawrence: University Press of Kansas, 2010), 1–26.

35. David A. Farethold, "Boy Scouts Leader Apologizes for Trump Speech's 'Political Rhetoric,'" *Washington Post,* July 27, 2017.

36. John Wagner, "Trump Blasts NFL for Not Adopting a Requirement That Players Stand during Anthem," *Washington Post,* October 18, 2017.

37. Des Bieler, "Cowboys' Jerry Jones: 'No Question' NFL Is 'Suffering Negative Effects from These Protests,'" *Washington Post,* October 23, 2017.

38. Rich Lowry, "How the NFL Lost to Trump," Politico, October 11, 2017, http://www.politico.com/magazine/story/2017/10/11/trump-nfl-anthem-goodell-flag-215701.

39. David Frum, "Why Cede the Flag to Trump?" *Atlantic,* September 24, 2017, https://www.theatlantic.com/politics/archive/2017/09/why-cede-the-flag-to-trump/540930/.

40. Jim Rutenberg, "Trump Takes Aim at the Press, with a Flamethrower," *New York Times,* August 23, 2017.

41. John Wagner, "Trump Campaign Ad Says His 'Enemies' Are Trying to Undermine His Progress," *Washington Post,* August 13, 2017.

42. Daniel W. Drezner, "Why Is Donald Trump So Bad at the Bully Pulpit?" *Washington Post,* August 14, 2017.

43. Nolan D. McCaskill, "Trump: 'I Hope' Hillary Runs in 2020," Politico, October 16, 2017, http://www.politico.com/story/2017/10/16/trump-hillary-clinton-2020-presidential-run-243807.

44. Amanda Erickson, "Trump Called the News Media 'An Enemy of the American People.' Here's a History of the Term," *Washington Post,* February 18, 2017.

45. Paul Farhi, "On Cable, 'All Trump, All the Time' Isn't Going Away—the Networks Are Addicted," *Washington Post*, August 10, 2017.

46. Eric Bradner, "Conway: Trump White House Offered 'Alternative Facts' on Crowd Size," CNNPolitics, January 23, 2017, http://www.cnn.com/2017/01/22/politics/kellyanne-conway-alternative-facts/index.html.

47. Mark Hensch, "Trump: 'I Love WikiLeaks,'" *The Hill*, October 10, 2017, http://thehill.com/blogs/ballot-box/presidential-races/300327-trump-i-love-wikileaks.

48. Matt Zapotosky and Devlin Barrett, "Attorney General Says Justice Dept. Has Tripled the Number of Leak Probes," *Washington Post*, August 4, 2017.

49. Glenn Thrush and Maggie Haberman, "Trump Is Criticized for Not Calling out White Supremacists," *New York Times*, August 12, 2017.

50. Michael D. Shear and Maggie Haberman, "Trump Defends Initial Remarks on Charlottesville; Again Blames 'Both Sides,'" *New York Times*, August 15, 2017; "Full Text: Trump's Comments on White Supremacists, 'Alt-Left,' in Charlottesville," *Politico*, August 15, 2017, https://www.politico.com/story/2017/08/15/full-text-trump-comments-white-supremacists-alt-left-transcript-241662.

51. Mark Landler, "Different Day, Different Audience, and a Completely Different Trump," *New York Times*, August 23, 2017.

52. Amanda Wills and Alysha Love," All the President's Tweets," CNNPolitics, September 25, 2017 (updated daily), http://www.cnn.com/interactive/2017/politics/trump-tweets/.

53. Mark Landler, "After a Disciplined Week in Asia, Trump Unloads on Critics," *New York Times*, November 12, 2017.

8. FOREIGN POLICY

1. "Donald Trump Explains All," *Time*, August 20, 2015.

2. Julie Hirschfeld Davis, "Trump Says Putin 'Means It' about Not Meddling," *New York Times*, November 11, 2017.

3. Julia Manchester, "Trump: I Want to Focus on North Korea, Not 'Fixing Somebody's Back,'" *The Hill*, October 7, 2017, http://thehill.com/homenews/administration/354419-trump-on-health-care-block-grants-i-would-rather-focus-on-iran-north

4. Nolan D. McCaskill and Louis Nelson, "President Trump's First 100 Days: By the Numbers," Politico, April 29, 2017, http://www.politico.com/story/2017/04/29/donald-trump-first-100-days-by-the-numbers-237701.

5. Jack Moore, "Trump Delays U.S. Embassy Move to Jerusalem in Victory for Arab Leaders," *Newsweek,* June 1, 2017.

6. Greg Miller, Julie Vitkovskaya, and Reuben Fischer-Baum, "'This Deal Will Make Me Look Terrible': Full Transcripts of Trump's Calls with Mexico and Australia," *Washington Post,* August 3, 2017.

7. Alan Rappeport, "Trump Talks Tough on Trade, but His Team Is Treading Lightly," *New York Times,* June 1, 2017; Meera Jagannathan, "Here Are All the Terrible Things President Trump Has Said about NAFTA—Before Deciding to Stick with It," *New York Daily News,* April 27, 2017; "Trump's Middle East Reset," *Week,* June 2, 2017; Mark Landler and Michael R. Gordon, "As U.S. Adds Troops in Afghanistan, Trump's Strategy Remains Undefined," *New York Times,* June 18, 2017; Michael D. Sheer, Julie Hirschfeld Davis, and Maggie Haberman, "Trump, in Interview, Moderates Views but Defies Conventions," *New York Times,* November 22, 2016.

8. Mark Landler, "From 'America First' to a More Conventional View of U.S. Diplomacy," *New York Times,* March 1, 2017; Thomas Gibbons-Neff, Eric Schmitt, and Adam Goldman, "A Newly Assertive C.I.A. Expands Its Taliban Hunt in Afghanistan," *New York Times,* October 22, 2017.

9. Peter Baker, "The Emerging Trump Doctrine: Don't Follow Doctrine," *New York Times,* April 8, 2017.

10. Susan Glasser, "The 27 Words Trump Wouldn't Say," *Politico Magazine,* June 6, 2017, http://www.politico.com/magazine/story/2017/06/06/trump-nato-speech-27-words-commitment-215231.

11. Glenn Thrush and Julie Hirschfeld Davis, "Trump, in Poland, Asks If West Has the 'Will to Survive,'" *New York Times,* July 6, 2017.

12. Penny Starr, "Trump: I'm a Nationalist and a Globalist," Breitbart, April 28, 2017, http://www.breitbart.com/big-government/2017/04/28/trump-im-a-nationalist-and-a-globalist/.

13. Jason Zengerle, "Rex Tillerson and the Unraveling of the State Department," *New York Times Magazine,* October 17, 2017.

14. Gardiner Harris, "Diplomats Sound the Alarm as They Are Pushed Out in Droves," *New York Times,* November 24, 2017.

15. James P. Pfiffner, "Organizing the Trump Presidency," paper prepared for presentation at the annual meeting of the American Political Science Association, San Francisco, August 31–September 3, 2017.

16. Donovan Slack, "Trump: Rex Tillerson Is Wasting His Time Negotiating with 'Little Rocket Man,'" *USA Today,* October 1, 2017.

17. Cristiano Lima, "Corker Unloads on Trump for Trying to 'Castrate'

Tillerson," Politico, October 13, 2017, http://www.politico.com/story/2017/10/13/bob-corker-rex-tillerson-castrate-trump-243771.

18. Carol E. Lee, Kristen Welker, Stephanie Ruhle, and Dafna Linzer, "Tillerson's Fury at Trump Required an Intervention from Pence," NBC News, October 4, 2017, https://www.nbcnews.com/politics/white-house/tillerson-s-fury-trump-required-intervention-pence-n806451; "Stephanie Rule: Tillerson Didn't Call Tillerson a Moron, He Called Him a F*cking Moron," https://www.youtube.com/watch?v=U4BCsB4YrbU; Randall Lane, "Inside Trump's Head: An Exclusive Interview with the President, and the Single Theory That Explains Everything," Forbes, November 14, 2017.

19. Michael Crowley, "Trump's Pursuit of Friendship with Putin Fulfills His Campaign Promise," Politico, July 7, 2017, http://www.politico.com/story/2017/07/07/trump-pursues-friendship-with-putin-240314.

20. Andrew Kaczynski, Chris Massie, and Nathan McDermott, "80 Times Trump Talked about Putin," CNN, n.d., http://www.cnn.com/interactive/2017/03/politics/trump-putin-russia-timeline/.

21. Aaron Blake, "Trump Contradicts His Son's Emails, Suggests Russia Preferred Hillary Clinton," Washington Post, July 12, 2017.

22. James Hohman, "Six Ways Trump's Putin Comments on Asia Trip Erode U.S. Credibility," Washington Post, November 13, 2017.

23. Susan B. Glasser, "Trump's Russian Schizophrenia," Politico, November 27, 2017: https://www.politico.com/magazine/story/2017/11/27/trumps-russian-schizophrenia-215869.

24. Michael Kranish and Marc Fisher, Trump Revealed: An American Journey of Ambition, Ego, Money, and Power (New York: Scribner, 2016), 276.

25. Greg Jaffe and Philip Rucker, "National Security Adviser Attempts to Reconcile Trump's Competing Impulses on Afghanistan," Washington Post, August 4, 2017.

26. Lee et al., "Tillerson's Fury at Trump Required an Intervention from Pence"; Matthew Lee and Jonathan Lemire, "How Trump's Advisers Schooled Him on Globalism," Washington Post, September 18, 2017.

27. Daniella Diaz, "A History of Trump's Thoughts on Afghanistan," CNN Politics, August 21, 2017, http://www.cnn.com/2017/08/21/politics/history-president-trump-remarks-afghanistan-tweets/index.html.

28. "Remarks by President Trump on the Strategy in Afghanistan and South Asia," White House, August 21, 2017, https://www.whitehouse.gov/the-press-office/2017/08/21/remarks-president-trump-strategy-afghanistan-and-south-asia.

29. Aaron Blake, "Rex Tillerson Totally Undercut Trump's 'We Will Win' Rhetoric on Afghanistan," *Washington Post,* August 22, 2017.

30. Josh Rogin, "In Private Remarks, Trump Opines on North Korea, Afghanistan, and Catapults," *Washington Post,* September 28, 2017.

31. Natalie Jennings, "Trump's Muscular but Vague Afghanistan Speech, Annotated," *Washington Post,* August 21, 2017.

32. E. J. Dionne Jr., Norman J. Ornstein, and Thomas E. Mann, *One Nation after Trump: A Guide for the Disillusioned, the Desperate, and the Not-Yet-Deported* (New York; St. Martin's, 2017), 130.

33. David Nakamura, "Trump Puts North Korea Back on State Sponsors of Terrorism List to Escalate Pressure over Nuclear Weapons," *Washington Post,* November 20, 2017.

34. Steve Coll, "The Madman Theory of North Korea," *New Yorker,* October 2, 2017.

35. See, for example, William J. Perry, "North Korea Called Me a 'War Maniac.' I Ignored Them, and Trump Should Too," Politico, October 3, 2017, http://www.politico.com/magazine/story/2017/10/03/north-korea-war-maniac-donald-trump-215672.

36. Peter Baker and Choe Sang-Hun, "Trump Threatens 'Fire and Fury' Against North Korea if It Endangers U.S.," *New York Times,* August 8, 2017.

37. Jordan Fabian and Max Greenwood, "Trump: Maybe the Threat on North Korea Wasn't 'Tough Enough,'" *Hill,* August 10, 2017, http://thehill.com/homenews/administration/346087-trump-maybe-threat-on-north-korea-wasnt-tough-enough.

38. Brent D. Griffiths, "Trump Tweets about North Korea's 'Rocket Man,' Dings Hillary Clinton Again," Politico, September 17, 2017, http://www.politico.com/story/2017/09/17/trump-tweets-about-north-koreas-rocket-man-242812; Edith M. Lederer, "North Korea Says Trump's Latest Tweet Is a 'Declaration of War,'" *Time,* September 25, 2017.

39. "Remarks by President Trump to the 72nd Session of the United Nations General Assembly," White House, September 19, 2017, https://www.whitehouse.gov/the-press-office/2017/09/19/remarks-president-trump-72nd-session-united-nations-general-assembly.

40. Austin Ramzy, "Kim Jong-un Called Trump a 'Dotard'": What Does That Even Mean?" *New York Times,* September 22, 2017.

41. Mark Landler, "After a Disciplined Week in Asia, Trump Unloads on Critics," *New York Times,* November 12, 2017.

42. James D. Fearon, "The Problem with the North Koreans Isn't That

We Can't Trust Them. It's That They Can't Trust Us," *Washington Post,*
August 16, 2017.

43. Jim Mattis and Rex Tillerson, "We're Holding Pyongyang to
Account," Fox News, August 13, 2017, http://nation.foxnews.com/2017/
08/13/mattis-and-tillerson-were-holding-pyongyang-account.

44. Jenna Johnson, "Trump on North Korea: 'Sorry, but Only One
Thing Will Work!'" *Washington Post,* October 7, 2017.

45. Evan Osnos, "The Risk of Nuclear War with North Korea," *New
Yorker,* September 8, 2017.

46. Felicity Vabulus, "Trump Is Pulling the U.S. out of UNESCO. The
Bigger Pattern Is the Problem," *Washington Post,* October 16, 2017.

47. Madeline Conway, "Trump Says He Can 'Live With' Either Two-
State or One-State Solution for Israel," Politico, February 15, 2017, http://
www.politico.com/story/2017/02/trump-two-state-one-state-solution
-israel-235054.

48. In 2017 the amount of land controlled by ISIS in Iraq and Syria
shrank from 23,300 square miles to 9,300 square miles, and its two main
urban centers, Mosul in Iraq and Raqqa in Syria, fell to a congeries of
allied forces that included the United States, the Syrian and Iraqi governments, Russia, and Syrian rebels. The Trump administration claimed
credit, in part because it gave American commanders on the ground more
autonomy, as did alumni of the Obama administration, who maintained
that Trump benefited from the strategy put in place by his predecessor. For
contrasting assessments of how much Trump contributed, see Linda Qiu,
"Can Trump Claim Credit for a Waning Islamic State?" *New York Times,*
October 17, 2017; and Jonathan S. Tobin, "Did Trump Beat ISIS?," *National
Review,* October 19, 2017.

49. Nicole Gaouetre, Dan Merica, and Ryan Browne, "Trump: Qatar
Must Stop Funding Terrorism," CNN, June 10, 2017, http://www.cnn
.com/2017/06/09/politics/trump-qatar-saudi-gulf-crisis/index.html.

50. Declan Walsh, "Trump's Bid to End Saudi-Qatar Stalemate Ends in
Recriminations," *New York Times,* September 9, 2017.

51. "I've seen in the Arab world, including the Palestinian world, the
high esteem they pay to a member of one's own family," said Jimmy Carter
(Maureen Dowd, "Jimmy Carter Lusts for a Trump Posting," *New York
Times,* October 21, 2017).

52. F. Brinley Bruton and Ali Arouzi, "Iran Nuclear Deal: Trump Drive
to Ax Pact May Alienate Allies," NBC News, September 16, 2017, https://
www.nbcnews.com/news/world/iran-nuclear-deal-trump-drive-ax-pact
-may-alienate-allies-n799446.

53. Trump's exceedingly unhappy decision to recertify in July is chronicled in Stephen F. Hayes and Michael Warren, "Getting to No: How the Trump Administration Decided to Decertify the Iran Nuclear Deal," *Weekly Standard,* October 16, 2017.

54. Josh Dawsey and Hadash Gold, "Full Transcript: Trump's *Wall Street Journal* Interview," Politico, August 1, 2017, http://www.politico.com/story/2017/08/01/trump-wall-street-journal-interview-full-transcript-241214.

55. "Remarks by President Trump to the 72nd Session of the United Nations General Assembly."

56. Eliana Johnson, "Trump Prepares to Wound Iran Deal—and Then Save It," Politico, October 3, 2017, http://www.politico.com/story/2017/10/03/trump-iran-nuclear-deal-243427.

57. Mark Landler and David E. Sanger, "Trump to Force Congress to Act on Iran Nuclear Deal," *New York Times,* October 5, 2017.

58. "Here's Donald Trump's Presidential Announcement Speech," *Time,* June 16, 2015.

59. Miller, Vitkovskaya, and Fischer-Baum, "This Deal Will Make Me Look Terrible."

60. Ana Swanson, "Trump's American First Trade Agenda Roiled by Internal Divisions," *New York Times,* October 20, 2017; "Trump Warns May Terminate NAFTA Treaty," *New York Daily News,* August 23, 2017.

61. "U.S. Hikes Tensions in NAFTA Talks with Call for 'Sunset Clause,'" *New York Times,* October 12, 2017.

62. "Trump Alarms Venezuela with Talk of a 'Military Option,'" *New York Times,* August 12, 2017.

63. Rebecca Savransky, "Colombian President to Pence: Military Intervention in Venezuela 'Shouldn't Even Be Considered,'" *The Hill,* August 14, 2017, http://thehill.com/homenews/administration/346433-colombian-president-to-pence-military-intervention-in-venezuela.

64. Rick Gladstone, "Trump Administration Defends Cuba Embargo at U.N., Reversing Obama," *New York Times,* November 1, 2017.

9. PROSPECTS FOR REMOVAL

1. Madeline Conway, "John Lewis: 'I Don't See This President-Elect as a Legitimate President,'" Politico, January 13, 2017, http://www.politico.com/story/2017/01/john-lewis-donald-trump-not-legitimate-president-233607.

2. Elise Viebeck, "Nearly 70 Democratic Lawmakers Now Skipping Trump's Inauguration," *Washington Post,* January 19, 2017.

3. The following paragraphs are based on Michael Nelson, "Presidential

Removal, in *The Presidency and the Political System,* ed. Nelson, 11th ed. (Washington, DC: CQ Press, forthcoming 2018).

4. Clinton Rossiter, *The American Presidency* (Baltimore, MD: Johns Hopkins University Press, 1987) 38, 194.

5. Benjamin Ginsberg and Martin Shefter, *Politics by Other Means: The Declining Importance of Elections in America* (New York: Basic, 1990).

6. Mark Hensch, "Trump Says 'Made Up' Russia Story Part of Decision to Fire Comey," *The Hill,* May 11, 2017, http://thehill.com/policy/national -security/fbi/333056-trump-made-up-russia-story-part-of-comey-firing.

7. Matt Apuzzo, Maggie Haberman, and Matthew Rosenberg, "Trump Told Russians That Firing 'Nut Job' Comey Eased Pressure from Investigation," *New York Times,* May 19, 2017.

8. Martin Finucane, "Comey Testimony Includes Good News, Bad News for Trump," *Boston Globe,* June 7, 2017.

9. Adam Entous, "Top Intelligence Official Told Associates Trump Asked Him If He Could Intervene with Comey on FBI Russia Probe," *Washington Post,* June 6, 2017; Adam Entous and Ellen Nakashima, "Trump Asked Intelligence Chiefs to Push Back against FBI Collusion Probe after Comey Revealed Its Existence," *Washington Post,* May 22, 2017.

10. Laurence H. Tribe, "Trump Must Be Impeached. Here's Why," *Washington Post,* May 13, 2017.

11. Burns, "Pledge to Impeach Trump, a Key Donor Demands of Democrats."

12. Bob Bauer, "A President's Words Matter: Deception of the Public and the Impeachable Offense," *Lawfare,* September 27, 2017, https:// www.lawfareblog.com/presidents-words-matter-deception-public-and -impeachable-offense; "A President's Words Matter, Part II: Impeachment Standards and the Case of the Demagogue," *Lawfare,* October 11, 2017, https://www.lawfareblog.com/presidents-words-matter-part-ii -impeachment-standards-and-case-demagogue.

13. Michael Collins and Daniel Connolly, "Rep. Steve Cohen Seeks to Impeach President Trump after Charlottesville," *Tennessean,* August 17, 2017.

14. "Articles of Impeachment against Donald John Trump, President of the United States of America," *Washington Post,* October 11, 2017.

15. Kyle Cheney and Heather Caygle, "House Democrat Pulls Trump Impeachment Measure," Politico, October 11, 2017, http://www.politico .com/story/2017/10/11/trump-impeachment-house-democrats-243674.

16. Michael Collins, "Rep. Cohen, Other Democrats File Articles of Impeachment against President Trump," *Tennessean,* November 15, 2017.

17. Burns, "Pledge to Impeach Trump, a Key Donor Demands of Democrats."

18. Amy B Wang, "Have Dirt That Could Impeach Trump? Larry Flynt Will Pay You $10 Million," *Washington Post*, October 14, 2017.

19. Anna Giaritelli, "McCain: Trump Scandals Have Reached 'Watergate Size and Scale,'" *Washington Examiner*, June 15, 2017; Cristina Marcos, "First Republicans Talk Possibility of Impeachment for Trump," *The Hill*, May 17, 2017, http://thehill.com/homenews/house/333803-first -republicans-talk-impeachment-for-trump.

20. Nicolas Fandos, "Hopes Dim for Congressional Russia Inquiries as Parties Clash," *New York Times*, October 22, 2017.

21. Peter Baker, Michael S. Schmidt, and Maggie Haberman, "Citing Recusal, Trump Says He Wouldn't Have Hired Sessions," *New York Times*, July 19, 2017.

22. Sharon La Freniere, Matt Apuzzo, and Aaron Goldman, "With a Picked Lock and a Threatened Indictment, Mueller's Inquiry Sets a Tone," *New York Times*, September 18, 2017; Michael S. Schmidt, "Mueller Seeks White House Documents Related to Trump's Actions as President," *New York Times*, September 20, 2017.

23. Dan Balz, "A Revelation Unlike Any Other in the Russia Investigation," *Washington Post*, July 11, 2017.

24. Peter Baker, "Trump Was Involved in Drafting Son's Statement, Aides Confirm," *New York Times*, August 1, 2017.

25. Matt Apuzzo and Michael S. Schmidt, "Trump Campaign Adviser Met with Russian to Discuss 'Dirt' on Clinton," *New York Times*, October 30, 2017.

26. Brendan Nyhan, "Why Trump's Base of Support May Be Smaller Than It Seems," *New York Times*, July 19, 2017; Gallup News, "Party Affiliation," Gallup Poll: news.gallup.com.

27. Rebecca Savransky, "Pence Responds to Trump Jr., Emails: He's 'Not Focused on Stories about the Campaign,'" *The Hill*, July 11, 2017, http://thehill.com/homenews/administration/341473-pence-not -focused-on-stories-about-the-campaign.

28. Jessica Estepa, "Coulter: 'At This Point, Who DOESN'T Want Trump Impeached?,'" *USA Today*, September 14, 2017.

29. Megan Trimble, "Trump Warns GOP Senator over Obamacare Repeal," U.S. News and World Report, July 19, 2017, https://www.usnews .com/news/national-news/articles/2017-07-19/donald-trump-warns-dean -heller-over-health-care-vote; Erica Martinson, "Trump Administration

Threatens Retribution against Alaska over Murkowski Health Votes," *Alaska Dispatch News,* July 26, 2017. For Trump's comments on Corker, see chapter 6.

30. "2018 Generic Congressional Vote," RealClearPolitics, November 8, 2017, https://www.realclearpolitics.com/epolls/other/2018_generic _congressional_vote-6185.html. The standard question is, "If the election for the U.S. House of Representatives were being held today, would you vote for the Democratic candidate or the Republican candidate in your congressional district?"

31. Elena Schneider, "Democrats' Early Money Haul Stuns GOP," Politico, October 23, 2017: https://www.politico.com/story/2017/10/23/2018 -fundraising-democrats-house-races-244044.

32. Aaron Blake, "5 Reasons the GOP Won't Dump Trump," *Washington Post,* October 14, 2017.

33. Dhrumil Mehta, "All the Cable News Networks Are Covering the 'Russia Story'—Just Not the Same One," FiveThirtyEight, November 6, 2017, https://fivethirtyeight.com/features/all-the-cable-news-networks -are-covering-the-russia-story-just-not-the-same-one/. Although Clinton played no role in this decision, suspicions were raised by news that donors related to the company executives had contributed millions of dollars to the Clinton Foundation. An FBI investigation in 2015–16 found no evidence of wrongdoing (Eileen Sullivan, "What Is the Uranium One Deal and Why Does the Trump Administration Care So Much?" *New York Times,* November 14, 2017; Peter Baker, " 'Lock Her Up' Becomes More Than a Slogan," *New York Times,* November 14, 2017).

34. By most accounts, the disability provisions of the Twenty-Fifth Amendment failed their first real test. In 1981 Reagan was seriously wounded by an assassin's bullet. While he was at the hospital undergoing major surgery, cabinet and staff members gathered at the White House in the absence of Vice President George Bush, who was returning from a trip to Houston. When White House counsel Fred Fielding mentioned that there was a constitutional way to "pass the baton temporarily" to the vice president, he was ignored, and when fellow staff member Richard Darman noticed that Fielding had prepared a document for the transfer of power, he took it away and locked it in a safe. Even as Soviet forces assembled at the Polish border, the main concern of those around the president was to maintain the pretense that he was strong and able (see Nelson, "Presidential Removal").

35. See, for example, George F. Will, "Trump Has a Dangerous Disability," *Washington Post,* May 3, 2017; and Ross Douthat, "The 25th

Amendment Solution for Removing Trump," *New York Times,* May 16, 2017.

36. Adrienne Lafrance, "Evaluating Trump's Psyche in Public," *Atlantic,* July 25, 2017.

37. John Gartner, "Mental Health Professionals Declare Trump Is Mentally Ill and Must Be Removed," Change.org, n.d., https://www.change .org/p/trump-is-mentally-ill-and-must-be-removed.

38. Philip Bump, "Senators on Hot Mic: Trump Is 'Crazy,' 'I'm Worried,'" *Washington Post,* July 25, 2017.

39. Austin Wright, "Corker: Trump Hasn't Shown Stability or Competence," Politico, August 17, 2017, http://www.politico.com/story/2017/ 08/17/trump-bob-corker-charlottesville-response-241751

40. See chapter 6, notes 24 and 25.

41. Sharon Begley, "Democrats in Congress Explore Creating an Expert Panel on Trump's Mental Health," *Scientific American,* August 16, 2017.

42. Bandy Lee, *The Dangerous Case of Donald Trump: 27 Psychiatrists and Mental Health Experts Assess a President* (New York: Thomas Dunne, 2017).

43. Eric Posner, "Trump Could Be Removed for Political Incompetence —Using the 25th Amendment," *Washington Post,* September 12, 2017.

44. Sophie Tatum, "Vanity Fair: Bannon Believes Trump Only Has 30% Chance of Completing Full Term," CNNPolitics, October 11, 2017, http:// www.cnn.com/2017/10/11/politics/donald-trump-steve-bannon-vanity -fair/.

45. Scott Lucas, "A College Lecturer Tweeted, 'Trump Must Hang.' He Doesn't Regret It," Politico, September 24, 2017, http://www.politico.com/ magazine/story/2017/09/24/cal-state-lecturer-tweets-trump-must-hang -215620.

46. Herman Wong and Lindsey Bever, "'I Hope Trump Is Assassinated': A Missouri Lawmaker Faces Mounting Calls to Resign after Facebook Comment," *Washington Post,* August 18, 2017.

47. David Von Drehle, "Trump Doesn't Seem to Like Being President. So Why Not Quit?" *Washington Post,* August 18, 2017.

48. Darren Samuelsohn, "Gore's Advice to Trump: 'Resign,'" Politico, August 17, 2017, http://www.politico.com/story/2017/08/17/gores-advice -for-trump-resign-241760; Saba Hamedy, "'Art of the Deal' Ghostwriter Predicts Trump Will Resign," CNNPolitics, August 18, 2017, http://www .cnn.com/2017/08/17/politics/art-of-the-deal-author-trump-resignation -prediction/index.html.

49. Glenn Blain, "House Dems Want to Formally 'Censure and

Condemn' Trump for Charlottesville Response," *New York Daily News,*
August 16, 2017.

CONCLUSION

1. Rachael Revesz, "Donald Trump Falsely Claims He Had "Biggest
Electoral College Win since Ronald Reagan,'" *Independent,* February 16,
2017; "Donald Trump Says Vladimir Putin Wanted Hillary Clinton to Win
Presidency," *Guardian,* July 13, 2017.

2. Jana Heigl, "A Timeline of Donald Trump's False Wiretapping
Charge," PolitiFact, March 21, 2017, http://www.politifact.com/truth-o
-meter/article/2017/mar/21/timeline-donald-trumps-false-wiretapping
-charge/; Jasmine C. Lee and Kevin Quealy, "The 382 People, Places, and
Things Donald Trump Has Insulted on Twitter: A Complete List," *New
York Times,* October 20, 2017.

3. Marc Fisher, "Donald Trump Doesn't Read Much: Being President
Probably Wouldn't Change That," *Washington Post,* July 17, 2016; Shane
Goldmacher, "Trump Refuses to Bend to the Office of President," Politico,
January 11, 2017, http://www.politico.com/story/2017/01/trump-presser
-highlights-not-backing-down-233488; Shane Goldmacher, "Trump Savors
Health Care Win: 'Hey, I'm President,'" Politico, May 4, 2017, http://www
.politico.com/story/2017/05/04/trump-health-care-win-238005.

4. Rachel Bade, "Ryan Defends Trump on Comey: 'The President's New at This,'" Politico, June 8, 2017, http://www.politico.com/
story/2017/06/08/ryan-defends-trump-on-comey-the-presidents-new
-at-this-239298; Jeff Shesol, "Can President Trump Learn on the Job?"
New Yorker, April 22, 2017; Burgess Everett and Rachel Bade, "Republicans
Lament an Agenda in 'Quicksand,'" Politico, July 20, 2017, http://www
.politico.com/story/2017/07/20/gop-lawmakers-despondent-as-recess
-approaches-240731.

5. Jane Mayer, "Donald Trump's Ghostwriter Tells All," *New Yorker,* July
25, 2017.

6. Joshua Green, *Devil's Bargain: Steve Bannon, Donald Trump, and the
Storming of the Presidency* (New York: Penguin, 2017), 239.

7. Michael Nelson, "Redivided Government and the Politics of the Bud-
getary Process in the Clinton Years: An Oral History Perspective," *Congress
and the Presidency* 43 (September–December 2016): 243–63.

8. Trump's approach to deal-making in business did not always work.
When he tried to renegotiate the terms for Frank Sinatra's concerts at

his new Trump Taj Mahal Hotel and Casino in Atlantic City, Sinatra instructed his manager, "Tell him to go f— himself or give me his number and I'll do it" (Eliot Weisman and Jennifer Valoppi, *The Way We Were: My Life with Frank Sinatra* [New York: Hachette, 2017], 175).

9. Michael Grunwald, "Trump's First 100 Days: What Mattered and What Didn't," *Politico Magazine,* April 26, 2017, http://www.politico .com/magazine/story/2017/04/26/trump-first-100-days-president-rating -accomplishments-215071.

10. Gabriel Debenedetti, "2020 Race Lures Sprawling Democratic Field," Politico, February 24, 2017, http://www.politico.com/story/2017/ 02/democrats-2020-presidential-field-235335; Shawn M. Carter, "More Signs Point to Mark Zuckerberg Possibly Running for President in 2020," CNBC, August 15, 2017, https://www.cnbc.com/2017/08/15/mark -zuckerberg-could-be-running-for-president-in-2020.html; Maureen Dowd, "Mark Cuban's Not Done Trolling Donald Trump," *New York Times,* October 27, 2017.

11. Erwin C. Hargrove and Michael Nelson, *Presidents, Politics, and Policy* (Baltimore.: Johns Hopkins University Press, 1984), chap. 4.

12. Michael Nelson, "Who Vies for President?" in *Presidential Selection,* ed. Alexander Heard and Michael Nelson (Durham, NC: Duke University Press, 1987), 120–54.

13. Robert C. Lieberman et al., "Trumpism and American Democracy: History, Comparison, and the Predicament of Liberal Democracy in the United States," First Draft, August 29, 2017.

14. "The Federalist Papers: No. 51," Avalon Project, http://avalon.law .yale.edu/18th_century/fed51.asp.

EPILOGUE

1. Carl Hulse, "For McConnell, Health Care Failure Was a Map to Tax Success," *New York Times,* December 3, 2017; Elana Schor and Heather Caygle, "Why Democrats Failed to Tank Tax Reform," Politico, December 16, 2017, https://www.politico.com/story/2017/12/16/tax-reform -democrats-obamacare-298958.

2. Jim Tankersley, Thomas Kaplan, and Alan Rappeport, "Fast-Changing Tax Bill Is Set to Clear the Senate," *New York Times,* December 1, 2017.

3. See, for example, Jonathan Easley, "Poll: Majority Oppose GOP Tax Bill," *The Hill,* December 13, 2017, http://thehill.com/homenews/ administration/364781-poll-majority-oppose-gop-tax-bill.

4. David J. Lunch and Damian Paletta, "Hours after Senate GOP Passes Tax Bill, Trump Says He'll Consider Raising Corporate Rate," *Washington Post*, December 2, 2017.

5. See, for example, Nancy Cook, "Trump Finds Success on Taxes Doing What He Does Best—Selling," Politico, December 18, 2017, https://www.politico.com/story/2017/12/18/trump-taxes-sales-congress-302241.

6. Jim Tankerlsey, Thomas Kaplan, and Alan Rappeport, "Republican Tax Bill in Final Sprint across Finish Line," *New York Times*, December 13, 2017.

7. Carol D. Leonnig et al., "Michael Flynn Pleads Guilty to Lying to FBI on Contacts with Russian Ambassador," *Washington Post*, December 1, 2017.

8. Karen Tumulty, "Trump's Best and Worst Day as President," *Washington Post*, December 1, 2017.

9. "Final Vote Results from Roll Call 658," House of Representatives, http://clerk.house.gov/evs/2017/roll658.xml; Cristina Marcos, "House Rejects Democrat's Resolution to Impeach Trump," *The Hill*, December 6, 2017, http://thehill.com/homenews/house/363544-house-rejects-democratic-resolution-to-impeach-trump. Two other CBC members voted present.

10. Michael D. Sheard, "Trump, Defending Himself after Flynn Guilty Plea, Says F.B.I. Is in 'Tatters,'" *New York Times*, December 3, 2017; Brent D. Griffiths, "Trump Slams FBI, Justice Department," Politico, December 3, 2017, https://www.politico.com/story/2017/12/03/trump-fbi-justice-department-clinton-276124; and John Wagner, "'I Never Asked Comey to Stop Investigating Flynn': Trump Goes on Tweetstorm about the FBI," *Washington Post*, December 3, 2017.

11. Maggie Haberman, Michael S. Schmidt, and Michael D. Shear, "Trump Says He Fired Michael Flynn 'Because He Lied' to F.B.I.," *New York Times*, December 2, 2017.

12. Maegan Vazquez, Gloria Borger, and Jeremy Diamond, "Trump Lawyer Says He Was Behind President's Tweet about Firing Flynn," CNN, December 3, 2017, http://www.cnn.com/2017/12/03/politics/flynn-firing-dowd-tweet/index.html.

13. Rick Gladstone, "U.S. Faces Blunt Criticism at U.N. over Jerusalem Decree," *New York Times*, December 8, 2017.

14. Eli Rosenberg, "Trump Should Skip Civil Rights Museum Opening, NAACP Says, Calling His Plans to Attend 'an Insult,'" *Washington Post*, December 6, 2017.

15. Seung Min Kim and Elana Schor, "Schumer, Pelosi Clash with Trump over Shutdown Talks," Politico, November 28, 2017, https://www.politico.com/story/2017/11/28/schumer-pelosi-cancel-meeting-with-trump-262853.

16. Andrew Restuccia, Sarah Ferris, and Helena Bottemiller Evich, "Behind Trump's Plan to Target the Federal Safety Net," Politico, December 11, 2017, https://www.politico.com/story/2017/12/11/trump-welfare-reform-safety-net-288623.

17. Josh Dawsey, Ashley Parker, and Philip Rucker, "From 'Access Hollywood' to Russia, Trump Seeks to Paint the Rosiest Picture," *Washington Post,* November 28, 2017; Billy Bush, "Yes, Donald Trump, You Said That," *New York Times,* December 3, 2017.

18. Ashley Parker and John Wagner, "Trump Retweets Inflammatory and Unverified Anti-Muslim Videos," *Washington Post,* November 29, 2017; William Booth and Karla Adam, "Trump's Retweets Elevate a Tiny Fringe Group of Anti-Muslim Activists in Britain," *Washington Post,* November 29, 2017; and Ian Pannell and J.J. Gallagher, "Video Trump Retweeted Did Not Contain 'Muslim Migrant' as Claimed: Official," ABC News, November 30, 2017, http://abcnews.go.com/US/dutch-website-muslim-migrant-video-trump-retweeted/story?id=51495780.

19. Akela Lacy and Kristen East, "Trump: Kate Steinle 'Killer' Re-entered U.S. through 'Weakly Protected Obama Border,'" Politico, November 30, 2017, https://www.politico.com/story/2017/11/30/kate-steinle-verdict-jeff-sessions-trump-274340.

20. Steve Coll, "Faking It," *New Yorker,* December 8, 2017; and Lindsey Bever, "Trump Suggested the 2001 Death of a Joe Scarborough Aide Is an 'Unsolved Mystery.' It Isn't," *Washington Post,* November 29, 2017.

21. Tumulty, "Trump's Best and Worst Day as President."

22. Josh Dawsey and John Wagner, "In Florida, Trump Banks on Economy Outweighing His Many Woes in Campaign-Style Speech," *Washington Post,* December 9, 2017.

23. Ashley Parker, "Trump Attacks Gillibrand in Tweet Critics Say Is Sexually Suggestive and Demeaning," *Washington Post,* December 12, 2017.

24. Eric Lipton and Danielle Ivory, "Under Trump, E.P.A. Has Slowed Actions against Polluters and Put Limits on Enforcement Officers," *New York Times,* Decemebr 10, 2017; Dawsey and Wagner, "Trump Banks on Economy."

25. Gallup, "Party Affiliation," http://news.gallup.com/poll/15370/party-affiliation.aspx.

26. Jelani Cobb, "The Worst Part of Donald Trump's Visit to the Civil Rights Museum," *New Yorker,* December 11, 2017, https://www.newyorker .com/news/daily-comment/the-worst-part-of-donald-trumps-visit-to-the -civil-rights-museum.

27. Resistance among not just Senate Democrats but also Senate Republicans led at least two politically extreme and professionally under-qualified judicial nominees to withdraw in December. Lydia Wheeler, "Three Trump Judicial Nominees Stumble—with Republicans," *The Hill,* December 17, 2017, http://thehill.com/homenews/senate/365175-three -trump-judicial-nominees-stumble-with-republicans.

28. Pence already was by some reports "ready to step in" to replace Trump at the head of the ticket during the *Access Hollywood* scandal of 2016. McKay Coppins, "God and Mike Pence," *Atlantic,* January–February 2018.

CPSIA information can be obtained
at www.ICGtesting.com
Printed in the USA
LVOW03s0839050118
561942LV00001B/1/P